WHO ME

Two Birds, Fifteen Cats, Two Dogs, One Hamster, Two Turtles and Goldfish

A MEMOIR

KATHY WHANG

PAGE PUBLISHING, INC.
Conneaut Lake, PA

First originally published by Page Publishing 2021

ISBN 978-1-6624-4150-9 (pbk)
ISBN 978-1-6624-4151-6 (digital)

Printed in the United States of America

To every one of them…
To my children and grandchildren…
To every life: past, present, and future…

CONTENTS

Introduction...7
Part I: Before
          Chapter 1:   Willie Whiskers 11
          Chapter 2:   Jet and Missy...............................36
          Chapter 3:   Just Jet 66
          Chapter 4:   Goldfish 89
          Chapter 5:   Tweetie Bird 111
          Chapter 6:   Prissy and Sooty..........................135
          Chapter 7:   Just Sooty 153
          Chapter 8:   George Washington 174
Part II: After
          Chapter 9:   Kathleen and Nicki Nicholas 197
          Chapter 10: Pepper and Ginger......................207
          Chapter 11: Amanda of Mill Valley.................222
          Chapter 12: Thomas, Tanya, and Baxter Baby.....236
          Chapter 13: Ebony......................................247
          Chapter 14: Amos, Andy, and Teaser the Bird 262
          Chapter 15: Molly.......................................281
          Chapter 16: Riley..296
          Chapter 17: Beatrice Blossom........................321

INTRODUCTION

Some say we are defined by the pets we keep…
Some say pets teach us about life and death…
Some say pets are essential to our wellbeing…
I say read our story and…

PART I

Before

Chapter 1

Willie Whiskers

Description: Willie Whiskers is black-and-white, but he would not be considered a tuxedo cat. His black spots do not cover him like a coat. His black is more like large poke-a-dots. One large spot runs down his back, and there are smaller ones running from the top to the bottom of his legs. The black never quite makes it to his paws, all four are white. He is shorthaired. Lean. Each ear is black on the outside and pearl pink on the inside. The black on his left ear spills across his left eye like a pirate's patch. His paw-pads and nose match the inside of his ears. His tail is black, tipped in white.

His most distinguishing feature is his whiskers—thick, white, and extremely long. He wears these like my dad wears his moustache, proudly. He knows he is handsome; you can tell by the glint in his very, very emerald eyes.

*****

Willie arrives in a cardboard box. Dad and Mr. Brown bring him home late after their office Christmas party. They are business partners, drinking buddies, and barbecue connoisseurs. My mom and Mrs. Brown are friends via their husbands' business connection, and their mutual tolerance of their hubbies' boyish antics and love of Scotch.

I am in the first grade. I have white blonde hair (always in pigtails) and blue eyes. It's the early fifties. My mom and dad are my world. I have a brother, but he's in the Army at Fort Ord. We are fifteen years separated, no brothers or sisters in between. Friends and family say, "Oh, Kathy's like an only child." I have many dollies; I especially love Tiny Tears. I have lots of coloring books and crayons. I go to church on Sundays and to school during the week at Park Avenue. What I really want is a kitten. Even an old cat would do. I make up stories about kittens, not lies, stories.

Tonight, I am going to bed early, not because I have to, but because I know Dad and Mr. Brown will be tipsy, loud, and huggy when they come in. Mom explains, "Boys will be boys," there's not much we can do about that. I don't want to be up when they arrive. I want to be in bed.

On Friday and party nights, I choose to go to bed right after dinner and hide under my covers. I use my sheets against the dad I am unfamiliar with. The dad that's been out with the boys.

Mom says Dad's just being silly. But it's different than when he is flipping pancakes that stick to the ceiling or when he dances around the kitchen in Mom's frilly apron. That's silly. Not troublesome.

Mom tucks me in and gives me an arm tickle. She doesn't ask if I'm sick. "Sleep tight, tomorrow's a new day. Bet we have pancakes."

I hear Dad and Mr. Brown come in the front door. My bedroom is at the front of our little house, right on the side of our covered porch. I lay still, eyes shut tight, ears wide open.

"Dottie," my dad calls to Mom. "Look what Carl and I found. It's perfect for Kathy."

I hear Mom move from the kitchen breakfast nook to the dining room, teacup rattling in its saucer. "Ralph, how was the party? Did they enjoy the hors d'oeuvres I sent? What's in the big box? Get it off the dining room table, I just waxed, you'll scratch the maple. O goodness, it's so dirty, and it's mewing."

"It's a kitten for Kathy. It was outside our building, hiding in the corner of the doorway. Carl and I didn't know what to do at first. Then I remembered what Kathy told her teacher. I told Carl this was meant to be. He found a box in the back dumpster and here we are." They slap each other on the back. *Whack, whack.* They are breathless and pleased with themselves.

12

Maybe I should get up and see this unexpected miracle. I've wished for a kitten forever and ever. I told my teacher I had nine of them at home in my bedroom. She called Mom to see if she could have one. Mom was embarrassed, exclaiming, "What an imagination!" My teacher laughed, assuring her that often six-year-old's make real their deepest wishes.

"Well, put the box on the floor in the kitchen, and let's have a look."

I hear the trio move to the kitchen, seems Mom wants them off the hardwood floors and onto the linoleum. Dad and Carl praise her appetizers, especially the mini cream puffs. They tell her all the office sends their thanks and wish her a Merry Christmas. The box is opened, one flap at a time, I can hear the cardboard sliding against itself. They must be afraid it will jump out. I hear mewing. It sounds scared. Then there's silence.

"It's scared. Here, sweetie, come out of the corner so we can have a look at you. You're alright. You're safe. Here, kitty," my mom coos.

I hear Dad and Mr. Brown move back to the living room for one last Scotch. Glasses clink. They make plans for the week ahead.

"Nightie, night, Dot. We'll see you next week for cards. Hope Kathy likes the little fellow, pretty sure he's a fellow." Mr. Brown, Carl, bumps the coffee table on his way to the front door. I hear him shuffle down the walkway to his car.

I want so to get up and see the kitty. What color is it? Where will it sleep? Will it live in my room? Will they make me wait until Christmas to have it? Wait until I tell my teacher. My eyelids won't stay open. I try hard to make them. I hear muffled chatter as Mom turns off the houselights and Dad locks the front door.

"Let's take him to our room. We can put a towel in the box for tonight. Tomorrow we'll find a basket. I'll put him next to my bed on the floor. What do kittens eat?" Mom whispers.

"Okay but let me take him out back first."

I am lost to sleep.

*****

13

I'm so cold.

"What's this, what's happening?"

Swish.

A big soft, furless thing scoops me up. It's not my mom. The grip is under me not at the nap of my neck. But it's gentle like her. It holds tight and then it lets go. *Plop.* I'm in a small dark place. Thankfully, it's warmer than the corner I was in. Maybe this will be a good thing.

Up, up I go. I slide this way and that.

I holler. "Where's my mom?"

I can't see in the dark. I slide from side to side. My heart beats faster and faster. I sink my claws in. Then I stop. My dark place lands on a firm spot.

"Carl, just put the box on the backseat."

I'm on a backseat in a box.

Ahead of me are voices. Loud, deep, fast speaking, somehow soothing voices.

"Won't my girls be pleased?" the voice, not called Carl, says to the other.

"They sure will be. I think we did everyone some good tonight, especially the little fellow in the back," Carl says.

"Are you sure he's a boy?"

"Yes, Ralph, he has quite a set for such a tiny one. Wonder how he managed to get all the way downtown, wonder where his mom is?"

Rumble, rumble, we are moving. I crouch down and plant my feet, shut my eyes, and hold my breath.

So here I am. On a backseat, in a box with Carl and Ralph.

Then I'm not. The movement stops. I am up again. I think Ralph has me. Then I'm going down. Light streams into my box. A face is peering at me with a gentle voice and a gentler hand. She rubs behind my ears. Ralph calls her Dottie. She's not my mom, but the feeling's familiar. I think I may be home.

Ralph takes me out into the night. He sets me on what I recognize as grass, although it's hard to tell in the dark. I hope he won't leave me out here. He directs, "Go pee, buddy." I sniff and squat. "Good kitty." He's pleased, I'm relieved. Back to the box.

Dottie strokes my back. I curl tight into a ball, warm against the towel.

I am lost to sleep.

*****

I can't wait to get up. I don't know why; I just know I must get up. Now.

My eyes open wide. The sun is barely turning the sky gray. Mom's up, she always beats me. I smell and hear the coffee percolating. If I move fast, I can catch it before it's done. I love watching the coffee color fall through the filter and change the water from tan, to brown, to black. Dad likes it black.

Kitty, Kitty!

A kitten.

Kitten, Kitten, Kitten!

That's it. I have a kitten. Slippers, robe, where are they? I push and pull them on.

"Mom, Dad. Where is my kitten?"

Mom laughs. "Guess the surprise is out." She winks at Dad.

Dad's propped in the corner of the nook, just unfolding the *Saturday Times*. Without looking up, he says. "Kathy, what about *Dick Tracy* and *Peanuts*? We always read them first thing before pancakes, you know that."

"Daddy, it's not Sunday yet, it's Saturday, and I know you have a kitty for me. I know, I know. I heard you and Mr. Brown last night. Can I have it now? Oh, please right now?"

"Oh, so you heard. Well, okay then. I should make you wait for Santa but guess that's asking too much."

"Go look on the back porch. Be gentle, he's in the big box by the washing machine." Mom adds cream to her cup and points to the back door.

The door is closed; there is a window in its top half. I can see the box if I stand on my tiptoes. I turn the handle slowly and creep in. I squat down next to the box; its top is open. I see my kitty.

15

Mom has placed two saucers in the box, one with water and one with something that looks like cream of rice. She says its baby pabulum and milk. She called the neighbor early, not knowing what kittens eat. The neighbor has cats, and she knows everything. She brought the pabulum over. She said, "This is what kittens eat."

My kitty is a tiny, tiny ball of black-and-white fluff. I can see the pink in his ears, and his nose is pink too. His has white whiskers that reach far beyond his kitten face, stretching wider than his body. They look like airplane wings or like he is carrying sticks in his mouth like a dog might.

He looks straight into my eyes. His are shiny and green. I reach in and stroke between his ears. "I will love you forever."

I feel Mom and Dad behind me. "What shall we call him?" Dad asks.

"Willie Whiskers. Just look at his whiskers." I carefully scoop him up and cuddle him close.

*****

"Good morning, little one," Dottie says. "Let's take care of business and give you something to eat." She lifts me up and kisses my nose. It's back to the grass.

I am placed on the back porch in my box. It is not as warm here as in the bedroom, but I feel safe. There's water and some sticky white stuff. My towel is folded. I am not sure about the white stuff; I dip my paw in and lick it off. It tastes okay. The gurgling in my stomach stops.

Ralph peers in. "Hey, buddy. How's it going? Kathy should be up soon. Hang on to your whiskers."

My whiskers indeed. I'm not sure what they are used for other than to get in my way, and now they have clumps of white goo hanging from them. I'm not sure of much. I don't know where my mom or littermates are. I don't know how I landed in the cold dark corner where Ralph and Carl found me. I do know, I am glad they came along. I am glad to have landed in this warm box with food and water and Dottie to look in on me. I hope Kathy is just as nice. I hope I can stay.

This must be her; she is smaller than the ones she calls Mom and Dad. Her face is round and pink like the pads on my paws. Her little hands chubby. She makes me purr, roll on my back, and beg for tummy rubs. I will love her forever.

*****

"He's wonderful, Dad, thank you so much. Can he sleep with me?"

"If it's okay with Mom. He'll have to be house-trained first. Right, Dottie?"

"Yes, once he learns to go to the bathroom outside and makes no mistakes, he can sleep with you."

"I can't wait to tell my brother and my best friend, Diana June, and Grandma and Grandpa. Thank you, thank you!"

Dad reminds me to thank Carl next time he's at the house.

"I will draw a picture of Willie Whiskers for Carl."

*****

I live in a two-bedroom bungalow in Alhambra, California. My water and food are on a red mat in the kitchen. I eat wet stuff that smells really good, much better than that white goo from when I was new. I sleep with Kathy in her bedroom which is blue, her favorite color. We often snuggle under her bedspread. I now have a basket on the back porch; the box is gone. I spend most of my time on Kathy's bed or on the back of Ralph's wingback chair in the living room. I take care of my business by meowing and standing by the back door. Someone always lets me out.

I have three yards: the front, the middle behind our bungalow, and the way backyard behind the garages that the landlady lives over. There are calla lilies to stick my nose in; they make me sneeze, and Kathy has to wipe off their orange dust that sticks to my fur. There are three trees to climb. I catch birds and mice. I do not take them to the back door; if I do, Dottie says, "No, no, no." I leave them by the incinerator for Ralph, who says, "Good old Willie, could you just keep to the mice and let the baby birds alone?"

Kathy dresses me in doll clothes. That's okay because she always fills a doll cup with milk for me. "Here's your treat, Mr. Whiskers." I purr in response.

Sometimes Kathy takes the doll's highchair to the kitchen. I eagerly jump in; Kathy pulls the tray down, and Dottie puts bits of buttered toast on it.

She quips, "Here, sweet Willie, here is your *buttied* toast." I will do just about anything for butter. I often paw Dottie's hand gently, no claws, hoping to get more. It works every time. Humans are so predictable.

Ralph takes naps on Sunday afternoons. He lays on his back on the living room carpet. I like to climb up on his stomach and nap with him. Well, I did until one hot summer day when his stomach made the worst noise. I thought something was trying to come out and get me. *Grrrrr*, it said. *Grrrr, grrrrr*. I went straight up in the air. Claws out, fur on end, eyes wide, and whiskers taunt. I came right back down on Ralph's round mound of a gut which was shirtless and exposed to the whirring fan on the coffee table. He sat straight up, jumped to his feet, and hollered just like the dog next door. He knocked the fan over and chased me around and around the room with Kathy's playhouse broom. Around and around.

He yelled, "That damn cat. Just wait, Willie, just you wait."

The front door wasn't' open or the back. I skittered down the hall, sliding on the wood floors and finally landed in a dark corner under Kathy's bed.

Dottie grabbed the broom from Ralph. She turned to face Ralph. Then helpless, she doubled over with laughter. "I'm so sorry, Ralph, but that's what happens when you nap plumb in the middle of the living room. Willie thinks you are furniture. Your empty stomach scared him to death, or was it that awful snoring. Poor kitty I'm not sure we will ever see him again."

"Honestly, Dot. Give a guy a break. I wasn't trying to scare him. Find the Bactine. Look at my stomach. We should have named him Zorro."

Kathy lifts the bedspread and peeps at me. "Poor, poor, Willie. Come out. Let's play dolls till dinner. Dad will be okay by then, promise. He's just loud, he wouldn't really hurt you. Mom wouldn't let him. After dinner you can go out and hunt mice. Okay? Please, kitty, come out."

*****

My parents love to entertain. We have all sorts of parties: birthday, anniversary, cocktail, dinner, and crazy eight parties. Dad's specialty is the backyard barbecue. Sometimes Mom and Dad invite family, sometimes just friends; on holidays they invite everyone.

This Sunday, we are having a special barbecue. We are going to meet Pam. My brother is going to marry her. He is bringing her from Monterey where they met in a bar. Bruce plays jazz there every weekend that he can get a twenty-four-hour pass. Pam lives in an apartment near Fort Ord, she's a model. She wants my brother to be a famous trumpet player or maybe an actor. Dad's not pleased; he wants Bruce to take advantage of the GI bill and get a teaching credential and play his trumpet only for fun. Her dad isn't happy either; he's a Hollywood producer. "B movies only," my mom says. "Mr. Fancy Pants," Dad says. Her dad wants her to marry a movie star. My brother just wants to play his horn.

Mom and Dad are trying to be kind and welcoming. Dad says, "We need to put our best foot forward, we owe that to Bruce. Maybe she is the one, and if not then that's for him to find out, not for us to say, told you so." Mom agrees. They have chosen to barbecue and have a picnic lunch in the backyard.

It's sunny, the sky is clear blue, a perfect Sunday afternoon.

Mom is making her famous potato salad, and Dad is grilling chicken basted in his secret sauce. Mom warns him. "Not too hot, Ralph, watch the peppers."

I am wearing my blue, seersucker sundress with bows at the shoulders and my new white scandals. Dad has one of his crazy Hawaiian shirts on and Bermuda shorts. (I wonder if he got the okay from Mom. She doesn't like him in shorts, he has knobby knees.)

Mom is in a peach shirtwaist; her skirt is flowing over layers of petticoats. Her wrists are stacked almost to her elbow with bangle bracelets: orange, white, lime, and sea blue.

We are all fidgety.

Bruce is the best brother ever. He sends me pen and ink cartoons of life in the barracks and plays "Somewhere Over the Rainbow" on his horn when he's home. I love that song; I love the Munchkins and Dorothy; she has the same name as my mom. Bruce is happy to sit with me and Willie for tea parties. He doesn't mind Willie in his lap, and he's the best at making milk tea; he puts three spoons of sugar in each cup.

I don't know if I will like Pam, but I hope she likes me. I want to be a flower girl when they get married. I have never been one. I've never even been to a wedding.

"Kathy, Ralph, they're here." Mom is calling from the living room. She's been watching for them out of the front window.

"Kathy, make sure Willie's on the back porch. We'll go in and out to the yard through the side door."

Pam is allergic to cats. Bruce has told that to Mom twice or maybe twenty times. Willie has to stay on the back porch so Pam won't get red eyes. I remove him from my bed and carry him to the porch. I shut him in. He immediately leaps to the top of the washing machine and then to the open window where he settles onto the sill. He makes the screen bulge. He looks happy, and he has a bird's-eye view of the backyard, the picnic table, and the smoking barbecue.

*****

I don't mind this spot, I've been here before, but I am not pleased about missing out on possible bites of chicken.

I can see my people. Bruce is here with a girl they call Pam. She's the reason I'm stuck here. Kathy had a serious talk with me; it seems that everyone is not fond of Willie Whiskers. That is perfectly alright, I'm not fond of everyone either.

I would prefer to be high in my elm tree, just an easy jump from branch to branch to the ground. And just a quick run from tree trunk to under the picnic table where I can rub against ankles and wait for fingers to offer bits of whatever is on the menu.

Maybe Kathy will save me a nibble. She is a very dependable little girl.

*****

Pam's okay. She's a tiny bit taller than Bruce. She tells me that's why she wears flats. She has really short dark hair like my brother's and red puffy lips. She holds tight to Bruce. He doesn't mind.

I'm not sure Pam likes picnics. She is bothered by the gnats that insist on joining us. It's warm and the glare of the sun makes her squint. "I should have worn a hat," she tells my brother. But she laughs at all my dad's jokes and answers all of mom's good-natured questions about how she and my brother got together.

She doesn't drink beer. Dad and Bruce do. Mom and Pam decide on vodka collins. Pam says, "A perfect choice for a hot day." Dad makes me a Shirley Temple; we even have red cherries.

Pam admires Mom's table; she thinks it's "so stunning for a pic- nic table." I think so too. The centerpiece is daises and red roses from our garden. Mom carefully arranged them in a big blue bowl she found at the dime store. The tablecloth is red checked. The water glasses are shiny, bright-colored metal (hot pink, carrot orange, sap- phire blue, emerald green, and canary yellow) from our Tupperware lady. Our plates are just white, but not paper, not today.

So far so good.

The chicken is grilled to perfection—golden brown and lightly bathed in secret sauce. Dad tests to see if it is done with a long fork. Poke. Juice spills out. Dad asks Bruce to hold the platter while he removes the chicken from the grill. Mom brings the potato salad, a relish plate, and hard rolls from the kitchen. There is lemonade, iced tea, or water to go with our meal.

We sit, pass food, eat, and chatter.

My brother smiles and hugs my shoulders. I wave at Willie.

Pam asks for a glass of water. "What's the matter, hon?" Bruce worries.

"I don't know. My lips are on fire."

Mom looks at Dad. Bruce looks at Dad. I look at Pam marveling that her lips are even redder than before.

"Too much pepper in the marinade," Dad admits.

Guess Pam is allergic to more than cats.

So much for first impressions.

*****

I am tired of watching from this window. A pecky blue jay is taunting me from the rosebush under the sill. The smell of chicken comes in waves through the screen.

When will this be over?

Finally, Dottie hugs Bruce. Pam kisses Kathy on the forehead. The five walk down the side of the house. Each trying to squeeze in one more goodbye.

Kathy has left bits of chicken on the picnic bench.

I love Kathy. Love, love, love Kathy.

Let me out. Now!

*****

There will be a wedding, and I will be the flower girl.

Mom and I pick material for my flower girl dress. It's pale aqua blue organza with flossed white flowers dotted across it. It will be lined in matching aqua taffeta. We will send the material and the pattern to my grandmother who lives in New York. She is a seamstress. She makes all the dresses for all the girls in our family. We send her material and patterns, and she returns boxes of dresses.

I will wear white patent leather Mary Janes and lacey ankle socks, white gloves and carry a small white wicker purse. Mom says I will be exquisite. I am pretty sure that means extra, extra pretty.

The morning of the wedding, Mom takes me to Adele's, her hairdresser. My hair is dressed in long finger curls like Shirley Temple's. Adele has a special wreath of baby's breath she attaches to the crown of my head with tiny combs. "It looks like a halo," Mom says. Mom has a new hat for the wedding to match her new suit. Adele puts her hair in a French twist to ensure that hat gets most of the attention.

Mom has told me that it will be a small wedding in Pam's family home in Beverly Hills. There will be family and close friends, mostly their family and friends. It's in May right after my brother is discharged from the Army.

The wedding is at three in the afternoon. We arrive at one. I expect a palace, like Cinderella's. I am disappointed. The house is small like ours. Theirs is Spanish modern, ours a California bungalow. There aren't any photographers and no movie stars.

Pam's sister, Lynda, meets us at the front door. She was a walk-on in *The Robe*. Dad says that's as close to a star that I'm going to get.

Lynda has long brown hair, nothing like Pam's pixie cut. She hands me a small bouquet of white roses laced with baby's breath just like my wreath.

"The wedding will be in the living room. When we are ready for you to lead the bridal procession, someone will come and get you, Kathy." She sits us in the front row. There are four rows of folding chairs. The living room couch has been pushed to the wall behind us. Lynda disappears down a nearby hall.

I am over the moon. Mom thought I might get to carry flowers; she was right. I'm so thrilled, so proud. I can't wait to walk in front of the bride to the tiny round table in front of the fireplace and join the minister and Bruce. (Mom says the minister is Episcopalian, not Methodist like us.) I am going to be the best flower girl ever.

Several women are busy in the dining room. I can see the cake. Soon they disappear down the same hall that Lynda did.

A grand piano stands in a corner of the living room. A young man, my brother's age, is sitting on the bench. I recognize him; he is a buddy of Bruce's from high school. He waves to us. He begins to play "Bridal Chorus."

Lynda is coming down the hall. Pam and her father are steps behind.

My brother appears from nowhere and stands to one side of the minister.

Everyone in the room stands. My stomach flips. My face turns pale, then hot and flushes pink. I look at Mom, she looks at Dad. The procession of three passes us and joins Bruce. I am still between my parents in the front row, not leading anyone anywhere. Tears are rolling down my cheeks. My flowers have fallen to the floor.

My brother raises his hand. "Just a minute, please." The music stops. "Kathy, come here by me. We can't forget the flower girl."

Dad picks up my flowers, squeezes my shoulder, and pushes me forward.

Wait till I tell Willie about this.

*****

We are moving.

They keep saying that. We are moving. We are moving. MOVING!

There are boxes everywhere. Lots of newspapers to dive into and hide under. Eventually they are pulled off of me and used to wrap plates, bowls, cups… I jump in and out of the boxes and run from one room to the next. What great fun!

Ralph says the boxes are giving me the crazies. I hope he doesn't get out that little broom again. Some boxes are almost full; they are easy to get out of. Some are empty, and I have to stand on my back legs and tip them over. A couple of times I've been caught napping in one full of sweaters or tablecloths. Dottie picks me up and places me on the back porch, sometimes on the back steps.

"Ralph, get Will and put him in the carrier. He can sit with Kathy in the backseat. I think we are ready to go. Meet you in the car."

Once again, I am in a box on the backseat. This time Kathy is next to me.

"Sweet Willie Whiskers, we are going to our new house. Don't be scared, we have your bowls and mat, and Mom says when you are used to the new house you can go back to sleeping in my room. The new yard is twice as big. There's an apricot and a plum tree. There are two old cats next door, Sister and Buster. I bet they will show you where to hunt. I'm a little scared about my new school and making

24

new friends, but I am not going to think about that until after the Christmas break."

Kathy sounds like I feel.

*****

We aren't moving much more than ten miles—Alhambra to San Gabriel. The cities are right next to each other.

Our new house, new to us, will be the second home Mom and Dad have owned in California. The first was in San Mateo. Before I was born and my brother was in grade school, they owned a house in Rochester, New York. They have moved all over the States because of my dad's job. Mom is hoping this will be the last move until they retire. They daydream about moving near the beach somewhere close to San Diego.

I heard Dad tell Carl the house on Bilton Way cost $12,000. Mom says that's a lot of money. It sounds like it to me. My allowance is $2.00 a week. I am nine years old.

The house has two bedrooms like our old one. There's a den for Dad and a formal dining room for Mom. There is a kitchen with a bay-windowed nook, big enough for a table and four captain chairs. There's a back porch like at our old house, but we are calling this one the laundry room. There are two bathrooms and two fireplaces. Mom and Dad are thrilled about the enclosed patio. They are going to make it into a lanai (garden room). It will have a tiny bar for Dad's scotch which he only drinks at home now. They will put a second TV in the lanai so Dad can watch baseball and golf without disturbing us gals.

On one side of the lanai is a small alcove which will be made into Dad's business office. His company is moving his desk and filing cabinets from the main office in LA, and they will install a telephone that only Dad can use. Dad will work from home when he is not out making sales calls. He will only go to the main office for meetings.

Mom is not sure about having Dad around all day. I heard her say. "He can be so demanding. I hope he remembers I'm not a secretary or waitress, and I don't answer telephones. Not unless he wants to pay me. If he plays his cards right, he may get coffee in the morning and a bologna sandwich for lunch." I'm pretty sure she is kidding; she would do anything for Dad.

I will be changing schools, but we will go to the same church. My new school has bike racks, so I can walk there, or I can ride my bike. Dad has already bought me a lock and a basket. I think it will be fun to ride my bike, but I'm going to walk until I see what the rest of the fourth graders do.

I will be starting the second half of fourth grade after the Christmas break. I have two weeks off. There is a problem though. I will be repeating California history in my new social studies class. The Alhambra and San Gabriel school districts share textbooks. At my old school I had just completed California history. I should be doing US history next. But the textbooks have been swapped. I will have to repeat what I have already learned. Dad is worried I will not learn everything I need for the fifth grade. Mom has asked a friend from church who was a teacher to help. She will tutor me on Saturdays.

It takes the entire Christmas break to get settled. Rooms are painted. Wallpaper peeled and replaced, and a grass carpet is put in the lanai. It's not real grass, it's not even green. It is dried straw, woven in square patterns. Willie is going to love to knead his claws in it. Wonder what Mom is going to do about that.

Mom has put Willie in our new garage. She says he must stay there for three days. His basket, food, and water are with him. We all visit him many times during the day. He also has a litter box. He has never had one of those before, but he knows exactly what to do with it. Mom said he would.

Mom put butter on Willie's paws, and she told Dad he will need to park in the driveway until we let Willie out.

"Butter on his paws? Mom, why?"

"Because he loves butter. He will lick his paws clean, and that will remove all the scent from the old house. Hopefully, then he won't try to get back to Larch Street. Sometimes kitties do that, try to go back home. He will need to learn the smells of his new home here on Bilton Way. That will take time. After he's been in the garage, we will keep him in the house for at least a week. Then we will let him out into the yard. We will have to go with him at first and watch him carefully. We don't want him to get lost in the new neighborhood."

*****

Have I been bad?

What is this dark place?

Why did Dottie put butter on my paws and not on the toast? Where's my toast?

It's going to take a long time to get this butter off. I hope my tongue doesn't break. I will have to lick between each toe twice. The butter has gotten all over me from sleeping in a ball. I love butter but not between my toes or on my fur.

What on earth do I do with this box of sand? Oh…got it.

They said, "We are putting you in the garage for a little while, it's for your own good."

"Seriously?"

So I'm in the garage with butter smeared on me and no toast and no grass.

Thank goodness there's a door with a window on the side of the garage. I can at least keep track of day and night. I've tried to slip out when they come in with the food and water, but no luck.

Kathy brings in bologna and tuna from lunches. Ralph found an old lamp and plugs it in during the day. I know it's not the sun, but it does help. Dottie can't stop saying how sorry she is. Nonetheless, I'm stuck.

I miss laying in the sun. I want to explore my new yard. Kathy says it's bigger than the old one. I can hear the birds, and I think there are some mice behind the garage. I hear a strange voice every night calling, "Here, Sister, here, Buster."

*****

Christmas break is over, and we settle into our new lives on Bilton Way.

Mom says it's not so bad having Dad home during the day. I think she likes having her morning coffee with him.

Willie has been released from his backyard dungeon and is doing great getting used to his new surroundings. He has three new friends: Sister and Buster who live next door and are very similar to their owners, Mr. and Mrs. Brown. And Inky who lives across the street and comes to visit him as soon as Lucy comes home from work and lets her out.

I've started school. I'm riding my bike. The school is big, and there are two of each class. That was confusing at first. There are lots of kids on my street. I see most of them at school. The twin girls two houses on the right of mine go to the Catholic grade school at the San Gabriel Mission. Lucille and Jeanie are my new friends. They don't live on my street but are close by, and we are in the same classroom. We walk to school together each morning. I have joined the Girl Scouts, Mom's a leader. Both Jeannie and Lucille are in my troop.

*****

I'm out, almost. I've moved to the house with my bowls, basket, and litter box.

It's interesting at first: smelling each room and piece of furniture; exploring cluttered counters, and cupboards that have been left open by mistake. There are still a few boxes that I dive in and out of. The most interesting thing is in the room they call the lanai. A sea of dry grass covers the floor.

"Have I died and gone to heaven?" No.

I take one step in, crouch, and dig my claws deep. Oh…lovely.

"Out, out, out," Dottie yells. The doors are slammed.

Oh, let me outside. Please. I need to scratch a tree or chase a bird. I need to pounce on any small jumping thing. I want to eat a bug.

At last, the door to the backyard is open, and no one makes a move to shut it.

"Halleluiah!"

*****

Summer comes, the first in our new home.

Dad puts in a shuffleboard court on the cement area between our back steps and the garage. He adds a big bright light over the back door so we can play year-round. He and I play just about every night after he finishes his work. The game is harder than it looks.

He is just about done with the patio that divides our backyard in two. There's a lawn that runs in front of the patio, and after it are fruit trees and camellia bushes. The previous owners left us a million camellia bushes. Mom says they are all prize winners. Our yard was famous for these flowers. The patio is made of rectangle-shaped pavers. Dad spreads gravel between each one. He goes to Pep Boys, his favorite hardware store, and treats himself to a new barbecue and Mom to a yellow umbrella for the picnic table. Both barbecue and table are put on the patio.

Mom picks plums and apricots from our trees. She carefully checks each piece of fruit to see if it is ripe. If it is, she gives a little tug, twist, and pulls. Before putting the fruit into her apron pockets, she makes sure there are no holes or bruises. She takes time every day to check for ripe fruit. She doesn't want the birds or raccoons to get the good fruit before she does. She doesn't bake or put up preserves, that's Grandma's territory, but there is always a bowl of our personal crop in the center of the kitchen table.

Willie has become more of an outside cat than inside. He is quite the mouser, leaving his nightly catch at the bottom of our back stairs that lead to the lawn. There is always at least one mouse without its head laying there. Dad puts them in the garbage can before Mom stumbles on them. During the day, Willie enjoys sunning himself in the middle of the shuffleboard court, often the cats next door join him. Their driveway is right next to ours. There is no fence between the drives, just a short hedge that I can step over and Sister and Buster can wiggle through. That's about as close as the three get.

The sunbathing party ends when the shade covers the court. They stretch and retreat, each to their own back door. Suppertime calls.

My friends and I ride bikes, make forts, and roller-skate. We like to ride or skate to the soda shop in the center of our neighborhood. Everyone calls our neighborhood the Village, because we have our own little town right in the middle where the main streets meet. There is a drug, grocery, and hardware store. A cleaner, a real estate office, and a soda and hamburger shop. If we are lucky, our parents will ask us to go and get milk or butter or electric tape. Then we get to keep the change for cherry cokes or root beer floats.

During the summer I don't have to be inside the house until the sun goes down. Then I take a bubble bath, call Willie, and we snuggle into bed and wait for Mom to read from my latest library book. Once Mom turns my lamp off, Willie and I talk about our day. I do most of the talking, he's a good listener. When my eyes get heavy and Willie no longer likes the covers on him, he jumps to the floor and heads to the lanai to get someone to let him out. I wonder what he does outside until Dad makes him come in. He's not allowed to stay out all night because once he did, and he was gone for three days. When he showed up, his white fur was gray, and his nose had a scratch across it. Mom said, "No more catting around, mister!"

*****

Buster and Sister live next door. They are brother and sister. These cats belong to Mr. and Mrs. Gregory. Dottie calls Mrs. G., Betty. Everyone, even Ralph, calls Mr. Gregory, Mr. Gregory.

Buster is bigger than three of me. He's an orange tabby, more rust than orange. His paws are enormous. He looks like Mr. Gregory, chunky and grumpy. Unlike Mr. Gregory, Buster has a bite out of his right ear. He doesn't meow, he says "MA." He spends his time sitting on the third step of his back porch. Now that it is summer, he joins Sister and me on the shuffleboard court to get a little sun. Mostly, he just stares at me. I don't think he likes it when I sprint across my lawn and up his oak tree after a blue jay or sparrow. He's too old to chase me, he just says "MA." I hope we become friends; he must know where the mice hide behind the garage.

Sister is a tortoiseshell; she has no tail. She's almost as round as Buster. She is docile and kind, like Betty. The other day I was chasing a grasshopper. It got away from me and flew over to Sister's driveway. She pounced and put her paw on it. I wasn't sure if I should follow. She just waited until I couldn't help but run after it. She raised her paw, she didn't hiss; she let me have the bug. Crunch.

The other day I took Sister a butterfly, a thank you. She was pleased and took it in her mouth. She placed it between her paws and watched it for a long time. She let it go.

My special friend lives across the street with Lucy and Alice; they are mother and daughter. Inky is their cat; they have no Ralph. Lucy works every day, and Alice goes to San Gabriel High. Inky is so black and shiny. She's tiny like a kitten, but Alice says she's eight. Inky loves me. Every evening when Lucy gets home, she lets Inky out and watches her cross the street to visit. I wait for her on my front porch. We sit together until Alice calls her home.

Ralph says, "Too bad she's fixed. We'd have some fine kittens."

I love Bilton Way. I'm glad we moved, buttered paws and all.

*****

We will have our first official barbecue on Bilton Way this coming Saturday. Dad has invited his business partners and their wives. I will be the only child there; everyone else's children are grown-up. I help Mom set and clear the table. I like most of Dad's friends; they always ask me how I'm doing and remark on how lucky Mom is to have me. They let me call them by their first names; Mom's says that's okay.

"Dad who is coming?"

"The usual crew. Johnny and his Dorothy, Carl and Eleanor, Leon and Mary, and two couples you haven't met."

My stomach takes a turn. Somehow, I thought maybe Dad wouldn't invite Leon and Mary. It was a silly hope. I know that Leon is one of Dad's biggest clients, and Mom loves Mary. But...

I worry about Saturday all Wednesday, plotting ways I might miss the barbecue or find a way to hide from Leon. I think I will ask Lucille if she can ask her mom if I can come to dinner and spend the night. Or maybe Alice can babysit me at her house. I'm pretty sure either one would be okay with my parents.

Finally, it's time to settle into bed with Willie.

"Willie, I don't know what to do. I don't like Leon. He always gets me alone, where I can't see Mom or Dad. He'll want to take a walk to the park or a ride to the store to get extra ice; then he asks if he can give me a shoulder massage or a back rub. Sometimes he touches my front. I say stop, but he does it anyway. I don't like it. He makes me promise not to tell Mom or Dad. He says it's our secret. He always calls me his princess. I am not his princess. I've tried hiding from him, but he always finds me. I try staying next to Mom or Dad, but they get busy. I don't know what to do. I know that it's wrong, but I don't know how to make it stop. I don't want to make Daddy mad at me."

Willie moves from under the covers. He sits up tall with his front paws pressed together, tail wrapped snuggly around him, whiskers at attention, looks me straight in the eyes and howls.

"What's going on in there? Is Willie sick?" Mom calls from the hall.

I burst into tears as Mom wraps her arms around me. I tell my story, one sob at a time.

She asks, "How long has this been going on? Why didn't you come to me sooner? Can you tell me what Leon has done?"

I answer between sobs. I can't get the words out fast enough. They tumble over each other, skipping out of my mouth faster than I can make clear sentences, piling up against the silence I have kept for so long.

"Oh, sweetheart, my poor baby. My sweet, sweet girl. I'm so very sorry."

At last there are no more words. The tears are endless. Endless.

Mom understands, nods her head, her face unreadable. She tells me the same thing happen to her when she was eleven and twelve.

She thanks me for being so brave and reminds me I can tell her anything.

"Promise?"

"Promise."

She finds my tissue box and places it between us. She blows her nose and helps me with mine. Willie is huddled in my bedroom doorway.

"I have to tell your dad."

"Oh, please no. Please."

"I have to. He needs to know. He needs to take care of this. Do you think you can sleep? Would you like a cup of milk tea? I will make it just like Brucey does."

"No tea, Mom, no book."

She tucks me in. There are extra hugs and kisses. She leaves the tissues next to me.

"Come on, Will, let's find Ralph."

Up early I find Mom and Dad already at the kitchen table, coffee mugs in hand.

My dad starts to speak but doesn't get past "Kathy." His eyes are wet; one, two tears escape down his cheek. I have never seen him cry. Mom told me he did once after he spanked me for being sassy to her. I was three. He left his handprint on my bottom. I have never been spanked again.

"Kathy, sit with Mom and me." He pushes the words out.

He says what Leon has done is wrong. He is going to talk to both Leon and Mary. He is going to make rules. I will never be left alone with either one of them. He and Mom will make sure of that. He says there are events that Leon has to be invited to, there is no way out of that. We will have to go through with Saturday. He explains that Leon is responsible for a great deal of his wages. Business is business. He apologizes for that. His face is so sad.

"Kath, this should have never happened to you. If anything like this or anything else ever makes you scared again, come to us as soon as you can. Okay?"

"Okay, Daddy."

We hug.

Mom has her head down; tears splash into her coffee. Willie is in the windowsill of the nook. The window is open. A warm breeze flows through the screen. It promises to be a beautiful day.

Saturday comes and goes. After that I seldom see Leon or Mary. When I do, Dad keeps me close.

Leon never apologizes. Mary does. She tells Mom this has happen before with their neighbors' daughter. She says, "Leon means no harm." Mom doesn't go with Mary to lunch or shopping anymore.

Daddy still loves me.

*****

Dottie's making toast. She butters it; I watch every stroke of the knife.

I jump from the sill to the floor next to her feet.

She feeds me one bite and then another and another. I don't have to beg.

Have I done something special?

"Willie, Willie, what would we do without you?" she murmurs. "Good old Mr. Whiskers, best kitty ever."

*****

I'm eleven when I start the sixth grade. Jeannie and Lucille are still my best friends. A new girl, Judy, joins us. She has freckles everywhere. She's from a private Presbyterian grade school. It only went through the fifth grade. She joins our Scout troop, and we become a fearsome foursome.

On Saturday, Judy and I take up roller dancing at our local skating rink. We went to a free lesson with our troop, and we decide we like rolling on the hardwood floor, dancing to the music, and best of all the flared skirts the girls wear. Jeannie and Lucille aren't interested. Judy and I wonder if roller-skating is in the Olympics.

Judy doesn't walk home with us; she goes the other way. She lives on the edge of our village. After school we often sit on the bench in the shade of the school and make plans for the weekend or dou-

34

ble-check homework. Judy is really smart. She always has the right answers. Sometimes we are late getting home. Our parents don't worry; they know who we are with. They ask only that we are home by four.

It's three forty-five. I know because for Christmas last year I got a watch with a red leather band. I wear it every day and wind it every night. Why is Mom on the porch?

"Hi, Mom, anything wrong? I'm not late."

"It's Willie."

Willie was hit by a car. He was chasing a big black crow across the street. They were both hit. The bird flew away, Willie didn't.

The driver of the car stopped. She went to Betty's house first. Betty looked at the cat lying in the street and cried out. "Oh, Willie." She followed the lady to our house.

"Where is he? Is he okay? Mom?"

"Kathy, Dad took him to the vet, but the doctor couldn't save him. We're both broken hearted. Your dad is back and in his office. Let's go inside."

We don't take Willie's death well. Not well at all. Betty doesn't take it well. Lucy and Alice don't take it well either. Even Mr. Gregory lumbers over to our back screen to tell me how badly he feels.

He mutters. "Willie was one great cat. Best mouser I ever saw."

Sister and Buster no longer sun themselves on the shuffleboard court. They keep to their backyard. Inky comes across the street daily looking for Willie. At first Lucy tried to keep her in, but she only howled until her front door was opened. She sits on our porch until Alice comes to carry her home.

There are no words. Willie was five years old when the car hit him. Half of my life, but just the beginning of his. Mom seldom makes toast anymore. If we have toast, Mom tears up just opening the butter dish. Dad mindlessly checks for mice every morning, always surprised not to find any. I hate going to bed. There is no comforting warmth next to me. Mom tries hot chocolate, extra reading time, and doubles up on the bubble bath. Nothing helps. Not even if she stays while I fall to sleep.

CHAPTER 2

Jet and Missy

Description:

Jet—Beautiful. Handsome. Jet is a black Persian mix. He has thick, long jet-black fur which is frosted in rust. His body is stout. If you watch him walk away, you are caught by the thought that he is wearing pantaloons and knee-high boots. The fur on his back legs puffs out until it reaches an inch or two above his back paws. His pantaloons are also fringed in rust. His face is perfect. Not flat, not pointy, like a cherub. You feel like you could pinch his cheeks. His whiskers are short and black; they poke you before you see them. He could be mistaken for a black bear cub.

If forced to pick a best feature, it would be his tail. It is a fantastic black plume, reminiscent of the feather found on a musketeer's hat.

He is gorgeous everyone says so. His eyes are yellow-green, flakes of rust circle his pupils. A beautiful, beautiful boy.

Missy—Petite, slender, feminine. Her sweet soul can be seen in her eyes which are a pale green.

She is Jet's littermate but doesn't resemble him in the least except for the incredible length of her fur. She is dove gray, but not her nose or whiskers. They are the color of clouds heavy with rain. Her fur is silky, not dense like Jet's. Her tail is long and sleek. Her face is heart shaped, finely boned. When she is sleeping her pink tongue gently protrudes and covers her lower lip.

Some would say she is ordinary. Not so.

*****

Sixth grade is a big deal. We don't move to a new school like they do in some districts; we stay in our grade school. I am excited that the sixth, seventh, and eighth grade classrooms are in a wing of their own; we are no longer considered the little kids. We remain in our assigned classroom, but some of the teachers move between the rooms teaching different subjects. I like that, you are not stuck with a teacher you can't stand, and Mom says this changing of classes will help prepare us for high school.

The only thing that doesn't change is the fearsome foursome. We have more homework. Book reports used to be about the plot and characters; now we have to add detailed information about the author's life and the time in which the book was written. English is no longer easy or fun. History is worse; maps and dates, dates and maps. Thank goodness Judy is still the smartest, and Lucille can read a globe. Jeannie and I would be in a lot of trouble without our other half.

Inky is still coming over to our front porch in the afternoon. I wish there was something I could do for her. She just sits on her haunches, front paws tucked under her chest with her head tilted down. Her ears are alert, they twitch now and again, but her eyes are closed. We don't know if she is sleeping or reminiscing.

Dad is working hard and goes on many business trips. His sales territory has gotten bigger. It includes all of Southern California, Nevada, and Arizona. Mostly he drives from client to client; sometimes he flies. There are two wonderful things about his traveling—the souvenirs he brings us, stuffed animals for me and turquoise jewelry for Mom, and he is always home by six on Friday nights; his boss never makes him travel on weekends.

Mom and Dad are involved in my school's PTA. Mom is still my Scout leader, and Dad is learning magic for a hobby.

Saturday will be the annual PTA's fundraiser. This year they are making money for field trips. There will be booths where you can win prizes and buy popcorn balls and cupcakes. There will be a cakewalk and a three-legged race. You have to buy tickets to play the games and get food. Dad is managing the goldfish booth. He has Mom doing the decorating for his booth. She is having fun cutting goldfish from orange construction paper and blowing up balloons. She is happy she doesn't have to bake a cake.

I hope to win a goldfish. Mom says we can keep it on the kitchen counter if I keep the bowl clean.

The fair is a success. Dad's booth makes the most money. No surprise, after all he is a supersalesman. Who wouldn't want to try their luck with Dad's encouragement? I tried, but not even one ping-pong ball would land in any of the fishbowls. I had twenty tickets, but no luck. Dad had to close the booth at eight o'clock. Five fish were left. Dad bought two for me, one for Jeanne, one for Lucille, and one for Judy. We helped him clean up the booth as a thank-you.

Mom finds a glass bowl in her china cabinet large enough for both the goldfish. We sit in the kitchen and watch them swim back and forth, round and round. I am amazed that they don't knock themselves out on the side of the bowl.

"Ladies, this is not what I call having a pet," Dad says. "They are cute and gold and fun to watch, but not something you can pet or hold on your lap."

"You're right, Dad. Do you think we could have another cat? I'm sure Willie wouldn't mind. And I think it would make us all feel better. I know I would."

Mom joins the conversation.

"Ralph, I think Kathy's right. It feels so empty here, like something's not right. Willie left a huge hole in our family. I was talking to Betty yesterday. She told me that the neighbors at the corner of Del Mar and Bilton have a Persian that is expecting kittens soon. She thinks it might be time for us to consider a couple of kittens. I agree."

"Dottie, are you really suggesting two?"

"Yes, that way they will have each other for playmates. They can curl up together in their basket and keep each other warm, and they will have company when we are on vacation. Betty says it's just as easy for her to come over and watch two as one."

"What do you think, Kathy?" Dad asks.

"Oh, that would be wonderful! Can we, can we? How soon can we have them? What colors will they be? Do you think we will be able to pick the two we want the most?"

The litter arrives two weeks after Mom and Dad say yes.

There are seven kittens in the litter. We get first pick. Betty set it up.

The three of us are allowed to look at the babies when they are just two days old. They are prunes. You can see slits where their eyes will open. Their tiniest of ears lay flat against their heads. They look like they are made from silk rather than fur. There is one black one, four variations on gray, and two black-and-white ones.

I pick the black one. Dad, a light gray. We are hoping they are a male and female; we won't know for sure until they are older. At this point we don't care; they are ours.

We have to wait six weeks before we can bring them home. Mom says that's okay; it will give us time to get all the things the kittens will need.

"Shall we pick names now?" I ask.

"No, let's wait until they are home and we have a chance to see what their personalities are like."

Dad and I think that's a good idea.

The weeks drag by.

The Andersons, the neighbors with the kittens, let me stop by on my way home from school to check on the babies. They grow fast. The black one is the biggest and the fluffiest. Mrs. Anderson says he (she's pretty sure) was born first. My dad's pick is the sweetest, letting the others crawl over her and step on her head. The mommy cat, Isabella, makes sure Dad's pick is first to feed. She is getting chubbier by the minute.

At last we go to get them. Mom found an old hatbox with a lid that we can use to carry the kittens. She's pretty sure the box once belonged to her mother. She lines it with soft flannel from one of my old nighties. Dad punches holes in the box top.

"Do we have to cover them up for such a short walk?"

"I don't want them to jump out onto the sidewalk. Better safe than sorry."

We head down the street. Mom stays behind making sure the laundry room is ready.

*****

"Mama, Mama. Where are you, Mama?"

"Don't worry I will take care of you. I will always take care of you."

"Promise?"

"Yes."

"You are the best brother ever."

*****

Two kittens are the best.

One minute they are rolling, tumbling, and tripping over each other; the next they are wound tightly together for a nap.

We come to a quick decision about their names: *Jet and Missy*.

Jet, because of his color and because of his speed. Once he gets going it is hard for him to stop. He got so carried away the other day running from my room to my parents' that instead of stopping when Dad met him halfway, he went right up his trouser leg. "Jesus, Jet, slow down I am not a tree trunk." Dad scolded him, detached him from his pant leg, and sent him on his way. Jet continued at *jet* speed the minute his paws hit the floor. He went straight under my parents' beds and summersaulted into one of Mom's high heels, slamming himself and the shoe against the wall.

"Easy on the landings, bud." Dad laughed.

Missy is an obvious choice for such a sweet, precious girl. Everything about her is a *missy*. Dad actually picked the name Missile to go with Jet. Dad is very interested in the space race. He is convinced that someday we will put a man on the moon, and we will do it before the Russians. Mom and I don't get the analogy, but it tickles Dad, so we gave in. We make Dad agree to call her Missy. Missile may be her official name (according to Dad), but we will call her Missy. We also suggest to Dad that he not share his naming reasoning with just anyone. Others might not get it. We don't want him to embarrass himself or us.

"Okay, ladies. Missy is a lot easier to say than Missile, so Missy it is."

Jet is the family's cat. Missy is Dad's.

*****

"Do you hear them calling? We'd better hurry or we will miss breakfast. It's the most important meal of the day you know."

"I do."

Here, Missy, here, Jet. Morning, noon, and night.

"Are those our names? Are you Missy? Am I Jet? Or is it the other way around?"

"I'm Jet."

"How do you know?"

"Because that is what Ralph called me when he shook me off his trouser leg."

"Well then, I must be Missy. That's good, I feel like a missy. Aren't we lucky to still be together? I don't think all of our littermates were as lucky. Our basket is so warm and toasty, especially since they let us sleep together."

"Yeah, it's great. Hey, hurry. There is no time to waste. There are birds and mice and those trees. I must climb and run and chase. Hurry let's get breakfast and get outside. Race you to the kitchen."

"You go ahead I'm not done preening. I know there will be plenty left. Kathy always makes sure my bowl is full. Don't forget, your bowl is blue and mine is pink. Go, get on with your day. I will be along once I've finished licking my paws. Something is stuck between my toes, so irritating. I won't be hungry until it's out."

*****

Dad's favorite chair is in the living room on the wall oppo-site our front windows. He can see what's going on in the neighbor-hood without being considered nosey. You can't see in our windows even when the lights are on because they are shielded by our covered porch, which runs the length of the front of our ranch-style house.

Dad says, "I can see without being seen."

His chair is a winged-back armchair covered in a sturdy brown tweed. It is good for his back. He has a curvature of the spine which makes sitting for long periods of time uncomfortable. Mom picked the chair because of his back, but also because she approved of its style. Mom loves decorating and collecting knickknacks, which she calls memory keepers. Each evening before dinner, Dad relaxes in his chair, has a highball, a smoke, and checks the business section of the newspaper. This is his weekday evening ritual. Missy has made some definite changes to this.

Missy perches herself on the back of Dad's chair. She looks like a gray pillow behind his head. Dad folds the paper and lays it on the end table; he opens a pack of cigarettes and removes the cellophane packaging. He no longer shoves the wrap into his pocket. He now carefully rolls it into a tight ball, the size of a gumball.

He whispers, "Okay, Miss Missy Missile, let's play."

He places the paper ball on his knee and flicks it with his index finger. It flies across the living room. Missy flies after it. So far not remarkable. Missy easily locates the cellophane under or on the sofa. She likes to take a couple of bats before securing it in her mouth. Bat, bat, bat. Now the remarkable. She returns to Dad sans cellophane. This game of fetch goes on until Mom insists we come to dinner.

"Now!"

*****

"Ralph is teaching me fetch."

"Isn't that what dogs do?"

"Well, it's a game Ralph and I do."

42

"Okay, happy for you. At least you're playing and not snoozing. You are awful lazy for a kitten. I must admit though that's a pretty cool trick. Not as cool as mine, but…"

*****

The kittens are soon cats. Big, busy cats. Playing and sunning. Inky no longer comes across the street. Missy sticks close to the house or where she can see Dad. Jet and Buster are hunting mates. Buster locates the prey, and Jet does the dirty work. They never eat what they catch. It is always deposited under the hedge between the drives. Dad is back to collecting it before Mom sees what the "boys" have done.

Like Missy, Jet has perfected a very un-catlike trick.

The first time he performed his stunt I was flabbergasted. He had been sitting on the picnic table. I had just crossed the lawn to the patio to offer him bits of cheese.

"Here, kitty, kitty. Jetty, where are you? I have a treat."

Just as I spotted him, he responded to my call with a leap from the table to the patio and hit me waist-high, did a backflip, and landed on his feet. We both glared at each other: me out of surprise and Jet out of being misunderstood. I couldn't believe what I suspected.

I called again, this time extending my arms like you do when you encourage a toddler to run to your embrace.

Jet is now ten feet away: watching cautiously, not sure he should risk more rejection. His back is to me. He acknowledges my voice and turns. He begins a slow trot toward me. He leaps with a motion that starts in his back legs and propels him upward. The motion ends with his front legs reaching for my shoulders. In an instant, he is in my arms. No claws. I cradle him. His purring is immediate, his cheek and nose reach for my chin, he leans in and so do I.

To make sure this isn't a mistake, Jet and I repeat this over and over and over. He continues to respond to my call by leaping into my arms even when the cheese is gone.

"Mom, Dad, come here. Quick, I'm in the back. Wait till you see this."

"Unbelievable, Dottie, do you believe this? I wonder if he will jump to me."

Jet isn't picky who catches him midflight as long as it's one of us. We amuse ourselves with this phenomenon almost every evening. It's a great crowd pleaser at barbecues. Betty tries to take a photo for the neighborhood paper, but it's impossible to catch Jet midair. She has many shots of Jet on the ground and in our arms but none of his actual flight.

*****

I knew they would like that. Guess that puts Missy and her cellophane ball in their place. Anyone can fetch, not everyone can fly.

*****

Dad's serious about learning magic. He takes classes from several working magicians at the famous Magic Castle in Hollywood. He can make goldfish turn into confetti. He can pour a pitcher of milk into a newspaper funnel, flip the paper funnel open, and expose completely dry newsprint. There are scarf, ring, and card tricks. He can make coins appear and disappear from just about anywhere.

Mom and I are his test audience. Missy is his assistant, always sitting at his feet while he performs. He is happy to entertain my friends, and they are happy to have him. He, of course, performs at our parties. He is really good!

I beg him to show me how he does the goldfish trick. But he refuses. He says that magicians are sworn to secrecy. You can't share tricks that you have paid to learn; that would be unprofessional.

My Grandma and Grandpa (my mother's parents) recently moved here from Rochester, New York. Dad said we'd better get them out here before one of them breaks a hip on an icy sidewalk. They live in Alhambra now, the city we moved from. Mom's sister (her only sibling) and brother-in-law and grown son (the baby of their five children) are also in Southern California. The three of them live in an apartment in Westwood. Their eldest son and family are making the move to California this summer; they will live in a new housing track in Chatsworth. This will be the most family we've ever had so close. Mom is planning a summer reunion.

Grandma and Grandpa live in a one-bedroom duplex. Mom is helping them set it up. They have started to go to our church; it is just a few blocks from them. They can walk or take the bus to Alhambra's main street where there is a Woolworths, Grandma loves their fabric; my favorite, Hamburger Heaven; and a JC Penny's where you can get just about anything. Grandpa is a walker, five miles a day, rain or shine. Walking downtown will be a breeze for him. My grandparents are great babysitters. I love going to their house. We play dominos, eat homemade bread and pies, and Grandma is helping me with my sewing. When we go on trips to the beach or Palm Springs, they come to our house to take care of the cats if Mrs. Gregory can't.

Judy no longer roller-skates with me. She lost interest and thinks ice skating is a better idea. I take private lessons now. I am about to be tested to move from intermediate roller dance to advanced. I will skate with a partner. I have been practicing with Mr. May; he owns the skating rink. I am required to perform three dance routines to specified music: a waltz, the swing, and a rumba. For Christmas, Mom and Dad had custom skates made for me. With the allowance I make from cutting our lawn, I buy skating skirts and matching boot covers at the rink's store. I am taking sewing classes at Singer on Saturday afternoons so soon I can make my own skating skirts and school dresses. I love to sew. Mom is pleased, like baking she is not interested in sewing. She says, "These talents you and Grandma have must have skipped a generation."

*****

Missy and I have been fixed. That means we will not be having kittens.

Dottie says it's for our own good. It will cut down on any catting around we may have in mind and hopefully will help prevent our early demise. She wants us to stay in our own yard and live long contented lives.

45

I have to tell you, getting fixed isn't a pleasant experience. First, you're pushed into a small box, then there's the car ride, and the strange-smelling doctor's office. The next thing you know, you're back in the box with a terrible headache and so, so sleepy. When you finally get your senses back, your people won't let you out of the house. And to top it off, you are sore in places that you shouldn't even talk about.

Poor Missy had it worse than me. They shaved her tummy. She's just now able to jump to her spot on Ralph's chair. He has been very patient. He carefully lifts her from her spot and puts her in his lap so he can rub under her chin and between her ears. They can't play fetch yet, so Ralph quietly reviews his paper while Missy naps. Ralph is saving cellophane balls in a bowl. He tells Missy, "It's okay, no hurry we will have plenty of time to play when you are feeling better."

I have given up jumping into arms. I am not sure how that would feel. For now, I am keeping my feet on the ground. No tree climbing either for a while. I feel like Buster acts—slow, very slow.

*****

Summer 1959 brings family, barbecues, and magic together.

Our backyard is beautiful in the California sun. If you step out from under the trees and look east, you see the San Gabriel's rise straight up cutting into the blue sky like castle steeples. Our grass is emerald green like in the Land of Oz. The bougainvillea covering the back of our house is beyond crimson. Mom won't let Dad trim it, not wanting to sacrifice even one blossom. The camellia bushes are gushing pink, red, white, and candy stripes of all three colors. Mom cuts these blossoms close to the bottom of the bloom and floats them in bowls of water. Every table has a bowl including the picnic table. Our fruit trees are trying to outdo the camellias; I think they are winning. Grandma comes to the rescue and shows us how to make jam out of our abundant apricot and plum crops. Jam making is a hot business on a summer day, but worth every sweet, sticky spoonful.

Grandma and Grandpa come every Sunday after church. Dad grills, we eat midafternoon, and then there's a canasta game until the sun leaves the backyard in shade. Missy, Jet, and I don't play; we watch from the hammock. I always go with Mom when she drives to my grandparents' home. If it's not too late, we have tea and sugar cookies at their house before we turn around toward home.

My cousins are settled in Chatsworth, and we are planning a special barbecue to welcome them. I am so excited because my second cousins are kids, not adults like my first cousins. They are twelve, eight, and three years old. Boy, girl, boy; King, Leslie, Greg. Preteen to baby.

This party will be a potluck. My Aunt Ruth, Grandma, and first cousin Pat are excellent cooks. We are depending on them to bring family favorites: custard pie, baked beans, and oyster stew. Dad will grill hamburgers and hot dogs, everyone's favorites. Mom has planned a fruit salad and will have all the condiments necessary for a successful backyard picnic. She is ready for the Easterners to tell her how much sweeter the fruit is from New York farms; this won't bother her in the least. She is in full agreement. There will be beer for the men, except Dad who will stick to scotch—on the rocks; Tom Collins for the ladies; iced tea for the teetotalers, Grandma and Grandpa; and for us kids Coke and 7 Up, a coveted treat.

My aunt, uncle, and cousin Bob arrive first. They have picked up my grandparents on their way from Westwood.

"Hi, Dorth, I am so happy that we are finally getting together."

"Me too, Ruth. I hope the kids all get along. Are they okay with cats? Our cats love a party, but I can keep them in if someone's allergic?"

"The cats are fine. I'm a little worried about King, he's taken the move hard. He may be sullen. Don't let it upset you. How are Bruce and Pam doing?"

"Oh, I understand. Ralph and I have moved so many times. It's always hardest on the kids. I know he must miss his friends and his Little League team. I understand he is quite good. Don't worry, it will take a while for him to adjust. Bruce is on the road doing some gigs in Seattle. Pam is busy doing whatever Pam does—not cleaning that's for sure. We haven't seen them in a while, that's a story for another day. I hope Leslie and Kathy get on. That would be so great for Kath, like having a sister."

"Mom, they're here."

*****

Missy, this is going to be a great party. They are all bringing dishes full of food. I heard someone say *oyster stew*. I'm not clear what stew is, but *oyster* I understand. I think if we time our appearance just right, we won't have to eat canned food tonight.

Jet, did you see the little one? That's what is known as a toddler. He's quick but clumsy like a puppy. Be careful, I bet he goes for your tail.

I wonder if Ralph will do the goldfish trick. Wouldn't it be super if we had oysters and goldfish for dinner? Do you think that might happen? Why does he always make the goldfish disappear? Why not make them appear and appear and appear.

I don't think that would be very magical; besides, where would he put them all? He only has a small bowl, just big enough for two.

That's my point, I would be happy to help him with that problem.

All you ever think about is your stomach.

And birds and mice and trees and bugs.

*****

I don't know much about boys, especially since my brother was already a man when I first remember playing with him. The boys at school are just the boys at school. I don't pay any attention to them. Alice says I will when I'm in high school. If King is an example of what boys are really like, Alice is wrong, I won't be interested.

King's a funny name. Mom says it's a family name. I think King takes his name too seriously. He is very standoffish, and he seems mad at us. Grandma says he's rude. I tried to talk to him about school and his move here, but he just ignored me. I think one of my cats must have his tongue. I'd like to crown him...

Leslie's great. She loves my kitties. She says that her dad won't let them have pets. I tell her she can share mine. She also likes to draw and do crafts like I do. She's younger, but it doesn't seem to matter, we can't stop talking. Our mothers have set up two weekends for this summer; first I'll go to her house and then she will come to mine.

Greg is the cutest. He's all smiles and antics. He has chubby cheeks and big dimples. He likes everyone. He chased the cats and caught Jet by his tail. He's toppled a number of drinks, spilled a bowl of potatoes chips, dumped cut-up strawberries into Aunt Ruth's lap, and banged his head on the picnic table. There were no tears, just the longest string of giggles. Dad said, "Hope he makes it to four."

Once the plates are scraped and the table cleared, Dad brings out his magician's table and dons his black satin cape. He performs his tricks to the delight of the family. The delight of everyone, but King.

King sits scowling on a chase lounge, huddled next to his dad, not impressed by fish made from confetti or disappearing water. Dad is not daunted; he is determined to make King laugh or at least smile. He walks up to King and pulls quarters from his ears: no response. Then pops paper flowers from behind his head: the slightest of smiles passes over King's mouth. Then Dad reaches down, and endless scarves unravel from the back pocket of King's shorts. All eyes are watching. King is silent. His cheeks begin to flush. He looks at Dad and is engulfed in rolling laughter that turns to giggles and ends with his arms around my dad's neck.

"How did you do that, Uncle Ralph? How did you do that?"

Dad ends the show by producing a carton of chocolate ice cream from under his cape. Mom brings sugar cones from the kitchen.

Hugs and kisses end the day. There are at least three rounds of goodbyes. And a series of dashing back-and-forth from car to house for missing items.

King shakes Dad's hand goodbye and asks, "When can we come again?"

*****

Oh, Jet, I'm exhausted.

From what? You spent the day watching the puck go back and forth on the shuffleboard court. How can you be exhausted? You were napping in the sun most of the day.

Don't be mean; it takes a lot out of a girl to spend the day in the sun. Heat can sap your energy, especially with all this long fur, and Dottie forgot to put out our water bowl.

Oh my, now that's a tragedy. All you had to do was wander to the front and take a sip from the leaking faucet by the yellow rose bush.

I, on the other hand, know what exhaustion is. It took me all day to beg six bites of hot dog, two oysters, a lick of custard pie, and sneak three pads of butter. I think I'm going to…

Puke?

*****

"Kathy, let's go. You better take a book and some paper and pencils in case you want to draw. Remember you won't be able to come into the room. You're not twelve yet, so you will have to sit in the waiting room."

"Okay, Mom." Nausea hits the back of my throat. My palms are sweaty and cold at the same time. I have dressed carefully in my dad's favorite sundress. It has a cobalt blue top, and the skirt is full with a pattern of multicolored blue and lavender flowers. Dad says it brings out the blue in my eyes. I have put my long blonde hair in a ponytail and twisted it into a bun on the top of my head. I am hoping someone will mistake me for twelve.

I want to see my dad and give him a bear hug. We love to bear-hug. It's a contest to see who can hug the hardest. Dad usually wins, but sometimes he lets me.

I was hoping we were going to bring him home from the hospital today. But Mom says we will be going for one or two more visits. She offered to let me stay home, but I don't want to be here alone.

"Mom, why can't Dad come home today?"

"Dr. Zell wants him to stay a few more days. He wants to make sure Daddy is headed in the right direction before he releases him. You know how Dr. Zell is, always cautious. He says Dad is doing well, but a few more days won't hurt. Better be safe than sorry."

Dad has had his first heart attack.

He was on an airplane coming home from a business trip in Arizona. Mom says they had to give him oxygen on the plane. When he got home and told Mom what had happened, she called Dr. Zell (our family doctor), and he had Dad go straight to the hospital.

I don't know what a heart attack is, but I can tell it is serious from the look on Mom's face and the concern from family and friends.

I have so many questions. "What if something happens to Dad? What will Mom and I do? Will we have to leave our house? Who will read the funnies to me on Sunday? Who will hold me on his lap and tell me everything will be okay? Who will do magic for us? What will poor Missy do?"

Tears fill in behind my eyelids, one or two leak onto the front of my dress. I find a tissue and wipe them away. I don't want Mom to see. I don't want to cry. Eleven is too old for tears. I inhale and try to push the tears back to wherever they came from.

"Come on, kiddo, let's get going."

Mom's face is pale, her mouth set in a deliberate smile. I see telltale beads of moisture resting on her nose; they always betray her worry. She diverts her eyes from mine and reaches for my hand.

Something goes silent and dark in my head, like when Mom turns the light off at bedtime and the flowered wallpaper turns gray and my dolls and treasures fade out of sight.

*****

Where is Ralph? The house is so quiet, and Dottie forgot to let Jet in last night. I've looked everywhere, where is Ralph? Kathy says don't worry, kitty. Worry about what? Is there something to worry about? I'm not worried, I'm sad.

I'm just going to sit in our chair. I am going to sit right where he sits and wait. I won't eat, and I'll keep one eye open when I sleep just in case he comes in late. I will be right here, right here on our chair.

*****

Dad comes home. Life is not the same. There are new rules.

1. *No salt.* Mom learns to cook without salt. She even takes on baking salt-free bread, which is something you can't buy at the store. Grandma comes over, and they experiment with different recipes finally settling on salt-free sourdough. Dad says that's the easiest to get down.

2. *No butter.* This is a tough one. Salt-free toast with no butter. Breakfast turns to oatmeal and cut fruit. I hate oatmeal, and I hate fruit. Mom says, "We are in this together." She puts brown sugar on my oatmeal, her only compromise. I hear her mutter, "I'm glad Willie missed this turn of events. He would have been devastated."

3. *No frying.* Mom boils and roasts, mainly we have chicken. Dad says, "When I'm feeling better, we will fire up the grill, they can't take that away from a guy." Mom warns, "No hot sauce!"

4. *No scotch.* Dr. Zell has known Dad for years; he tries to soften the blow and suggests a small glass of red wine before dinner. He says that red wine is good for the circulation. Dad's not a fan of wine. He elects to stop drinking, cold turkey.

5. *No more smoking.* This is the hardest rule of all. Dad tries, but his nerves get so bad he shakes. Dr. Zell is concerned that the cure is worse than the disease. He tells Dad to start by just cutting back. Dad goes from a pack a day to one cigarette after each meal and one before bedtime. We celebrate when he cuts down to just one in the evening. I'm sure this cigarette is for Missy's benefit as well as for his.

Dad spends the first couple of weeks home in bed. Missy is allowed on the bed, something that hasn't been permitted before. She sleeps curled against his side, only getting up when he does.

Dad is slow to get up and about. He sits on the edge of the bed to put his shirt and trousers on. Mom helps him put on his shoes and socks. He catches me watching and shuts the bedroom door.

I feel lost, unable to get my balance. Will it ever be the same? When will my daddy be back?

"Kathy, sweetheart, I know this is hard for you to see Dad like this. Getting well from a heart attack is a slow process. Daddy can't help but feel down. He doesn't like that he has changed our lives; it makes him sad. And he doesn't like that he doesn't feel like himself; that makes him even sadder. Like you he wants our lives to go back to the way they were. I think they will if we work together and are patient. It won't be easy, but I think we can do it."

Mom's words reduce me to tears. She moves me away from their room toward mine. We sit on my bed, my head in her lap. She moves my hair away from my face, her hands are soft and warm. Jet finds us and lays in the doorway, watching, waiting.

One afternoon, Dad calls from his bed.

"Find us some champagne, that's like wine, right? Get Kath some soda. Let's have a toast. I am getting up and heading to my office."

Mom was quick with the glasses. I don't know where the champagne came from, but she found it and a bottle of black cherry soda, my favorite. Mom brought the party to Dad on a tray. We all sat on the edge of the bed.

"Here's to a new day and to my girls."

We guide Dad down the hall and through the lanai to his office. His mail is piled high, and Mom had stacked all his phone messages on the corner of his desk. He sits down and gives his swivel chair a spin. "Okay, let's get started. What's for lunch, Dottie?"

Missy and Dad go back to their nightly game of fetch.

Bear hugs are back. I let Dad win.

Mom stops gathering Jet's nightly catch. A task she distains.

We have pancakes Saturday mornings, often Dad pulls a bouquet of paper flowers out of Mom's apron pocket.

*****

Ralph's back, Jet. Everything is going to be alright now.
I hope so, Missy, I hope so.
Ralph thinks I'm too thin. Dottie told him she will make sure I eat more. If I don't, she will take me to the doctor. I don't want to go to the doctor, I am going to eat a lot. Want to race to the kitchen?
Always!
Tonight, I'm going to find an extralarge mouse, special for Ralph. Buster is on the lookout; he's pretty sure we can find one in the ivy under the plum tree. Maybe this time I will leave it right by Ralph's office, so he can't miss it when he steps out to watch the sunrise.

*****

I turn twelve in October. I love that my birthday is in the Halloween month. Sometimes I have pumpkin pie instead of cake to celebrate. I'm in the seventh grade.
We have health class every Wednesday; we are learning about boys and girls and what makes them different. Thank goodness they separate us. The boys go with the vice principal and the girls with the school nurse. The mysteries of life are embarrassing enough without sitting through the *Did You Know* film together.
Afternoon recess is weird on Wednesdays. The boys huddle together and watch us as if we were strangers. The girls are no better. We gather at the tetherball court, chatter and giggle about our new knowledge. Lucille wishes we were back in the fourth grade, clueless. Judy can't wait to be in high school and have a boyfriend. I'm hoping that when I tell Mom about the film, she will say not a word of it is true. It takes till Friday before we can have a decent game of kickball, boys against girls.

Mom tells me it is true. I pout in my room. She brings me Hawaiian punch and chocolate chip cookies. It doesn't help.

As predicted by the *Did You Know* pamphlet, I start my period at the average age of twelve. I'm horrified, nothing Mom says makes me feel better. I read about Anne Frank, and I don't have a clue why she thought this was such a wonderful thing. I think it's the worst. Mom insists I go to school.

For whatever reason Mom tells Dad. I could die. How will I sit across the table from him at dinner? Mom says I can't stay in my room. "Life goes on."

"Kathy, come set the table."

I cut through the den to the kitchen, instead of going through the living room where I know Dad and Missy will be. Bad decision. Dad is sitting on the couch flipping through the *National Geographic*. We avoid eye contact. I notice wet spots on the glossy picture of a panda eating bamboo.

"Dad, are you alright?"

"Oh, I'm fine. It's just the pills I take. Sometimes they make me sad."

I continue to the kitchen. "Mom, Dad's crying. Do you think he's okay? He says it's his pills."

"It's not his pills. He just can't believe that you are growing up. It makes him sad."

That was the third and last time I saw my father cry.

*****

I love our life, Jet. It's perfect.

I love our yard. The apricot tree is my favorite. You should climb with me.

*****

It's eighth grade, I'm thirteen. I will graduate in three months. I am excited and ready for high school.

Saturday is painfully sunny. Odd for March. The sky is a brilliant blue, there are no clouds. Dad makes his famous corn fritters instead of pancakes. We cover them with warm syrup. Dad says it reminds him of his folks' farm and gathering syrup from their grove of maple trees. He takes me to my skating lesson, and afterward, he takes Mom and me to lunch at Hamburger Heaven. He's just home from a business trip and is anxious to catch up with his girls.

I'm standing at the kitchen sink, looking out the window at Sister who has her paw on a lizard. There's a commotion in the back of the house. It's coming from the lanai. Mom calls my name. Her voice is unrecognizable: flat, firm, insistent. "Kathy, go get Mrs. Gregory. Tell her I need her, it's your dad."

I jump the knee-high hedge between the driveways and bang on Mrs. Gregory's door. "My mom needs you…" Before I can finish, she grabs my hand and drags me back across the hedge. Her hands shake as she struggles with our screen door. She pushes me through the laundry room and into the kitchen.

"Kathy, sit here at the table. Don't move till I come back."

Minutes pass…or is it hours? The house is silent, holding its breath. I hold mine.

Mrs. Gregory returns, her cheeks wet. Mom is calling Dr. Zell.

"Mrs. Gregory, what's wrong?"

"Sweetie, call me Betty." She takes me by the shoulders and hugs me so hard it hurts. She is not a hugger.

My dad suffered a massive heart attack. He dropped dead in the lanai. Just like that, dead. His last words: "Dottie, can you come here?"

I feel like oversifted flour. Like tiny particles adrift. What I know is stripped away. What I don't know is everything. I had no warning, no say, no chance to make things right. I'm abandoned. Lost.

People. In and out.

Arrangements.

A viewing. A funeral. My room my only refuge. Jet and Missy my only comfort.

Grandma cooks. Grandpa walks. I watch.

Everyone expected my dad's death.

"He was living on borrowed time. Clogged arteries, curvature of the spine impeding a lung, and a major heart attack. What would you expect? It was bound to happen," they tittered.

Everyone saw it coming, everyone but me.

My mom directs friends and family in and out of the house, to and from the funeral parlor, and back from the cemetery for tea, coffee, and bake goods.

Friends shake their heads in wordless sorrow. They promise casseroles. They say, "Call us anytime, let us know what you need."

Business partners group in a corner of the den and quietly divvy up Dad's lucrative sales territory.

When noticed, they shake my hand and say, "Be a good girl. You have to take care of your mom now."

What? I'm just a kid. My head screams: who's going to take care of me?

Time creeps forward. I'm stuck. Friends bring my homework. They stay as long as they can stand my silence. I am not good company.

After two weeks at home, Mom insists I return to school. She talks to my teachers and asks that they don't tell me how sorry they are; their concern will make me uncomfortable, and "Kathy is afraid of crying in front of everyone." No one talked to the kids; their concern is overwhelming. First day back, Mom comes for me at noon.

Mom is convinced that activity is the key to my recovery. She signs me up for tennis. Together we figured out how to start the lawn mower; Dad always started it for me. We learn to fire up the barbecue. Mom returns to mouse duty. She insists on shuffleboard each evening. We try to get Missy to play fetch. That was something she only did with Dad, so we aren't too hopeful. Arm in arm, we watch Jet and Buster start their twilight hunt out of the kitchen window. Betty waves from across the drive.

I prepare for my eighth-grade school graduation. Grandma makes my dress from lavender dotted swiss. It has an empire waist, bell sleeves, and a slim silhouette. Mom calls it sheath style. She assures me it is quite appropriate for an almost high school student.

My grandparents, my aunt and uncle and cousin Bob, the Gregorys, and several of my father's business friends join my mother for my graduation. They sit on the bleachers in our school auditorium. I enter, they wave. My aunt has her handkerchief to her mouth, and Grandpa dabs his eyes. There's so many of them, I'm embarrassed. I feel my father smile as I step forward and accept my diploma.

*****

I worry about Missy; she won't move from Ralph's chair.

*****

Summer 1962. My mother makes Fourth of July breakfast. Its Dad's corn fritters. She does a great job, just like… I thought the tears had stopped, but no. Mom wraps me in her arms. "We are going to be just fine. Syrup? It's maple."

Being a freshman is exciting, mostly scary. Lucille and I meet each morning and walk to our lockers together. I've memorized my combination, but I write it down on a scrap of paper and tuck it in my wallet just in case. The high school is huge compared to our grade school; the kids are from all around the valley. Each class is full of new faces. The YMCA sponsors service clubs: Lucille, Judy, and I join the same one. Jeanne joins with a group of girls from her church. We all plan to try out for the drill team in the spring; you can't actually be on the team until your sophomores.

Mom moves my grandparents into our house. She is lonely; the house seems too big for us, empty. I'm not consulted. Mom assures me that it will be better for all of us.

Grandma and Grandpa move into my room. I move in with Mom. My mother and father had twin beds. Dad was an insomniac; his tossing and turning drove Mom to distraction, and twin beds solved the problem. I take her bed, and she takes Dad's. We redecorate the room. She lets me take on the project of refinishing the furniture. I antique five pieces in harvest gold. It's a kit we found at the hardware store. We are impressed with ourselves and with the furniture results. When I have friends spend the night, Mom sleeps in the lanai.

Jet moves from the laundry room to the foot of my new bed. He comes in at eight now; he no longer stays out till the wee hours. No one is up at 3:00 a.m. to let him in. His buddy Buster is going in earlier too. Betty says, "Buster is relieved not to have to keep up the night owl charade for Jet. He's much too old for that."

I do my homework in the kitchen. Grandpa smokes his cigars on the patio and his pipe in the den. Grandma puts her sewing machine where my desk used to be. Mom turns Dad's office into a tiny guest room. Dad's desk, file cabinet, and phone are gone. His company came and took them away. His company car is gone also. I miss that big red station wagon coming up the drive signaling Dad's return from a client, signaling the nightly shuffleboard game, signaling him.

Mom takes a job as church secretary. She says she needs to get out and about. I think she's bored. She works from one to four every weekday afternoon. She answers the phone, prepares the weekly bulletin, and keeps the minister's calendar. On Sundays she straightens the pew pockets and arranges the altar flowers. She joins the choir just before the Sunday service begins.

I go to church and Sunday school because Mom makes me. That's just the way it is. She says when I'm eighteen I can make my own choice. Ever since I learned that my Sunday school teacher didn't come to my father's funeral because he didn't see the point since my dad never came to church, I know what my decision will be. To set the record straight, I inform my teacher my dad couldn't sit for an entire hour on a hard pew because of his back. The man just stared at me. Mom said, "Christians are human too. We can't expect too much." I have no expectations.

I give up skating to prepare for drill team tryouts.

Mom hires a gardener. We need someone to keep the trees and bushes trimmed and fertilize. I only know how to mow, and Mom is fine on a stepladder but not on the ten-foot one Dad used for trimming.

I become one of many neighborhood babysitters. My street is my territory. I fund Christmas and birthday gifts, burgers and shakes at Bob's Big Boy, and a pair of coveted baby buck oxfords with my babysitting money.

The family down the street has three boys, one still in diapers. I babysit them almost every Friday and sometimes Saturday night. Their dad walks me home. I tell my mom he hugs me too tight when saying goodbye. She calls them and explains I can't sit for them anymore. "Three boys are just too much for Kathy to watch."

Mom takes Missy to the vet. We've tried everything to get her to eat. We've offered canned tuna and boiled chicken. No luck. The vet gives her a shot to perk up her appetite. It works for a few days. Mom takes her back. She comes home without her. "The vet believes the kindest thing to do is to let her find Ralph. I agreed."

I scoop Jet into my arms and hope he will understand. Grandpa motions me to bring Jet and sit next to him on the couch. He puts one hand under Jet's chin, the other around my shoulders. I like the feel of his starched white shirt and his embrace. I am glad my grandparents are living with us.

Mom takes Missy's dishes to the kitchen. I hear her on the phone.

"Hello, is this the Salvation Army? I have a chair to donate."

*****

I don't understand. Nothing is the same, except for that annoying blue jay in the plum tree who insists on dive-bombing me.

Everyone is out of place or in someone else's. I don't know where Missy and Ralph went too. They're just gone. And I'm not.

*****

It's four in the afternoon, and Grandpa hasn't returned from his walk. He is usually back by three, right before I get home from school.

Grandma asks if I will call Mom, she's worried. Grandpa is very punctual.

"Mom, can you come home early? Grandpa isn't home yet."

"Sure, I'll leave in a few minutes. Tell Grandma I'll drive down his usual route on my way home and look for him."

Fifteen minutes after I call, Grandpa walks in.

"Fath, where have you been?"

"Oh, Muth, I just got a little lost. I had to sit awhile to get my bearings. I'm home now, stop scowling at me."

Grandma wipes her hands on her apron, unties and drapes it over a kitchen chair. She gives Grandpa an icy stare from her ice blue eyes and leaves the kitchen without a word.

"We were worried. Are you okay? Mom's on her way."

"Goodness, Kath, I didn't mean to alarm anyone. I just got a bit turned around. I am after all ninety-three. I hope Muth gets over her mood and starts dinner, I'm starving."

I hear Mom come up the drive. I beat her to the back door.

"He's here."

The alarm washes out of her face, replaced by a smile.

We return to our routines. Mom gets me off to school in the mornings and goes to work in the afternoons. Grandma is making me a wool plaid pleated skirt for fall and bakes bread each Saturday morning. Grandpa walks, smokes his pipe, and allows himself one cigar a day. Mom says he doesn't smoke his cigar; he chews it. Nasty. I make the drill team. I am looking forward to marching in the camellia parade. I'm told it is the next best parade to the rose parade. Now a sophomore I have been elected treasurer of my Y Club. I'm working up the nerve to ask Tim (a crush since grade school) to the Sadie Hawkins dance. Lucille and I are planning a slumber party. Jet spends his days on the front porch following the sun from one side to the other, and his nights on any available lap. When the TV is turned off, he knows its bedtime and plants himself on my bed with his back against mine.

I still walk home from school with Lucille and sometimes Jeannie joins us. One afternoon, Jeannie stops, shifts her books from one hip to the other, and calls for a huddle. We haven't huddled in a long time.

She whispers, "Hey, guys, my dad is building a bomb shelter under our garage."

Lucille's eyes get bigger, browner, and rounder. "He's doing what? Where? Can we see? Why?"

"He's digging, well, he has guys digging a bomb shelter under our garage. He says we are supposed to say it's a wine cellar. I'm not supposed to be telling you. I think he's gone crazy. My mom has a list of what to stock it with. There will be bunk beds and a bathroom like on a boat. My little brother asked Dad if he could have a campout in it with his Cub Scout troop. My dad got red-faced and told him that this is a family secret, and if he told anyone he would be in big trouble."

"Geez, why are you telling us?" Lucille asks.

"Because I had to tell someone. It's bizarre and scary, and Mom and Dad won't talk to me about it."

I am quiet, trying to sort through this secret. Lucille and I know what a bomb shelter is. They are popular with those who believe that the Soviet Union and the US are headed toward a nuclear war. In school we have regular "duck and cover" drills just in case.

I am not sure I am happy that Jeannie has shared this with us. It makes all the gloom and doom too real.

Now that my dad has died, I tell Mom everything. I can't help it. I just do. She is my personal counsel on everything, bad or good. I'm relieved when I hear her come through the back door. I quickly turn off the TV, silencing American Bandstand and catch her in the laundry room.

"Mom, Jeannie's dad is putting a bomb shelter under their garage. She says it's a secret. She told Lucille and me on the way home from school, and we aren't to tell anyone. What's the big deal? Why is it a secret?

"Oh my, you've had quite a day! Not everyone is building a shelter. We aren't, and we won't. They are actually called fallout shelters, because they are meant to protect people from the radioactive dust that falls from the sky after a nuclear bomb explodes. The people putting these shelters in are nervous that if something were to actually happen and their friends and neighbors didn't have a shelter, they might try to force their way into theirs. Most privately built shelters, like Jeannie's, are only meant to house the family that built it. Only enough food and water are stored in them for the family to live underground until it is safe to come out. The government suggests people should remain inside for at least two weeks. People want to keep their shelters secret so they won't be pressured to share."

"That sounds mean. Why aren't we going to build one?"

"Kathy, I don't believe we will have a nuclear war. I believe that we will find common ground with the Russians. After all, that would be best for both countries. Neither one of us wants a bomb dropped on us. Why would we? I believe Kennedy and Khrushchev will work this out. Does that make sense?"

"I guess so. But I would love to see inside Jeannie's shelter. Sounds creepy. Mom, if they ever drop a bomb on us, I think we should just sit on the back steps with Grandma, Grandpa, and Jet and watch the show. I wouldn't want to live in a radioactive world anyway."

She nods and stifles a laugh. "Sounds good, now let's deal with the problem at hand, dinner."

Jeannie never brings the bomb shelter up again, either do Lucille or I. In our US history class, the subject of nuclear war and bomb shelters comes up. The three of us are silent, our eyes examine the engraved hearts and meaningless messages on the pine tops of our desks.

Weeks after Grandpa went missing, he announces that he feels tired.

"Muth, I won't be walking today. I'm worn-out. I think I'll go back to bed."

And he does.

Days later, he is still refusing to get up. Grandma seems miffed about serving meals in bed, coxing him into his chair so she can change sheets and guiding him down the hall to the bathroom. She is not used to him not taking the lead in their daily lives. She asks Mom to call Dr. Zell.

"Ladies, there is nothing medically wrong with Nathaniel. He is as he says worn-out. As long as he is eating and able to get to the bathroom, there is nothing I can do. Get him up when you can and keep me posted. I will check in with you next week if I don't hear from you before."

Muth adores Fath; you can't always tell but she does. She is quiet, and he is gregarious. He is outgoing, she is not. Grandma assumes her role as caregiver with love and kindness. She tucks any irritation with her new role down where we can't see it. I don't think she is irritated as much as surprised that her beloved of sixty-plus years is the first to slow. She gives him a bell to ring and pats him on the hand. "Just ring if you need anything." He rings and rings, and she answers and answers.

Grandpa rallies for his ninety-sixth birthday. He's up and dressed in his usual starched white shirt and charcoal gray slacks. He has added a pair of burgundy suspenders; his pants are a little loose. The entire family comes to watch him blow out his candles. Mom and I have put all ninety-six on his cake. It takes forever for us to light them and keep them lit. Grandpa's bald head shines in the candlelight, strangely like a halo. His cheeks are rosy. Stories are told. Jokes made.

Smiling he addresses his adoring crowd. "This is the biggest darn bonfire I have ever seen." He inhales and in one breath blows all ninety-six candles out. He needs no second breath, no do-over; he gets it right the first time.

Grandma stands stick straight next to him, holding his hand, beaming with pride. Her mouth in a Mona Lisa smile. He kisses her forehead before cutting the first piece of cake.

Six months after his party, Grandpa passes away. Quietly in his sleep. We worry that Grandma may follow in Missy's footsteps.

The death process is the same: arrangements, viewing, funeral, well-wishers, casseroles, shaking heads in disbelief.

I don't get it. Grandpa was ninety-six. Ninety-six. Why all the angst? He had a wonderful life. A long life. It was his time. My dad was fifty-five. Fifty-five. He was just at the crest of his life. A life cut short. His timing horribly wrong. I just don't get it.

I refuse to go to the viewing, no more wax dolls for me. I try to stay home from the graveside service in pretense that I will help with the post-grave reception. Mom doesn't buy my less than heartfelt offer.

She understands my reluctance but argues. "Life creates situations that demand us to respond for the sake of others in spite of our own feelings. It doesn't seem fair or right. I get that, but you need to go for Grandma and Grandpa; they deserve your presence. They didn't take your dad away. That was life's mistake not theirs."

I go. I listen. I pray. A prayer of desperation.

*****

Another one gone. Willie, Ralph, Missy, Grandpa. Who's next?

CHAPTER 3

Just Jet

Description: Jet is still like a black bear cub: fluffy, stout, lovable. His face and paws remain velvety; his pantaloons and tail are still edged in rust. He has a kind face, and now his eyes are a deeper green. His black nose is always wet. On his cheeks and the bridge of his nose are tiny flecks of white, like someone salted him. You must look closely to see any sign of aging and then it's fleeting, just a shadow of what's ahead.

Unlike Missy, Grandma rallies and turns her grief into a flurry of baking and sewing. Mom and I are relieved and happy to be the beneficiary of her redirected energy.

Grandma is not a talker. I think it's because she is hard of hearing. Mom disagrees. "That's just who she is, quiet, reserved. Some people think she's aloof. Not really, she prefers actions over words."

I am convinced that Mom loves Grandma more than me. She caters to her. She sets the thermostat to Grandma's preferred temperature. It doesn't matter that sweat covers my nose. She checks locked doors that don't need checking. I know they don't need checking because I just checked. Mom insists we check again; Grandma is sure we've forgotten. Mom makes us go to early service at church, that way Grandma can sit with her ancient friends in the front row. They spend the first fifteen minutes of church vying which hearing aid wand works best. They should be praying. Just once, couldn't we sleep in? Isn't that really what Sunday is for? Grandma can't stand loud music unless of course it's a church hymn. Mom makes me turn the stereo volume so low I might as well turn it off. Mom doesn't seem to care at all about my feelings.

"Kathy, she's old. This is the least we can do. She's my mom. I don't love her more, just different. Someday you'll understand. Relax, you have a whole life of sleeping in and loud music ahead of you."

Jet likes Grandma more too. He moved off my bed to hers. Like I don't need his comforting warmth. Even worst he chooses her lap instead of mine. I guess he prefers to watch Lawrence Welk rather than listen to me chatter on the telephone. On Saturday mornings he begs bacon from Grandma, never once coming to my chair. The other day I caught the two of them in her bedroom rocking chair; eyes shut, snoring, in the middle of the day.

I pick Jet up, look him in the eye, and ask, "Who do you love better?"

He replies with a single *murp* and forces his way to the floor.

*****

I like my ladies. Sometimes they are grumpy. Dottie mumbles under her breath, "Three women in one house is dangerous business." I can see her point. It's a good thing the house is big enough so they each have a spot to hide. Eventually, they come together over Grandma's fresh baked bread or Dottie's latest church gossip or Kathy's imitation of Jeannie's little brother trying to *Twist*.

Dottie offers me buttied toast each morning. She lets me sit on the empty chair at the kitchen table. Sometimes when it's just her and I, she lets me put my front paws on the table and eat the toast bites right off her plate.

Grandma is patient; she never rushes me out the door or off her rocker. She always has time to rub behind my ears and under my chin.

Kathy's a teenager. I think that means self-centered, impatient, and pouty. But that's okay, she's still my favorite. She dances with me in the living room. I let her hold my front paws, and we sway back and forth to Herb Alpert. She sneaks me squirts of Reddi-wip. She sits with me on the back steps, and we watch the blue sky turn black and the stars pop bright through the plum tree branches. I used to sleep with Kathy, but I had to stop. She *dream walks.* She kept propelling me off the end of the bed with her left foot.

I'm a very lucky cat. All my ladies love me best.

*****

My brother comes home.

Bruce and Pam are no longer together. They are divorced. Bruce says Pam broke his heart. Since she left, he has been bouncing around Washington, Oregon, and California. He plays his trumpet in bands booked in jazz bars and dance emporiums. He's been ghostwriting for Spike Jones and arranging scores for independent filmmakers.

"Mom, can I come home for a while? I wasn't able to when Dad passed. I feel awful about that. But I'm between jobs now. I miss you guys. I could help around the house. Mom, I'm not sure what I should do next. I can't believe Pam left me."

"Of course, we miss you too. Come and stay until you get back on your feet."

Grandma and I are not clear on what "back on your feet" means, but we are anxious to have Bruce home and hear about his adventures.

Bruce moves into the nook in the lanai. He moves drums, an upright piano, and stacks of records and music books into our garage. Mom parks her car on the aging shuffleboard court.

Bruce sleeps late, practices nightclub routines during the afternoons, looks for work in the evenings, and comes home at the crack of dawn. He spends hours on the telephone. Mom flips when she sees the first phone bill. Bruce promises he will pay her back once he gets a gig. He tells her the calls are necessary to find work. The music business is all about who you know; calling people is part of the game.

He gets some club engagements. He is known for handwriting musical scores, an art similar to calligraphy. Clients pay for original scores to be handwritten before they are mass-produced. He gives piano and guitar lessons. There is not an instrument he can't play. To supplement his income, he takes on odd jobs as handyman and house-painter. These are jobs he can do during the day so he can pursue music at night. He is able to pay rent, help with food (he loves to eat), buy cigarettes and beer. He begins to help Mom with the phone bill.

*****

I was just getting used to life with my girls when Bruce arrives.

He calls Dottie, Mom. That makes Kathy his sister. Like Missy and me. But he's way older than Kathy. Different litters, I guess.

Bruce moves into the lanai. There's a bed where Ralph's desk used to be. There are shoes, shirts, pants, a cool leather jacket, and a tux. There is no closet in the alcove, so Dottie finds a small dresser and puts it where Ralph's file cases were. She finds a dress rack so he can hang what needs hanging. It's really the rack Grandma uses to hang dresses after she steams them. She doesn't mind.

"Bruce, you can use the little bathroom off the den. That was your dad's. That will give you a little privacy. It has a nice shower."

You should see the stuff he moves into the garage. Wow... He keeps his trumpet in a black case lined with red velvet. He puts the case under his bed. I know, I've been under there and looked. I would love to take a nap in it.

I'm pretty sure all the instruments are a surprise to Dottie. Pretty sure she hadn't planned to have an entire band in her garage.

"Hope this is okay, Mom?"

"Okay for now." She gives him a squeeze. His face relaxes.

Bruce keeps the hours of a cat. Which is really cool, because now I can stay out late, just like in the old days. We often come in together around dawn and sleep till noon.

He looks like Ralph. Dark brown-black hair. Round brown eyes. No moustache though.

He talks to me like he would to one of his buddies.

"Hey, Jet, how's it going. Any mice tonight? If you are quiet, I think we can score some cheese from the fridge. Just follow me. We'll have to tiptoe; the girls are asleep."

Funny telling me to tip toe. Why do you think I have these pads on my feet?

We share cheese, milk, Reddi-wip, and even scrambled eggs just before the sun comes through the dining room windows and settles on the back wall of the kitchen.

Bruce always has a pair of sticks in the back pocket of his pants. Often, he takes them out when we are having our early-morning snack. I sit across from him at the table, watching. He takes the dish towel and folds it once, twice into a rectangle, and lays it on the table. *Tap, tap. Rata tat tat. Tap, Tap. Rata tat tat tat.* The quiet thumping and the shadows of the sticks on the wall make my eyes heavy. I curl into the seat of the chair.

"Hey, buddy. We better get to our beds before the sun does. Sweet dreams."

Grandma loves to feed Bruce. She cooks and bakes all of his favorites.

He teases that she is going to make him fat. "Gram, no one likes a fat horn blower. Come on let's have a little waltz around the kitchen, then I can have one more piece of your apple pie."

Grandma and I are delighted that Bruce has come home.

*****

I remember that I love my brother. I remember that he took me to Miss Mary's preschool in his old black jalopy and would pick me up and take me home for milk tea and cookies. I remember that he serenaded me with "Somewhere over the Rainbow." I remember him saving *my* day at his wedding. I remember twirling around with him on the lawn by his barracks when we celebrated my sixth birthday at Fort Ord. I remember.

I don't remember this man, this musician, this cool cat. This stranger. He looks familiar. He remembers the same stories I do. But his time away and my growing up have created an empty space between us. We want to pull closer. We are struggling to find common ground: me at fourteen, him at twenty-nine. I want to have a brother. I am tired of being an only child.

Judy is over the moon for my brother. She treats him like a rock star.

"I can't believe you have a brother that's a musician. So cool. So cool. He's dreamy. Do you think he will be famous? Maybe I could take guitar from him. My dad bought me one for Christmas, I can play a few chords."

Judy has changed her route home from school so she can stop by my house every afternoon; that's when Bruce practices in the garage. It's at least a mile out of her way and in the opposite direction; she insists the walk is good for her. She likes to watch Bruce play and compose. She sits and peers at him from our back steps. "Oh, he's so talented. I love the way he writes the inky black notes on the heavy manila score sheets. Dreamy…" She'd stay there forever if Mom didn't shoo her away when she gets home from work. Judy watches the garage like she is watching television. Creepy.

"Judy, he's almost thirty." I try to reason with her; she is embarrassing me and my brother, and Mom is getting tired of finding her on our steps every afternoon.

"I know I can't help it. He is so cool. I wish I could see him perform."

"That's ridiculous. How would you get into a bar?"

"There are ways. I'd ask your neighbor across the street, Alice, she'd know. She's eighteen, and I hear she's been places you'd never guess."

This nonsense lasts for about two weeks. Mom tells Judy, "You can't come over to our house unless I'm here to supervise. So weekday afternoons are out. I have to work. You are welcome on Saturday if I'm here, and if it is okay with your mom. Have her give me a call."

Bruce is relieved. Me too. Judy stops speaking to me.

"What's with Judy?" Lucille asks.

"She's mad about my brother. Literally. She has a crush on him. My mom says her fawning over him is inappropriate. Mom told her she couldn't come over anymore unless her mom and mine agree. I think Bruce should have a vote too. Pretty sure it would be no."

"That's weird. Judy can be so weird. I think she's boy crazy. She is in love with anything with pants, that's what my mom says. Poor Bruce. Hope Judy gets over it soon."

"Me too."

My brother is charming, handsome, and at loose ends. That's what my mom calls it, loose ends. I think life is more than he bargained for. With Dad and Pam gone, he has no buffer.

Mom and I aren't sure which loss has affected him most, Dad or Pam. He seems drained of his usually infallible optimism. His initial whir of activity and plans for success are fading. He loses focus on his music endeavors. He chain-smokes two to three packs a day. He moves from just beer to whiskey. Mom buys food one meal at a time so he can't empty our refrigerator and cupboards before daily meals are made. He is demanding, arguing with Mom that she should buy his cigs and liquor. He loses the few gigs he had. He stops his handyman jobs. He's sullen, that's what Mom calls it. We are careful not to make him angry; everything makes him angry. He brings women home for overnights. He thinks nothing of sneaking them in and then having them stay for breakfast. Grandma is mortified; she serves his guests reluctantly, giving them the silent treatment with their coffee and toast. Mom locks the phones with a gadget which renders the dial motionless. Police knock on our door at eleven at night, demanding Bruce's whereabouts so they can serve him a warrant for (a million) unpaid parking tickets. When she confronts him, he says he sold the car so what's the big deal. He won't understand that the tickets and his responsibility don't disappear because the car does. Mom gives him chance after chance to "get his act together." He promises to change but doesn't. Mom tries to get him to talk to Dr. Zell, he refuses. She suggests our minister. That suggestion makes him stomp out of the lanai to the garage. Scotch with a beer chaser in hand.

Pushed to her limits, Mom changes the locks on the doors, packs his suitcase and duffel with what he hasn't hocked, and puts them on the curb in front of our house. She calls him a cab and gives him two months' rent for an apartment she has found for him in North Hollywood.

"Bruce, I have Kathy to raise. Woman of the night and police banging on our door aren't the right way to do it. I love you, but I can't have this going on in front of Kathy, and certainly not in front of Grandma."

Grandma, Jet, and I watch from the dining room window. We are shocked. Who is Mom anyway?

He leaves quietly. "I get it, Mom, I do."

Mom cries late at night when she thinks I'm asleep. So does Grandma.

I'm numb. I want to love my brother. I hate him for what he's done to Mom. I want the brother of my memories, not this cool cat. Not this scary cat.

*****

Wow, hey, buddy, what's going on. Don't leave. We cool cats need to stick together. What about our nightly hunts?

Guess I'll just go find Buster to hang with. Boring.

*****

Drill team moves from intricate marching patterns performed on the football field to quick-paced dance routines confined to the gym's center court. The original team of sixty girls has been reduced to twenty-four; these girls comprise the spring team. SGH moves from football to basketball.

I am on the spring team. I can't believe my luck. The chances of making this elite group are slim; you are up against incumbent juniors and seniors. I don't even know how I had the courage to try out. The routine is tricky, and instead of performing in groups of four, you perform individually. The judges take an entire weekend to decide who's in and who's out. I couldn't believe it when I saw my name on the list.

The spring team practices first period; this practice is in lieu of a traditional gym class. In my case, in lieu of soccer. (Thank God! I hate shin guards, so dorky.) From drill practice I go to chemistry then to history. I love history because it's followed by lunch, and because we have a new teacher from Los Angeles, Mrs. Black. She is part of an exchange program. We can't tell if she is Negro or Indian (from India not Native American) or a mix of some sort. Her skin is deep brown, but her features are Anglo. Lucille is emphatic that she is a Negro. She claims her mom heard the principal telling the PTA president that she was Negro.

Mrs. Black treats us like adults. She is very different from our other teachers. When she talks to us, she looks us in the eye. If we ask why, she asks us why not. She is the only Negro on our campus, student or teacher. Having a Negro on campus or even close enough to touch is a novelty. We spend hours discussing her looks and her last name. We wonder if she has made up her name to make a point about the current movement to use the word *black* instead of Negro. We should just ask her. No one has the courage.

We have a cluster of Mexicans who hang out on the shaded side of the cafeteria. They aren't in any of my classes. Well, that's not true, several of the girls have been in home ec with me. The boys all smoke and carry cigarettes rolled up in the sleeves of their white T-shirts. Some of the girls smoke too, but not like the guys. They all keep to themselves. In the halls when they pass, they always look down. I've tried smiling and saying hi to them, but there is never a response. Even Olivia a friend from grade school won't say hi anymore. She used to come to play at my house; she has wonderful stories about Mexico and her grandparents. Her mom showed us how to keep our hair shiny by wrapping it in a towel with boiled onions. It worked, but pretty smelly. Olivia and I loved playing dolls and drawing. The majority of the Mexicans live across Del Mar Boulevard in a small well-kept neighborhood the adults call the barrio. Some of the kids call the Mexican kids *beaners*. Judy explains to me in her most superior voice that *beaner* comes from the fact that their diet consists mainly of beans. I'm not sure I get it; I think that's a stupid thing to call anyone.

We have a handful of Asian students, mostly Japanese. They are the top students in all our classes. They participate in student government and all the academic clubs. My friend Vivian is Japanese; we were Girl Scouts together, and now she is in my Y Club. She has younger twin sisters and a baby brother. I love her brother. He's just one-year-old, and he looks like a doll my mom and dad brought me from San Francisco's Chinatown. His black hair is stick straight and pokes out all over his head. It looks like a shiny black halo. I told my mom when I have kids, I'm going to have a little boy that looks just like him. She gave me the funniest look and said, "Well, we'll see about that." Vivian and her sisters go to Japanese school every Saturday. When we have Y Club activities on Saturday, she can't attend, so we try to do our service projects on Sunday. Vivian is the smartest person I know. If I ever have a little girl, I think I will name her Vivian. She also lives across Del Mar toward the city of Monterey Park. Her dad is a gardener; her grandparents owned a farm near San Jose before the family moved here.

It's the Friday before next week's Thanksgiving break, November 22, 1963. We are thirty minutes into history and the horrors of Donner Pass. Lucille is explaining in a low whisper how her family is going to make it to Mexico and back during the break so they can spend Thanksgiving with her cousins. "Yes, they celebrate Thanksgiving." She hisses at me. "They're from here."

The classroom phone rings. Mrs. Black goes to the side wall and lifts the heavy black receiver. Mrs. Black turns white. Literally. We watch her replace the receiver in its cradle. She turns and faces us. "Okay I want you all to move to the auditorium. Take your books. No chatting. Don't stop at your lockers. The principal has an announcement to make." We respond with silent obedience.

Lucille and I gather our things. Mrs. Black's demeanor is detached. We walk down the outside hallway and filter in with other students as they exit their classrooms. We move across senior court toward the school auditorium which stands center campus. No senior stops us; there is no resistance to this underclassmen transgression. It's like we are all sleepwalking, and it's not even lunchtime. Lucille and I are gripping one another's hands. I want to go home. I want my mother.

What? What just happened? I replay the principal's words in my head.

"At 10:30 a.m., Central time, our president, John F. Kennedy, was shot in Texas during a motorcade. He was taken to a local hospital and has been pronounced dead. I have decided to end the school day. Please return to your own homes. Let the school nurse know if there is no parent at home. She will contact a PTA member to make sure you have a safe place to go. We will contact your parents this evening regarding Monday's schedule."

What? My mind is stuck. I am grasping for comprehension, but it is out of my reach. Tears are rolling down Lucille's face; her hand trembles in mine or mine in hers.

Students disperse from the auditorium. In twos and threes, they radiate out from the school toward their homes. No one stops to make plans or stuff books in lockers. Tonight's game is forgotten. We move with purpose like ants headed to the safety of their nest.

Mrs. Black is directing students out of the back gate; the gate Lucille and I use. As we pass, she reaches out to us. Like Lucille, her cheeks are streaked with tears. She enfolds us in her arms. "It's alright, girls, we will be alright. Go straight home." Lucille begins to sob. Mrs. Black shares her tissues. I find my voice and beg Mrs. Black to come with us. "Thank you, but I need to stay and help clear the campus. My husband is on his way."

"Lucille, do you think the Russians will drop the A-bomb?"

"I don't know. How can our president be dead? What happens now? Johnson is next in line. Right? How will he be made president? Oh my god, what will happen to us?"

"I don't know. I wonder if my mom and grandmother know. Let's hurry. Maybe the news will tell us something."

"Your mom's home, right? She hasn't gone to work yet?"

"I'm sure she's home. Here's your street, shall I walk you to your house?"

"No, I'm okay. Call me tonight if I don't call you first. I wonder if Jeanne is in her bomb shelter."

My mother and grandmother are camped in front of the television. The sound is turned up so Grandma can hear. Mom gives me a hug; I sit next to her on the couch.

"Mom, what does this mean? What will happen to us, to our country? Do you think we will go to war?"

"I don't know, I just don't know."

For three days we live in front of the television. The black-and-white images of the grieving family and nation sapping the color from our blithe existence on Bilton Way.

A suffocating gray-black mist holds us in disbelief through Thanksgiving. The neighborhood is hushed; no one talks above a whisper, or maybe it's our ears that refuse to hear.

On December 2, 1963, I go back to school. Mom goes to work, and we celebrate Grandma's eighty-eighth birthday (DOB 12/1/1875). Grandma lets Jet lick the frosting off the candles. Grandma's wish: *better days.*

The nightly news changes from grief to asking why, how, and what next. The seniors go back to harassing anyone who trespasses on their court, and my history class has a new substitute.

*****

What's wrong with my girls? I can't get their attention. They seem fascinated with the TV. My box needs cleaning, and I'm hungry.

I been meowing at the back door, and no one pays attention. I'm going to have to resort to clawing the corner of the couch. Don't think I won't, my claws are sharp from the plum tree.

Here comes Dottie. I knew my claws in the knotty brown fabric would get her attention.

"Oh, poor kitty, so sorry. We've neglected you. Our best guy. Our best kitty. Here, let me make things right."

Well, it's about time. I push my weight against her legs. I hear the can opener whir. I pass in and out of her legs. I am careful not to trip her as she finds a clean bowl. I ratchet up my purring. I can be very loud and rumbly. (Contrary to sage opinion, purring is not just a reflex; it's the way we cats vocalize love. Scientists don't know everything. Certainly not about cats.)

I love Dottie.

*****

It's junior year. I get my driver's license, but it takes two tries. Mom says I can drive her car when she's not using it. She's only working three days a week now, so some days I can drive to school. Wait till I tell my friends.

"How *bitchen* is that!" Lucille is over the moon. She drives her dad's old Studebaker but has to share it with her older sister.

"Oh God, don't say that word in front of my mom. I'll never get the car."

"Oh, I wouldn't, my mom doesn't like it either. What prudes. Everyone is using it."

"Except for you and me."

I am a candy striper at the local hospital/convalescent home. I'm thinking of becoming a nurse. Mom was almost a nurse, but Dad came along. She had to return all her uniforms and books. In her day, you couldn't train to be a nurse if you were married. Lucky for me, she chose Dad. I wear an orange- and white-striped cotton jumper over a white blouse. My grandmother washes, starches, and irons the jumper each week. I look very professional. I make beds (with perfect square corners), read books to kids, and bring the magazine cart around for the adults. I help keep track of Mr. Jones who wanders the halls and sometimes gets into other peoples' beds, one woman in particular. I'm embarrassed. He's ninety-five, I think he must be a little crazy. When he's not in the wrong bed, he's a sweetheart.

I am doing well in all my classes except French. I beg Mom to let me switch to Spanish. I am sure I can make up the two-year basic college requirement if I start now and go to summer school. But Mom's like a dog with a bone on this subject. She insists I take French. Grandma's father was French Canadian. "One more year won't hurt you, Kathy, then we can chat together." Mom knows all of twenty words in French which she has already taught me. But she has a dream of cultivating her French heritage. She doesn't understand that my French teacher, Mrs. Kunkel, hates me.

Mrs. Kunkel has hated me for almost three years. She enjoys embarrassing me. Like the time I was asking Larry to show me where we were in our textbook. She pointed her boney little finger at us and accused us of being too cozy (in French of course); or the time I misspelled a verb and she yelled, "Mon Dieu, Mon Dieu." You would have thought I knocked down the Eiffel Tower.

We are beginning to talk about college at school and at home. And finally I am sort of interested in boys, rather they seem interested in me.

I have memorized the grid that the California university system gives outlining the units, grades, and subjects required for admission. Mom insists we consider the local state Christian universities: Azusa Pacific, Biola, Pepperdine, etc. It's a church thing. The youth group takes the juniors and seniors each year on a Christian university tour. Mom and I are still at odds about church, especially the youth group (which I distain.) I have decided it's easier just to acquiesce (my new favorite SAT word) and go on the tour than to irritate Mom. She rarely gets irritated, she's so even-tempered unlike me. She's emphatic about so few things. I owe it to her to participate. I know in the end she will send me where I want to go. I have decided on being a physical therapist. That leaves me just one choice, UCLA (the University of California at Los Angeles). I meet all the requirements including extracurricular, and my grades are just shy of straight As. (I hate Madame Kunkel. Hate. Hate. Hate.)

Boys. I think something may be wrong with me. I don't see what my friends see in them. I don't know what all the fuss is about.

Lucille is boy crazy now, just like Judy.

Last summer Mom took Grandma, me, and Lucille to Huntington Beach for two weeks. Mom rented a two-bedroom apartment just a block from the ocean. She wanted to take Jet, but the owners of the apartment were insistent—no pets.

During our stay, Lucille invited a family friend to join us for a day. He's the crush of her life. She talks about him nonstop; they've known each other since they were toddlers. Both our Moms say okay to the visit.

Lucille's plan is to have her crush all to herself. He is bringing a friend for me. They were going sailboarding; the boy and I are to stay on the beach. This will be my first blind date. Her crush rearranges her plans. I end up with him in the middle of Newport Bay on his sailboard. We float around in the sun for three hours. Lucille and his friend are left on the beach.

I thought Lucille might go home then and there and never speak to me again. She stayed, tightlipped.

I have to admit her crush is dreamy: blue eyes, blonde, tan, very surfer-like. He makes my stomach flutter and my checks blush. All we do is talk and listen to his transistor radio. He's eighteen, I'm fifteen. He asks if he can call me when we get home. "Yes, I'd like that." I didn't tell Lucille that part.

Lucille calls her mother and tells her what happened. The crush and I are forbidden to see or talk to each other.

My mother thinks the entire incident is absurd. "Absurd, really absurd." Even Grandma is miffed. Lucille isn't engaged to the boy, is she?"

I didn't know what to think or feel. "Boys are a lot of trouble."

He calls me one evening.

"I wish it were different, Kathy. Don't tell anyone I called. Wish things were different. Don't forget our song, 'Wonderful Summer.'" (1963, Robin Ward)

"I won't." I can't. Every time I hear it on the radio warmth, swells from my stomach to my throat and causes a grin. So stupid, wonderfully stupid.

Days later I realized this was my first breakup.

Lucille and I aren't the way we were. There's an empty space between. My second breakup.

Judy is into college boys. She takes extra courses at LA State in the evenings to strengthen her college entrance chances. She sets me up with my second blind date. I try to get out of it, but she claims it's already a done deal. I don't know what to wear or say. We go to a coffeehouse somewhere near Pasadena, the Icehouse. I should be excited; it's the place everyone wants to go. The couples are holding hands huddled over candlelit tables. Judy and her date follow suit. I'm not. I won't. I wish each second, minute, hour would pass at the speed of light. If I could I would push the hands of all the clocks around and around. Ticktock, ticktock. The night drags, I'm a drag. Finally, the ride home. I stiffen anticipating the kiss. No way out. It's awful. I'm awful.

Judy calls in the morning, "The guys want to do it again next weekend. Okay?"

"No."

"What is this boy thing," I worry to Mom. "What is wrong with me?"

"Nothing is wrong with you. You just aren't ready. Give yourself some time. Relax. There's really no hurry. And you don't have to like every boy you date. Be picky, it's okay."

"But girls only talk about boys and dating, dating and boys. I have nothing to add, it's getting embarrassing."

I'm told by a football player in my science class that one of his teammates wants to take me to the junior prom. Surprisingly, I'm flattered and even anticipate his call. But no call is received.

Lucille explains, "You, dummy, you were supposed to let his friend know you'd say yes when he asked."

"Oh my god, this is all too much. I don't get it. I'm doomed."

So, no prom. I'm relieved that I won't have to deal with any after-prom nonsense, especially the inevitable silence at the front door; but I just may have missed my only chance to go to prom, a prom, any prom. Shit.

Judy is no help. She is absorbed with her now-steady college boy, whom she has no intention of even mentioning the prom to.

"How juvenile," she says to me on the phone. "Seriously, why would anyone want to go to prom? We are too cool for that. Cheer up. You've gone out with a college guy, and you are only a junior, that beats going to the prom any day."

*****

Each night when the lights go out and my girls settle into their beds, I make my rounds.

I check my bowls in the laundry room, hopeful for an unexpected leftover. Sometimes there are chunks of cheese or pieces of bologna or a dab of tuna salad. I love a surprise.

I pad through the lanai and make a stop at my box. I pay close attention to the moon as it shines through the floor-to-ceiling windows. I like the shades of blue it casts on the floor. I can see the spider respin its web in the corner of the outside doorjamb. So careful every night to reconstruct the previous pattern. Each night she's busy at her task unless it rains. I admire her tenacity.

I double-check to see if Bruce has come back, I wish he would come back.

I pad down the hall to Dottie's and Kathy's room. They are usually asleep by the time I come to check on them. I'm careful not to wake them. I titter on each bedside table and lean close to feel their breaths go in and out. I pick my way from table to table, bed to bed avoiding reading and water glasses, Kleenex boxes, and dog-eared magazines. Watching them makes me purr. I would like to rub my head against their cheeks and receive a loving push away. When I'm satisfied they are deep in dreams, I leap onto the rag rug, avoiding the wood floor. My paws make a thud on the wood; I don't want that.

I pounce through the bedroom door from rag rug to hall runner. I dart around the floor heater, careful not to let it hiss at me. I scurry down the hall to Grandma's room. She snores, me too. I sleep in her rocker. It's a stuffed one. She leaves my blanket in the seat of the rocker; it's made from someone's old flannel PJs. It's worn thin from washing. There are flowers on it, faded, I don't mind. I like the smell; BENGAY, lavender water and me from last night. Grandma folds it in a perfect square and smooths the wrinkles flat. I put my paws on the seat edge and jump to my spot; this makes the chair give a gentle rock, pleasing. A few kneads at the blanket edges. Then I curl myself in a ball; once, twice until I'm just center seat. Settled, my tail slides under my chin.

"Night, cat."

"Murp."

*****

I am accepted at UCLA. As congratulations, Mom takes me to Hawaii for fourteen days. It's the summer between my junior and senior year. Betty takes care of Jet. Grandma goes to my aunt's and uncle's. It's just me and Mom.

Mom lets me have a bikini, a Hawaiian print of olive and cream. It has a matching sarong that she insists I wear to and from the beach. We buy muumuus and grass hats; we sun on black and green sand beaches. We go to the obligatory luau, eat pig and poi, and listen to Don Ho sing "Tiny Bubbles."

There is a nightly parade of tourists on the board/cement walks separating the giant hotels from the sand and ocean. It's a steady flow of families, couples, off-duty military with a handful of locals, and the ever-present pearl-in-the-shell vendor. Incomprehensible conversations swirl around our ears. Faces are relaxed, the humidity makes them glow. I am shocked when we cross paths with families from my high school community. "Small world." Mom notes. Indeed.

We visit all the islands; we see all the beauty: volcano to jungle to foamy ocean waves. We are immersed in loveliness. Aloha.

More than once we are stopped by Asian sailors. They politely ask my mother if she will take their picture with me. Mom consents. I blush. Snap. Snap.

"Well, that's embarrassing. Suppose it's the bikini?"

"The bikini and your blonde hair and blue eyes."

"Really?"

"Yes, really. You are very pretty. Don't get a big head. Beauty is only skin-deep."

"Oh, Mom."

Senior year.

Home from Hawaii, blonde hair now green from my last dip in, surprise, an over-chlorinated pool, I'm face-to-face with leaving home and growing up. I don't want to talk about it. I prefer to focus on the deluge of senior activities.

Our Y Club has an awards banquet. I've been treasurer, secretary, and president. Pins and sweater patches are handed out. We will continue to meet and wear our sweaters each Monday for the remainder of the year. I'm very proud of my patch full of pins.

No longer on drill team, I help to welcome the new members. We seniors teach the newbies the basic routines. Another banquet is held; we honor our coaches and the girls that have been our team captains. New junior captains are chosen. Applause, tears, melancholy.

I drive my mom's huge white Impala to our senior luncheon in Los Angeles. Judy, Lucille, Vivian, and Susan go with me. We look like we are ready for high tea with the queen of England. I wear a blue stripe seersucker suit, wide brim white hat set so it shades my right eye, white pumps with three-inch heels, and carry a white leather clutch. I do an excellent job of driving the freeway into LA. Mom has shown me how to use the Thomas Guide. Things get tricky once we exit and get on the surface streets. I drive down a one-way street the wrong way. Drivers pull to the sides of the road as the girls scream and point me to the Statler Hilton garage.

(I remember the Statler Hilton. My father took me there for lunch when I was five. He worked in Los Angeles on Olive. Mom dressed me in a gray wool suit, and I wore white gloves and black Mary Janes. Mom said Dad and I made quite the pair. We visited his office first; everyone got up from their desks to say hi. Carl was there, he gave me a pen. When we got to the hotel, we went in an elevator. I was scared especially when the doors shut. Daddy held me tight, his hands atop my shoulders. When the doors opened, we were faced by a sea of gray carpet and a room full of round tables covered with white tablecloths. Someone led us to a table. Dad said, "We have reservations." The waiter unfolded the napkin at my place and put it on my lap. I was the only little girl there. Dad was so proud, I was too. We beamed at one another. He had steak, and I had a club sandwich. I didn't spill, and neither did he.)

"Guys don't tell my mom I went the wrong way on that street. She'll never let me have the car again. I am so sorry. Don't tell your moms either."

Promises made.

The rest of the luncheon was a blur; the trip home was without incident, thank God.

There are dances, the prom (I don't go, although a family friend offers to take me), senior pictures, club and activity pictures, last brown bag lunch in senior court, and locker clean out. More blur.

Reality hits when the registration packet from UCLA arrives. Mom has to fill it out for me. I'm no help. Unable to sit still at the dining room table, unable to focus on the forms that spew from the envelope, I sit frozen, my pen midair.

"Kathy, go sit on the couch. I'll do it. Sit right there. Watch the Loretta Young Show. She always has a good movie. I'll call you if I have a question. We need to get this done and in the mail." Mom looks worried.

Cap and gown, royal blue. Graduation. All-night party. Breakfast at Norm's. Yearbook signing. Blur. Blur. Blur.

The summer sun is bright, hot, comforting. Just like last summer and the summer before. Jet's the same—crazy over mice, cheese, and buttied toast (just like Willie). But the rust on his face is being replaced by little white speckles. He is looking very distinguished. Mom's the same—working, gardening, and leading various church activities. Grandma's the same—sewing, baking, and rocking. I'm not. In two months, I'm going to college, living on campus, without Mom, Grandma, Jet, Lucille, or Judy.

I am scared to death.

*****

Lots of "hurry up we gotta go, we'll be late" going on around here.

Kathy's has new shoes; they make her taller than Dottie and Grandma but less steady.

Lots of things in bags. Lots of bags. I love the bags. I dart in and out and pounce on them when they slide off the bed. Leap and grab, fly down the hall and back. Up on the bed, twirl and down on floor, oops caught in a handle. Yikes, trapped. I shake. I can't get loose. Let me go. It won't, it's going to win. Spin, spin, spin. Hiss.

"What is going on? Calm down. I'm right here. I got you. You just have to relax, kitty, and I'll get you untangled. There you go, all better. Leave the bags alone. Go. Mom and Grandma are making toasted cheese sandwiches in the kitchen, bet they have saved a piece of cheese for you."

*****

UniCamp, UCLA's orientation for incoming students. An indoctrination to campus life.

Mom is convinced this will relieve all my worries. We read the welcome pamphlet. This program will introduce me to the campus, the library system, the student union, book buying/selling, class scheduling, and life in the dorm.

We pack the car for my three-day stay. I have anticipated all the activities listed with just the right outfit; having the right outfit always makes me feel better. We get off the freeway at Westwood Boulevard. I read the directions to Mom as we navigate our way past the veterans cemetery and up the Eucalyptus-lined streets toward the dorms.

"That's fraternity row." I point to the left. One huge house after the other labeled with Greek letters. There is no activity; the street is quiet, waiting for pledge week.

Mom follows the UniCamp guides; they direct us into the parking lot below Sproul, the dorm I will be staying in for camp. We join a line of cars inching their way toward a group of official-looking young people (students I'm guessing). They direct her to stop and motion her to stay in the car. They wave me out. Stunned, I gather my purse and orientation materials, hand Mom the map, and open my door. A young man wearing a UCLA polo shirt smiles. He grabs my suitcase out of the trunk and slams it shut. He directs my mom to follow the exit signs. She looks startled. She drives out of the lot.

"Wait." She's gone.

The boy in the polo shirt escorts me and my bag to a shuttle.

"Welcome to UCLA UniCamp. Have a great weekend. Go Bruins!"

"Hi I'm Hilary. I'm from Mount Washington, near Silver Lake, east of downtown LA. My dad's an architect, mom's a designer. I have two brothers, both younger. I'm Jewish, not practicing, what are you? This is my bed, that's yours. I took this side of the room, but happy to switch if you like this side better. I'm so excited, this will be great fun. There's a *welcome* in the floor lounge in fifteen minutes. Let's be early, okay? Here's your orientation packet. It's huge, right? Well, I guess we have a lot to know."

"Hi I'm Kathy."

I couldn't ask for a better roommate. Hilary is everything I'm not, confident, worldly, and a UCLA connoisseur. Her dad and mom are alumni. She's going to be a fine arts major, minor in English lit. Her first teddy bear was a Bruin. In less than an hour after her arrival, she has met everyone on our floor, knows their names and their backgrounds. She enthusiastically introduces me to her new friends and happily takes me under her wing. I'm relieved, happy to let this human whirlwind introduce me to college life. Go Hilary!

Back home, orientation behind me: I laugh with Mom about how she deposited me in the parking lot and didn't even look back, wonderful Hilary, a boy I met from Alhambra High who took me to the orientation dance, and how she was right, I am now ready for college.

"Do you think you and Hilary will stay in touch? This boy, is he nice? Were you able to get the classes you want?" Mom is full of questions.

"Yes, Hilary has invited me to spend a weekend at her home as soon as we get settled in our classes. She's decided to commute, since she lives so close. She wants to take me to the Los Angeles Music Center; her family has season tickets. The boy, Tom, is nice, quiet. He knows a lot of the kids from my church group. He wants to take me to the first football game. I need to stop by the athletic office and pick up my student ticket. We are hoping to sit in the card section. All the students want to sit there. I can't wait. Oh gosh, the class thing was a mess. I'm so glad the camp counselors helped us. I was able to get everything I needed. After I move into my dorm, I'll go get my books. I know where the lecture halls are. Hilary and I scoped that out."

*****

She moved out. Emptied the closet, took her pillow, and left. Gone. So it's me and Grandma and Dottie. I'm considering sleeping on Kathy's bed, Dottie looks sad. I'll start in the rocker and move to Kathy's bed just before dawn. That's my plan.

The day she left, we sat on the back steps. She dripped on me, big wet soft tears. I didn't know what to do. I leaned in and put a paw on her arm. More tears.

"I'll be back, sweet Jet. Make sure Mom's okay. I love you so much, you are the best kitty ever."

Big black boy cats don't cry. They can't, it's physically impossible. We can, however, mope. I like to curl into a ball and shut my eyes tight, usually under a bush or bed. Cheese is the only cure. Grandma and Dottie are clear on that.

*****

CHAPTER 4

Goldfish

Description: Orange. White. Silver. Gold. Sometimes spots: black, brown, or white. Eyes, black. Mouths open and shut: O, -, O, -, O. Fins, scales, waving tails. Best feature, they keep swimming until they don't.

I move into Dykstra. It's the first dorm on your way up the hill where the majority of on-campus students live. Dykstra is followed by Rieber, Sproul, and Hedrick. Each dorm overlooks the student athletic field. This field is where all intramural sports are played. To get to campus you have to walk alongside of the field on an asphalt path. I'm disappointed. I thought the school's football team practiced there. I'm told that field is somewhere else, hidden away from the general student population. My walk to and from campus won't be as scenic as I'd planned.

I am taking my final load up to my room. Tuesday, Mom and I made a trip together. We took her Impala. The humongous trunk was crammed with books, toiletries, a typewriter, a desk lamp, and linen just in case Mom felt the dorm's issue wasn't up to snuff. This trip I'm on my own. I've parked my Mustang in the dorm's loading zone. I'm trying to hurry before I get a parking ticket.

"Nice car '64?" a random male student asks.

"Yes."

For my seventeenth birthday, family friends worked with Mom to give me this miracle midnight blue Mustang. The card included "from Dad." The paint has metallic chips; it looks like a bottomless pool of navy blue water in the moonlight. I love it. There are bucket seats and an automatic stick shift between them like a race car. The car was rescued from the junk yard and refurbished by these family friends. They own a car restoration company. They called Mom.

"Dorothy, we are sure Ralph would approve. We want to do this for Kathy in his memory. We guarantee it will be reliable and very cool."

Mom gave her okay. Her only qualm was that it was a Ford. My dad was a Chrysler man.

Every time I turn the key, I think of my dad. I see the tilt of his head, his moustache just so and wonder if magical paper flowers wait to surprise me.

"You're lucky girl. Need a boyfriend?"

"No, thanks." I laugh and shut the trunk.

My wardrobe is excessive. This is my fourth trip to my room today. Grandma has been sewing all summer, me too. I have a ridiculous amount of back-to-school clothes.

"Good god, how many trips is that? I've never seen so many clothes. You know they aren't going to fit in that cubby of a closest they give you." Comments a floor mate. "You know you don't have to wear a new outfit every day. This is college not an audition for *Seventeen*."

She's right. There isn't room. I push and shove. No luck, I return the excess to the trunk of my car. I will take the extras home next weekend. I move the car to the student lot and walk back to the dorm. I hope my roommate shows up tonight. We start classes Monday, and I have just two days to get the lowdown from her. My move-in packet says she's a senior. I am sure she can fill in any blanks that Hilary and I have missed.

My roommate arrives in time for dinner. She is a nursing student and a Rhodes scholar. She plays the saxophone and is in a jazz quartet. Her name is Darlene.

Darlene is knowledgeable about everything UCLA. She's serious, seems older than her years. She's from San Pedro. Her family is. They seem very religious and very strict. Her dad is a longshore fisherman. He is away for months at a time. Her mom calls her almost nightly. I am pretty sure Darlene is an only child.

Darlene is engaged to Burt; he plays in the UCLA marching band, a tuba. I think they met over their music. I get the feeling that her mom would prefer Burt to be Portuguese.

I share a little about my brother, his musical genius, his trumpet, and love of jazz.

Darlene asks if I play an instrument.

I explain that my dad would not let me play an instrument. He was afraid, like my brother, I would choose art over a practical life endeavor. He was proud of Bruce's talent, but worried about how he was going to make a living. Dad was unmovable on this subject despite my mom's wish that I play the piano.

Darlene takes me under her tutelage. She cautions me on what I should worry about: all parties and all boys. She says not to worry about grades, there won't be As until sophomore year; professors that ramble, buy the lecture notes; and being homesick, everyone is first quarter.

I tell Darlene about Jet.

Darlene has never had a pet.

"I miss my cat. I was thinking maybe it would be fun to have a couple of goldfish. They would make the room homier."

"Fish as pets?"

"Why not?"

"I'm a fisherman's daughter. I might eat them." She almost giggles.

I table the fish idea.

*****

It's very quiet here. Grandma can't see or hear, so when Dottie is at work she just rocks in her chair; no stereo, no TV, no giggles on the phone. Even when Dottie's home, there is more quiet than not. There are just us three at the kitchen table. I miss Ralph, Missy, Grandpa, Bruce, and Kathy.

"Buster, do you ever get lonely?" We are sunning on my front porch. He rolls over on his back, closes his eyes, and sticks his front paws straight up and his back legs open and out, not a pretty sight. All you can see is his enormous white gut. I wait, no answer. Guess he's asleep. I move down the steps to the rose bush, hoping to find a grasshopper or a moth to bat.

Buster rolls to his side and squints into the setting sun. "I don't know lonely, my people are always where they are supposed to be. Sister is always where they are, and I'm always nearby. So I'm no help. I don't know what I'd feel if one of them was somewhere else. But I do know that Kathy will be back. Dottie told Betty she will be back. Cheer up."

"Hope you're right. Everyone who left before hasn't come back."

"Don't worry, come and lay in the sun with me."

*****

The dorm is divided into wings, male and female. Separate elevators. Shared cafeteria, front desk, and downstairs lounge.

Our floor is a collection of girls morphing from child to adult. They are giddy to thoughtful. There are ponytails to daring blonde Afros. Everyone is an advocate; whether for a husband, social reform, an A in biology, or a Friday night date. It's loud, busy, and dramatic.

Darlene is one of a few seniors on the floor. Most floor mates are freshman and sophomores. The majority of junior and senior women have been filtered out to sororities or apartments. I'm dumbfounded by the large number that have married or are cohabitating with boyfriends. I try to wrap my mind around girls my age setting up housekeeping, starting families. It's crazy to me. I'm a fish out of water.

When there isn't a football game at the LA Coliseum or a Friday night date, I couldn't talk my way out of, I go home. I study better at home: so quiet there, Grandma makes my bed, and you can still see the faded image of the shuffleboard court on the driveway.

Things are where they belong, where they should be. More importantly Mom's there.

I have Psych 101 in Franz Hall Mondays, Wednesdays, and Fridays at 11:00 a.m. The lecture arena holds close to three hundred students. It's like being in a theatre, but the stage is on the ground level, it's not elevated; no one looks up at the professor. We surround him in sweeping semicircles. We enter the room at the top, and he enters at the bottom. P-101 is a basic elective for many of the medical science majors; physical therapy falls into this category. Darlene tells me it is an easy four units. "Take it, get it out of the way." I sit in the middle of the middle tier of seats. I take the first empty seat I see. I'm never in the same seat twice, but I'm always in the middle. I like these large classes; they let me be just another face in the crowd. I like being anonymous. From my vantage point, the professor looks like a miniature in a dollhouse. I have to wear my glasses. Everyone seems self-propelled, interested only in their notebook and the blackboard down below. No one ever sits in the same seat. It's impossible to recognize students from one lecture to the next. Except for the boy who sits in front of me. He is always in front of me. Strange, a coincidence, I guess.

I am carrying sixteen units: four subjects—math, English, biology, and psychology. It's only between psychology and English on Wednesdays that I have time to have lunch in the student union. I like to sit in the lounge next to the student bowling alley; it's small and out of the way, perfect for people watching.

"Excuse me. I think we have the same P-101 lecture in Franz Hall. I wonder if I could buy you a cup of coffee," says the boy who always sits in front of me.

I focus on this boy who has sat down next to me on a wood cube posing as an end table. He's cute, very preppy. I like preppy. He's wearing a light gray collared shirt, tucked in. He has on dark gray slacks, not jeans. His dark black hair is parted on the side, thick and shiny. He is on the shorter side, but not too short for my five-foot two-inch height. His eyes are dark almonds; his skin warm brown. My instinct is to say no, but...

"I recognize you; you sit in front of me. I don't drink coffee."

"What do you drink?"

"Tea."

"Well then, how about tea?"

"Okay."

"I'm Jim. Do you like sugar?"

I nod yes. "I'm Kathy."

"Okay, I'll be right back. Promise you won't run off."

"Promise."

Jim and I are a couple. One coffee, one tea. Simple. Meant to be?

Being a couple has many advantages in addition to the obvious first love experience. I don't have to be polite in managing my possible dates anymore. It's a simple response, "Oh thanks, but I have a boyfriend." No one's feelings are hurt, and I don't end up with a groper or moron.

Using the line *I have a boyfriend*, I stop the daily calls from the boy that I met at orientation. The one that took me to the Gary Beban post-football bash in Topanga Canyon. The boy who expected me to jump into the sleeping bag he conveniently had in his trunk. "What do you think we were coming up here to do? Just party?" he asked, blurry eyed. I wanted to tell him I certainly didn't have a slumber party in mind, especially a surprise one. I just wanted to meet Gary, our famous quarterback. I wasn't here to get blotto and lose my virginity.

Jim lives in Hendrik. He's a sophomore, majoring in physics. He's romantic, well-mannered, considerate, and attentive. We are well matched in our naivete.

Jim's paying for his college. He works part-time in his dorm's cafeteria and some nights in a hospital library. He has a student loan. I'm funded by Mom and a Social Security benefit given because of my father's death. I'd rather have a student loan.

In the dorms you can move your meal plans between dining halls. Jim and I eat dinner together two or three times a week. I pack lunch every morning in my cafeteria: tuna sandwiches, chocolate chip cookies, and chips. We meet at Royce Hall most days and sit on the concrete walls framed by brick arches and share the brown bag fare. We study together most nights in libraries throughout the campus; when not in a library we study in Dykstra or Hedrick's lounges. Of course, we don't always study, but we are always together.

*****

Humm. What's all the fuss? I'm under the kitchen table watching feet go back and forth from stove to refrigerator to sink to dining room.

Kathy's been home for three days. Dottie says it's her Christmas break. Dottie and Grandma have been cooking and cleaning and whirring around. I am trying to keep my paws tucked close under my chin to avoid getting them stepped on. I've been in and out of Kathy's suitcase. I've sniffed her books and papers, and I've managed to sleep with her the last two nights. She still loves me best, she told me so.

The fuss Dottie explains to no one in particular as she gives the pot roast another poke is that tonight we are going to meet the *boy*.

The boy? What does that mean? I'm feeling queasy. I wish I had time to consult Buster. When the *boy* comes, I may just stay under the table. I may just watch, find out what the boy is up to. See how he smells.

*****

The doorbell rings.

"Hi, come on in."

Jim's at the door with a large potted poinsettia. The plant has three fire engine red blooms. Mom and Grandma are at my heels. I back them up a bit so Jim can get from the entrance hall to the living room.

"Mom, Grandma, this is Jim, Jim Whang.

"Hi, so happy to meet you. Mrs. Locke, this is for you and Grandma Patrick and Kathy of course. Merry Christmas."

"Oh, how nice, Jim. Poinsettias are a family favorite. Come, sit."

Grandma sits next to Jim on the couch. She can't stop smiling at him. Mom places the poinsettia on the fireplace and heads to the kitchen for drinks and another poke at the pot roast. I sit on the other side of Jim. I spot Jet peeking at us from the doorway of the den. He is almost invisible with his dark fur framed by the shadows of the room behind him.

"Jim, this is Jet. Jet, this is Jim. Come over here, Jet. Jim knows all about you. Come sweet kitty. Jim meet the best kitty ever."

*****

Jim reaches out to me and waits for me to smell his hand. He smells good like my Ralph, Grandpa, and Bruce. He's very young like Kathy. He's dark to her light, like I was black to Missy's gray. I let him rub my head. I can't resist leaping into his lap. He doesn't seem to mind. He continues to stroke between my ears.

Grandma says, "Get down, silly old cat, you'll make him all furry."

Kathy says, "Oh, thank goodness, Jim and I were worried you might not like him."

I purr and settle in.

*****

Dinner's a success. Pot roast and Yorkshire pudding. Mom knew what she was doing when she picked that menu. Jim's never had Yorkshire pudding. It's Grandma's specialty. He tells her it's a new favorite. More smiles. He offers to help with the dishes, but Mom assures him that is her and Grandma's forte. She ushers Grandma to the kitchen and Jim and I into the living room.

"Thanks for coming and for the poinsettias, love the three blooms. Very clever. You were a hit."

"Your mom is great and so is Grandma. I'll be back tomorrow." He walks to the kitchen door and thanks Mom for dinner and waves at Grandma. He will spend the night at his Uncle Caesar's house in

Monterey Park, just minutes away. Tomorrow we will repeat similar introductions with his family.

I watch him walk across the porch to his car. He blows me a kiss. Buster is in the middle of his driveway, watching.

"Hey, big guy. You must be Buster. I'll see you tomorrow."

I go to the kitchen. I give Mom a hug.

"What do you think, Mom?"

"He's cute and really well-mannered. I like him." A bemused look crosses her face.

"Mom, what is it?"

"Oh, I was just thinking about Vivian's little brother."

Until that moment I hadn't thought about Jim being Asian. I hadn't put much thought into our relationship, just heart. It became so obvious in a split second; I was beguiled by this beautiful Asian boy. I bend over and scoop Jet into my arms. "Oh, Jet, I just might get my childhood wish after all."

Jim and I are loyal to UCLA sports. After the Christmas break, we move from football to basketball. We stand in long lines of students waiting for the Pauley ticket office to open each Wednesday. The tickets are free for the student section, but its first come, first served. Basketball tickets are harder to snag than those for football. Pauley is large for a college basketball arena but can't compete with the amount of seating in the coliseum. Because of the team's win record and a chance to see the famous John Wooden, basketball tickets are always at a premium. Jim and I are always in line at 6:00 a.m., and we manage to attend most home games.

Lew Alcindor lives in my dorm. The top floor of the men's wing has been renovated to house the basketball team. I hear the beds are extralong, and their lounge is equipped with pinball machines and televisions; that's the gossip. I think they must eat up there too. I never see the team in our dining hall.

The other day I stood next to Lew. I didn't know it at the time. We both were at the front desk. The night clerk was handing him his mail. I came to his waist and felt the need to duck as he stretched his yards-long arm out to receive his mail. I glanced down to make sure he was attached to the ground and not somehow floating above me.

I had to catch my breath. He was grounded alright by enormous, gigantic, humongous feet. Darlene was waiting for me by the elevator. She caught my eye; she was waving hysterically, not at all like Darlene. Once I had my mail, I moved toward her wondering what's wrong. I'm careful to back away from the front desk to avoid any possible backward motion from the unbelievably big feet.

"That's Lew Alcindor!" Darlene gasps. "You were standing right next to him. Right next to him. We have to call the guys."

I called Jim as soon as Darlene hung up with Burt.

"Of all the times not to be with you. I can't believe your luck. Did he say anything to you? I can't believe you didn't recognize him."

"Well, I couldn't see his face, just his belt buckle. And I'm sure he had no idea there was anyone next to him. After all, if he looked my way, he wouldn't have seen me." I laugh at the thought. "He was asking for his mail. He's soft-spoken, very polite, not at all like some of those guys on the team. I wish I had said hello."

*****

Jim and Kathy are at our house almost every weekend. Dottie and Grandma love having him to cook for. They alternate between old favorites and new recipes from Dottie's church group. The group, Grandma says, is about to publish their own cookbook. It's important to test all the recipes.

I never thought laying in the sun would be so satisfying. There's a perfect spot on the front porch where the sun seeps onto the cement and remains for hours. I let its warmth soak deep into my fur, I can feel it in my bones. Lovely. I still like to paw bugs, especially roly-polies, until they move. I just don't want to chase them more than a foot or two. I'd rather sleep in Grandma's rocker than stay out at night waiting for mice. Besides, Betty keeps Buster and Sister inside at night now, so it's lonely outside in the dark. Betty and Dottie agree we are all too old to be on the hunt. I think she's right.

Dottie has been cooking me special food. She picks me up and looks me in the eyes. "Kitty, are you okay? What's going on with our crazy old black cat? You've been awfully quiet lately. It's not like you to be so nappy."

I purr in response. I love that she picks me up and holds me like a baby. I don't mind being on my back in her arms. She rubs the tip of my chin, making my eyes squint shut. I tilt my head forward, forcing her hand to find the back of my ears. She scratches gently. It's good to be me.

*****

"Jim, I've decided to commute next year."

"That makes sense, I know you miss your mom. I think we will do better with our studies if we aren't together all the time. Mark and I have decided to get an apartment. We like rooming together, but we are both sick of the dorm. It will be cheaper and less restrictive. I have a lot of night labs scheduled this fall, and I hope to get more hours at the library. It will be great not to be constantly checking in and out. Are you worried about the commute, all that time you'll be on the road?"

"I am hoping I can get all my classes and labs set on an MWF schedule. Since I changed my major to psychology, I shouldn't have so many physical labs. They always seem to fall on Tuesdays and Thursdays. An MWF plan should be doable. That way I only have to drive three days a week."

(UCLA eliminated the physical therapy major in my freshman year. They argued it was not an academic endeavor, too practical for a university. My counselor suggested psychology as an alternative. He said all my units, past and present, would transfer, and I could still graduate in four years. Also, the psychology major will meet all requirements in most postgrad physical therapy programs if I still want to pursue that career.)

Sophomore year starts as planned.

Jim and Mark's apartment is small and sparse, almost as small as their dorm room. Mark's mom cleans and stocks it with food. The boys move in and immediately begin a wall of empty beer cans. They hope to complete the wall by fall finals. Mark tries to convince me its pop art. Any privacy Jim and I might have hoped for in an apartment versus a dorm is swallowed up by numerous friends looking for the same thing. Mark and Jim can't say no; couples are always crashing at the apartment. Mark spends a lot of time at the library, and Jim and I are more comfortable going out than staying in.

I get my perfect MWF schedule. But the commute is tougher than I imagined. I creep along with the other drivers, bumper-to-bumper in and out of Westwood. What I thought would be an easy forty-minute drive is a torturous hour. I park off campus and get to class via a shuttle. It often runs late, me too.

My beautiful midnight blue Mustang gulps gas at the rate of five dollars a week. I get holiday and summer work at Robinson's department store in Pasadena. That will help with the gas and books. I will be in the toy department for Christmas.

I love being home, I feel pampered and safe. But I miss the inclusiveness of campus life. I miss Jim.

Again, I change my mind, I am moving back to campus winter quarter.

My biggest hurdle returning to dorm life will be getting a room in the middle of the school year. My mother has a connection through church who might be able to help. She says he operates a mission on skid row and does youth work with both USC and UCLA. He may be able to help with housing.

Grandma and I kid Mom about him; he seems bigger than life to me. I can see him preaching in a tent somewhere or on a box in Pershing Square. He came to the house once, brought flowers. Mom was gracious but firm, "Thanks, but we need to stick to church work."

Mom cautions. "Ladies, we are running out of time. It won't hurt to see if he can help. It's that or stay on your aunt's couch. She would love it, but would you?"

"Okay, but I'm not going to any youth groups or volunteer at any soup kitchens. Room or no room."

I get a room in Mira Hershey. I like to think I was just lucky.

The dorm is really old. I'm pretty sure it's the first woman's dorm at the university. It sits right across the street from sorority row. (That's where Jim's sister lives. She's a senior.) Parking is limited. Jim will park my car at his apartment. He has an assigned space; the car will be safer there than trying to park it on Hilgard.

The quarter starts on Monday. I only have the weekend to get settled and meet my roommate. All I know about her is that she is a sophomore too.

Jim helps me move in. My room is on the third floor, and there are no elevators in Hershey. We climb the stairs four times piling boxes in the hall outside my room.

I knock on my door, no answer. It's locked, so Jim hands me the key. The room is typical: two beds, two desks, and two closets. Matched sets on either side of the room. One-half of the room is definitely lived in—the bed's unmade, clothes protrude from the closet, and the desk is piled with books, candy wrappers, and a container of paint brushes. My side is empty except for a stack of bedding on the mattress.

There's a knock. We turn from emptying boxes to find the RA (resident assistant) in the doorway.

"Hey, Kathy, sorry your roommate isn't here to welcome you. Off to a rally or something. She's an art student, should be back Sunday night."

"Okay, thanks." I relax. "I guess I can wait one more day."

"Kathy, I stacked the empty boxes in the hallway. We can take them down when we leave. Your clothes are in the closet, the ones I could squeeze in. You will have to find a place for the rest."

"Thanks."

"Let's go out to dinner, skip the cafeteria one more day. Hamburger Hamlet okay?"

"As long as I get custard Lulu for dessert."

"Of course."

Midnight. Sunday.

The door flies open, light floods the twelve-by-twenty-foot space. A girl's silhouette is framed in the doorjamb.

"Oh my god, I forgot you'd be here. Sorry, hope I didn't scare you."

My sleep-fogged brain focuses. Before I can respond, she pushes her luggage into the room. "Go back to sleep. We'll talk tomorrow."

I roll over, happy to accommodate.

Alice is my height, short. She's full-figured, I'm not. She has saucer-sized eyes as black as her ebony skin. Her hair is slicked back, very vogue. My blonde hair and blue eyes are reminiscent of the little Dutch Boy that put his finger in the dam. She is a dynamo of words and movement. Her persona is huge, brilliant. I'm reserved, cautious. I feel faded next to her.

Alice informs me that our floor is all Black. I will be the first and only white resident. I feel like an intruder.

I can't wait for Jim to meet her. She can't wait to meet him. She seems fascinated that Jim is part Korean and part Caucasian. She is even more curious about his parents when she learns that his mom is from the South and his dad is full Korean born in Hawaii.

Alice has four close friends on the floor; they join her each Tuesday morning to hang out in the room before going to class. Alice invites me to join them. I am hesitant.

I am nervous, five black girls and me. How is that going to work? Alice is convinced it will. She insists. I yield.

The girls stick to Alice's side of the room. They sit shoulder to shoulder perched on the edge of her bed. They drink coffee, I drink tea. Two of them are majoring in psychology like me. One is a math major. One's undeclared. Alice is the only artist. Tuesday after Tuesday, we sit and stare. Alice works hard to initiate conversation.

The ice breaks. They accuse me of hating all blacks. I accuse them of hating all whites. They want to touch my hair, and I want to touch theirs. We compare our palms and the bottoms of our feet; they are the same pink flesh. They are incredulous when they learn my boyfriend is part Korean. They want to know if my family's pissed, and they don't believe me when I say no. We creep toward common ground. We discover we've all been in a church choir; love Sidney Poitier, Paul Newman, and Johnny Mathis; hate the USC Trojans, prefer pizza to burgers; and can't stand this all-women dorm.

We get down to what matters. One Tuesday it's makeup. We share mascara, eyebrow pencil, eye shadow, lipstick, and blush.

Alice is rolling in silent laughter across her bed. Tears are streaming down her cheeks. Her bare feet beat the air.

My biggest nemesis is carefully applying my dark circle cover-up under her eyes in perfect pink half-moons.

"What's the problem, Alice?"

Alice sits up and convulses once more into silent laughter. The rest of us are widemouthed.

Donna looks at us and then in the mirror.

"Well, guess this just isn't my color."

We relax into our Tuesdays. It's close to finals; sometimes we study, mostly we talk.

It's Thursday, and I'm returning from a study group on campus. Surprise, the girls are in our room. Their faces seem tight, their postures worried.

"What's up?"

Alice fills me in. "Dr. King's been killed. I hear there may be trouble on campus tonight. I think you should go home or to your aunt's."

"Why should I go?"

"Because I want you to be safe."

Jim takes me to my aunt's; it's closer than the drive to San Gabriel. I give Alice her phone number. Alice will call me when I can return.

As a precaution, campus is locked down. My aunt and I watch the TV to see if UCLA makes the evening news. There are some black and white images of picketers along Bruinwalk. I call my mom to let her know where I am and what's going on.

There is no violence, a few demonstrators with placards.

Alice calls. I return the next day.

*****

This will be the third time Dottie pulls me out of the ivy. This will be the third time she takes me to the doctor. I don't want to go. I don't want another shot. I just want to go to sleep and dream about the mice Buster and I've caught, the butter I've licked and the cheese I've stolen, Grandma's rocker and her steady snoring at night, how it feels to sit on Dottie's lap when we have a fire in the fireplace, how

I used to leap into Kathy's arms and hear her delighted giggles, the snotty old blue jay in the plum tree, Bruce and our midnight chats, sweet Missy, Ralph, and Grandpa's pipe smoke floating across the backyard.

*****

"Kathy, your mom called. She sounded funny, kind of upset. You better call her back."

"Hi, Mom. Alice said you called. Anything wrong?"

"Hi, sweetie. I have some sad news, and I thought you should know before you and Jim come for the weekend."

There's a tightness in Mom's voice, I'm sure there are tears behind it. I know it's about Jet; he keeps hiding in the ivy, and Mom keeps taking him to the vet.

"It's Jet, I had to put him to sleep. The vet said he could give him another shot, and that would perk him up again, but he didn't think that was really fair. He felt Jet was anxious to go."

I hear Mom put her hand over the receiver; there are muffled sobs. I take the time to wipe the tears from my cheeks.

"Poor old kitty. Mom, you did the right thing. He's with Missy and Daddy now. He'll be so happy, really he will."

"I know. But I'll miss him so. He was the best."

For Easter, Jim gives me two goldfish in a large bowl with rocks and a small castle in the bottom.

"This is for your room. I've already named them, hope that's okay."

"Oh, what a kind gift. I love it. Alice will too. I bet I know their names."

"You do?"

"Jim and Kathy."

"Forever, I love you."

Jim and I are in Hershey's downstairs lounge. We have been arguing about who's doing what over the summer. He's applied for a physics internship out of state, and I'm not looking forward to going back to Robinson's. The idea of him abandoning me for an entire summer is unbearable. I try to see it from his point of view. If he gets chosen it will look great on a résumé. He would be sure to get picked up by one of the aerospace companies or an engineering firm. I don't want to be selfish, but my emotions are.

"Are you trying to tell me something? Don't you want to be with me?"

Jim is shocked at my reaction. So am I.

"Yes, of course I do. I love you, you know that. I want to marry you. But I also want to take advantage of this opportunity. It could make a big difference for both of us.

Jim doesn't get the internship, but he does get a motorcycle. Now he can come and go from school, work, my house, his house, anywhere with complete autonomy. No more relying on me or begging the car from his sister. I'm scared for his safety, but the smile on his face as he pries off his helmet in my driveway is priceless. I don't even mind the smell of gasoline that wafts around him for hours after.

Junior year I'm back in the dorm, this time Sproul. Alice is immersed in art projects and demonstrations. She hasn't decided where to live yet; she moves from one friend's apartment to the next. She is gravitating toward rooming with some other art students in Santa Monica. My roommate is my old high school friend Judy. She has transferred to UCLA from Pasadena Junior College.

The goldfish have made it through the summer. Judy and I put their bowl on the bookshelf between our desks. They are in front of the large window that traverses the width of the dorm room. We are on the sixth floor; our drapes are open most of the time. We have no fear of Peeping Toms because we are fields away from other dorms. It's like living in a tree house. If you squat down and look through the bowl, eye level with the fish, they seem to be swimming in the blue sky with clouds for rocks and black birds and sea gulls for fellow sea creatures. The fish express their delight by mouthing a million Os as they swirl around in their glass globe.

Judy tries to convince me the fish need to be renamed. She thinks the names *Jim* and *Kathy* are lame, sappy.

"Their names are so childish. So uninspired."

"Their names are not negotiable."

"But Chaucer and Macbeth would be so cool, so cerebral." Judy is an English lit major.

"No, Judy."

*****

"Okay that does it, why don't they ask what we would like to be called. Do they think we are stupid or something? Geez, we get no respect."

"Well, we are just fish; no hands, no legs, and barely a neuron for a brain."

"Point taken."

"What do you think our names should be?"

"I think Nugget for me and OJ for you. Keep it straightforward, you are orange and I'm gold. Why would we want human names, names that have no connection to what or who we are?"

"And you think Nugget and OJ do? If your theory is correct, then it should just be Gold and Orange."

Nugget takes a deep dive and hides under the bridge of the castle.

"I see you under there," mouths OJ. "Better come out, it's dinnertime, and you don't want to sulk too long and end up with soggy shrimp flakes. That's the worst."

*****

Jim has two more quarters before he graduates. Neither of us is sure what happens next; we know we should have a plan, but we don't. We focus on fall finals and the Christmas holiday; our immediate future more manageable than our great unknown.

I go home to study for finals and to make my bridesmaid dress for Darlene and Burt's wedding, which will follow days after Christmas. I like the quiet and the minimal distractions of Grandma's cooking and Mom's Christmas preparations.

WHO ME

I arrive home on Friday in time for dinner. It's just me and Grandma. Mom's at choir practice. Grandma has made my favorite, turkey soup. She made broth from our Thanksgiving turkey. She froze a batch for my return. She's a whiz in the kitchen despite arthritis in her hands, deafness, and minimal eyesight.

"Hi, Kath. I made your favorite."

"It smells wonderful." We sit down at the kitchen table.

There is a strange tang to the soup. The taste isn't bad, just different. I think it must be an overdose of her secret ingredient, dill.

"This is great, Grandma, thanks. Have you been cooking all day?"

"No, not really. I just had to add a few vegetables and seasoning. The rest was easy."

Mom arrives as we are finishing. Grandma goes to the stove and ladles a third bowl. Mom hangs her coat, gives us both a hug, and joins us at the table.

Mom and I begin to catch up. The chatter makes Grandma antsy; she pats my hand and moves to the sink.

"I'll just get at the dishes."

Mom winks. Grandma is always more comfortable at the sink.

Mom whispers to me, "The soup tastes a bit off. The carrots look odd. Do they look odd to you?"

We examine the carrots. Mom smiles and leans in.

"They aren't carrots they are oranges, Mandarin oranges. She must have mixed them up. She used oranges, not carrots."

"Mom, don't tell her. She'll be upset. She worked so hard. I thought maybe she couldn't see how much dill she was using."

"It's our secret. Glad Jim didn't come tonight."

"He would have been fine. You know he loves anything Grandma or you cook. He would have thought Mandarin oranges very gourmet. I hear he has a date with her to learn how to make Yorkshire pudding."

Jim will spend Christmas Eve with his family. I will meet him at his house Christmas Day afternoon. This will satisfy each of our family's traditions.

Jim and I have a special date planned the weekend after finals. That will be our Christmas, Jim and Kathy's. A movie and Mexican food. Jim's borrowing his uncle's car so he won't arrive smelling of gasoline. I plan to finish the bridesmaid dress for Darlene's wedding by Wednesday and then I'm going to indulge myself and work on my holiday outfit—a cranberry velvet double-breasted jacket and a gray-black tweed miniskirt. I've had the material for weeks; I can't wait to tackle it.

Jim is extravagant with me. He never lets me pay for anything; he always opens my door (car or otherwise) and never lets me follow him through one. I don't know how to reciprocate. Last Christmas he gave me a beautiful watch, so delicate and sophisticated. For his gift I made him a poster of his favorite pool player, Willie Mosconi. For my birthday, he gave me a pearl promise ring: two pearls set in a white gold infinity setting. I made him cutout cookies, heart-shaped, frosted in red for his birthday. They were from a secret family recipe but in no way comparable to a promise ring. I can't compete. I suggest that we don't do Christmas gifts this year.

"We need to save our money. Fees are going up next quarter."

"Okay, I get it. I promise no gifts this Christmas."

Our date is perfect. It is close to 1:00 a.m. when we tiptoe up the drive to the back stairs. Mom has left the door unlocked. Jim has asked if he can have a cup of tea before heading back to his uncle's.

I put on the tea kettle, and we sit down at the kitchen table.

"I miss Jet. Remember how he would join us. I think he worried that I kept his girl out too late. Wish he were here."

Jim has removed his sports jacket and is holding a brown paper bag, the size that you pack your lunch in. He slides it toward me.

"What's this? Jim, no gifts remember."

"Open it and take a look."

I unfold the top and peer in. Dumbfounded I pull out a black velvet box. I know, I should know what's going on, but I don't. I really don't.

"Here let me help." He flips open the box. "Will you marry me?"

It's a diamond ring. I can't put my thoughts into words or get my words to my mouth. Surprise has silenced me. I hear myself squawk...yes.

The tea kettle whistles. I turn the stove off. No tea is made.

"I should wake up mom, she should be the first to know."

"She knows. I asked her for her consent weeks ago."

Our winter break is no longer just about finals, Christmas, being a first-time bridesmaid or making next quarter's spending money at Robinson's. It's about the rest of my life.

I wake Mom once Jim leaves. I'm giddy. She's not.

"Mom, aren't you excited for me? Jim said you gave your consent."

"Of course. It's just..."

"It's just what, Mom?"

"You didn't tell me. When Jim asked me, I was caught off guard. You've always tell me everything."

"Mom, I had no idea. I mean I knew we would be married at some point, but I didn't know when. We never discussed when. I thought you knew that."

"Oh, I did, of course I did. I love Jim. I guess I'm just not ready to lose you. I'm always losing someone. I just thought we had more time."

The morning brings a deluge of engagement chaos. Mom's been calling friends and family since seven. Grandma is already planning what she refers to a trousseau. I'm holding a cup of tea in my hands trying to digest the past twelve hours. Mom hands me a plate of pancakes and wraps me in her arms.

"Syrup? Sorry I was so gloomy last night. Hurry eat, then run next door and show Betty that ring and give her the good news. She'll be over the moon."

Jim and I drive to his home in Dominguez Hills to make our announcement. His younger sisters are enthusiastic, begging to be flower girls; his dad is all smiles, his face washed with pride. His older sister is reticent, she has a date she is getting ready for. His mom seems pleased, insisting on trying on my ring and wanting to know the price and the carat count.

Jim's Korean grandmother is the one who makes me feel this is my family. She holds my hand between her soft-skinned, warm palms. An enormous smile pushes her cheeks up into her eyes making them appear like half-moons. Her skin is mocha in color, lined with life, and vaguely dusted with freckles. Jim's dad says, "From working in the pineapple fields." She is four foot ten inches, a widow, confident in English as a second language, committed to her Savior Lord Jesus, and a resident of East LA living in bungalow Jim's grandfather bought her from his time on the railroad. She asks if I go to church. I tell her I go to Marengo Methodist in Alhambra. She's delighted, explaining she goes to a Korean Methodist church close to her house. She declares, "Jim to be the luckiest boy in the world to have found a good Christian girl." She will teach me to make kimchi.

We make it through finals, Christmas, and Darlene's wedding.

We are married March 23, 1969, at Marengo Methodist. It's the Sunday after winter finals, the eighth anniversary of my father's death and Jim's parents' twenty-fifth wedding anniversary. It's a candlelight ceremony. My brother walks me down the aisle. My mother says, "I do" to the question "Who gives this woman?" Alice, Judy, and Cousin Leslie are my bridesmaids. Mark is Jim's best man.

Our grandmothers pose for the photographer. They both wear blue dresses and have pink roses in their corsages. They smile and hold hands. *Click.*

CHAPTER 5

Tweetie Bird

Description: She is sky blue. A parakeet, not at all like the yellow cartoon character from my childhood which is her namesake. She is quiet and reserved, shy. Her wings and tail are tipped in gray. Her head much bluer than the rest of her. Her chest is almost white, her beak cream and her three-toed feet the color of hay. Her pinpoint black eyes see more than their size. She nods off to sleep like a baby, eyes hooded then shut, when the dreams come you can hardly tell where they've gone. She can chirp and rarely squawks. Her best quality: she's there for us.

We return from our north, up-the-coast honeymoon in time for spring quarter. I will finish my junior year as a married woman, and my husband will graduate in June.

Jim and I set up housekeeping. Our apartment is in the back of a huge complex on Sunset Boulevard across the freeway from campus. Our address is Brentwood.

We start with a rawhide couch and recliner from my mom's den; a king-size bed, a wedding gift from Jim's parents; a drop leaf table with two chairs from the Goodwill on Santa Monica Boulevard; a coffee and end table from our landlord's basement; and lamps and silverware from gifted books of Blue Chip Stamps. Our kitchen and bath are completed with wedding and shower gifts. Jim's dad brings light bulbs and toilet paper. A friend loans us a stereo; we buy a television and set it on my mother's hope chest.

The goldfish are with us. We put their bowl on the kitchen windowsill. Their dorm view of blue sky is replaced by a cement wall. We do our best to make them comfortable in their new surroundings; we hang strings of clear green plastic beads in the window—our intent is to create the look of seaweed.

*****

"How about that ride over here?"
"How about this window? How about these beads?"
"Do you think Jim and Kathy are hippies?"
"No, they have too much stuff, and they aren't barefoot."

*****

Finances are tight. Jim continues his part-time work, and when not in class, he is at the UCLA placement center searching for a full-time job, one that will "please" start right after his June graduation. My mom is covering my living and school expenses until I graduate. We save gas by taking the bus to and from campus. We promise each other no "fun" shopping until Jim has a job. No new clothes for me and no albums for Jim. We discover that we both like to cook, we eat in.

On Saturdays, we spend the day in pajamas under afghans and quilts we've managed to acquire from our used-to-be homes. We sit on the floor, backs against the couch, and share warm chocolate chip cookies and fresh lemonade. We watch black-and-white cowboy or military movies. Anything with John Wayne is a favorite.

Sundays we head to one mom or the other. We count on leftovers of fried chicken or pot roast to get us through the beginning of the week. On Wednesdays, we grocery shop in a local store in Brentwood Village. The irony does not escape us that we are poor college students shopping in a gourmet market in the heart of westside wealth. But the store is close, and we can walk. We don't buy cheese or wine, so our weekly bill isn't much more than from a typical grocery store.

Jim gets a job with Lockheed at their Palmdale facility. He will be an administrative assistant in the engineering division. The Palmdale plant is developing the L-1011, a jumbo passenger jet. Because of his degree, he will be a salaried employee. He starts one week after graduation. In celebration, we dress up and go to a rooftop restaurant with an ocean view in Santa Monica. We buy our fish a bigger bowl and add a pirate ship. Jim treats me to yards of material and two new dress patterns, and we add the Beatles "Yellow Submarine" to his growing album collection.

A real job, a real paycheck, and man takes his first step on the moon (July 20, 1969). We are married five months almost to the day that Armstrong puts his feet on moonrock and struggles to plant the US flag. I'm twenty and Jim's twenty-one. I start my senior year in October.

I'm not sure I trust the fuzzy marshmallow man on the TV. How can this be true, man, a real man on the moon. I'm overwhelmed with the thought of flying through space, of seeing the earth as a ping-pong ball, of having my beloved Mr. Moon exposed as a rock pile. Does Armstrong care that his one step will change childhood forever? That we won't look up anymore and see that silvery face looking down on us, keeping watch until the light of dawn. Jim's watching me. I refocus on the television and push my reverie toward the thought of how pleased my dad would be about this man on the moon.

"Jim, can you imagine doing something like that?"

"Not really, it's surreal, right? I can't wait to hear what they will be saying at work. One of our divisions designed and built the solid propellant launch escape motor and the pitch-control motor for the Apollo. I'm sure the office will be celebrating."

"Whoa. I have no idea what you are talking about, but it sounds impressive."

"I'm amazed at all the people that are involved in the space effort. It's not just California or Florida, it's people all over the States."

Jim drives the Mustang to work. I take the bus to campus.

The bus runs along Sunset Boulevard toward the north edge of UCLA and then dips down Veteran and enters the campus at the medical center. Each morning we work our way to the center of campus where the bus deposits us at the entrance to the student store. I love this ride. We pass various-sized mansions, rolling lawns, a Rolls-Royce or two, meandering tree-lined driveways, gardeners unloading mowers from trucks, the gated side streets of Bellaire, the student lot where Jim and I parked until the campus police threatened to call my mother, and the dorms where we fell in love.

"I am sure my ride is not as scenic as yours," Jim laughs. "At least I don't think so. Can't see much in the dark."

Jim's drive is two hours, going and coming.

Each morning he drives north through the San Fernando Valley. It's dark as he passes the abandoned oil pumps east of Newhall and the horse ranches of Acton. He winds through the bristly, scrub-dotted hills to the flats of Palmdale. The monolith hangar that houses the L-1011 rises from the desert floor, the only thing visible as Jim passes the cutoff to Pear Blossom. He enters the facility's parking lot, already host to a hundred cars belonging to the third shift. He wanders the lanes, finds a spot, shows his badge to the security guard, and grabs a coffee from the food truck.

At night he reverses his arrival, swapping coffee for a bean burrito.

We fall into a pattern: work, study, eat, sleep, repeat. Saturdays and Sundays, we hide under the covers until we are forced out by family or friends.

During our first summer, Jim takes me on a tour of the L-1011 facility. The hangar is enormous, the plane's gigantic but dwarfed inside its aerospace barn. The orange, blue, and white coveralled laborers are mixed with the white shirts and neckties of the engineers. Jim beams as several men greet him. I'm introduced. We visit the smaller cubed building in front of the hangar; this is where Jim's office is. There are miles and miles of runways; they seem to melt into the desert floor.

My tour includes Palmdale. It's flat, desolate with no oasis in sight. There are scattered apartment buildings and houses that remind me of those on a military base. The main street is sparse: a diner, hardware store, feed and grain, and a midsized we've-got-it-all store of some sort. Jim says the engineers that live here are referred to as desert cowboys. They live on the outskirts of town on sand-dunned, tumbleweed ranches. Some have horses, most have dune buggies. Their properties boast boulders and yuccas. Yuccas I recall are those biblical trees that provide no shade.

"Jim, this is awful, we can't live here. You don't want to live here, do you?"

"No. My boss says most employees, those without sand in their veins, live fifty miles south in Newhall or in one of its neighboring suburban developments. It's still a long drive, but better than living here. That's where we will look."

"Jim, come here."

"Oh no, we must have left the window open. I'll take care of it."

"It's my fault I forgot to check last night."

I can't stop the tears. They splash into the toilet, just like our dead fish. Jim is somber as he shuts the lid. He delivers a short eulogy.

"Bye guys. We're sorry. Jim and Kathy rest in peace."

Flush.

I turn twenty-one in October right after my last fall quarter starts. I've only had screwdrivers mixed in dorm coffee cups, a couple of gulps of beer at the football games, and a few sips of Mom's Tom Collins at parties. I'm not virtuous; I just don't like the taste of alcohol. Jim decides I should find out what my capacity is. Now that I'm twenty-one, I should know my limits.

The Saturday after my birthday, Jim sets us up at our Goodwill table with a bottle of bourbon and two shot glasses.

"Okay, let's get serious. We will trade shots until you can't do anymore."

"Okay, what if I last longer than you?"

He laughs. "That will never happen. Never. Ready. Begin."

"Jim, how many is that? I don't feel anything yet. Well, maybe a little sleepy. I don't like the way it burns as it goes down."

Jim looks at me. His smile is less than bright, and he is already flushed pink, an undeniable sign of his Asian heritage.

"That's four."

We continue.

"Okay that's enough. I need something to eat. Jim, Jim, are you okay?"

Jim is slumped over in his chair, right cheek flat on the table. His left hand holds a full shot glass, slanted, ready to spill. I remove it from his hand and move him to the bedroom. He makes no protest as I tuck him into bed.

I giggle. I have a few potato chips and a stale donut. I promise I will never speak to anyone, especially Jim, of my incapacity or is that capacity to drink.

We sleep in. Jim offers to take me to brunch. I opt for pancakes.

Weeks later, Jim receives a letter from the draft board. His number has been called. He is being asked to report.

"Mom, what will we do? Go to Canada? This is unbelievable. My God, Jim can't go to Vietnam. We're just kids, dumb kids. We should have had a plan."

"Kathy, calm down. Worst case you move back in with me. It's Jim we need to worry about. Isn't there a marriage exemption, or something about being the last to carry the surname?"

"I'm not sure, maybe. They are always changing the rules. He used to qualify under the college exemption, but now that he's graduated, that doesn't count. He's going to talk to his dad. His dad will know what we can do. Maybe working for an aerospace company will make a difference."

Jim and I lay awake and second-guess all possibilities. Jim's never considered a military life. He's proud of his dad's service in the Korean War, that he received numerous honors and retired with the rank of captain. We enjoy his dad's privileges on the naval base in Long Beach. Dad lets us take his big old Pontiac with his rank/service sticker on the front bumper. It's magical. The guards snap to attention, salute, and wave us through. Jim carries a family pass which allows us access to the base's theater and commissary; first run movies for twenty-five cents and household goods including food at deep military discounts. This is what we know about military life, the trappings. Going to fight, holding a gun, being apart for longer than a day is beyond our comprehension. Jim is scared to death and so am I.

"What did your dad say? Is there anything we can do?"

"He is talking to the Veterans Administration. He has some contacts there. He is sure they will be able to help."

"Is he okay with you not wanting to go?"

"Yes, he's been to war, he doesn't want that for me."

We wait. Dad comes through with the best possible and surest plan.

Jim gets a medical deferment, he's asthmatic. He had asthma as a child and "fortunately" was treated for an attack after the age of eighteen. We obtain his medical records. Jim meets with the draft board. Three weeks later it's official—he is permanently deferred. We take his dad and mom to dinner. We should do more, but how do you thank someone for saving your life.

June 1970, my last final. I close my blue book, gather my pencils and purse, stand up, and crunch. My glasses have fallen from my lap, I've stepped on them. I bend down and gather the remains. I'm so irritated. I don't have time for this. I'm to meet Jim at 2:00 p.m. in front of the student union. He has taken the day off to take me to Palmdale to test for a typist job with Lockheed. If this works out, we will have two incomes, work in the same building, and share the commute.

I'm not thrilled about being a typist. But it's my only option at this point. My degree is useless without a master's or preferably a PhD in a specific field of psychology. I want to work. I have no desire to go to graduate school. I certainly don't want to sit around waiting for "hubby" to get home. And there's the problem of being a woman—that limits my choices. Men can get most any professional job with a degree in most anything. They start at the bottom of a company's career ladder—become a trainee and they are on the path to success. It's taken me six months of job searching to gasp this phenomenon. This reality is right up there with smashing my glasses, highly irritating.

My typing skills are minimal. I can eke out a term paper on the typewriter, but that's with a whole lot of liquid paper. The idea of taking a timed test and being allowed only three errors sets my stomach churning. Jim's mom comes to my rescue. She is a medical secretary, typing transcripts from surgical procedures. Her typing is excellent. She manages to get instruction books and tests from her personnel department. She explains how typing tests are given and drills me until my skills are almost guaranteed to pass a basic test.

I'm wearing the dress I made for Easter. It's light gray, patterned with large impressionistic pale pink flowers. It makes me feel grown-up. I have white two-inch-heeled pumps on. The color of my nylons is "sun-kissed." I am ready. I am confident.

"Hi, sweetheart, you look great. How was your final? We better get going. Your appointment is at four."

"Jim, I need to throw up. And I smashed my glasses, hope I'm not jinxed."

"Hey, Mom, Kathy passed her test. She's in. She's going to be right across the hall from me supporting the engineers designing the plane's S-duct. They think her math and science background will help her understand the terminology and the equations she'll be typing. She will start at grade 3. She'll have to punch a clock, but she's employed!"

"Thank you so much, Martha. I couldn't have done it without you. We want to take you and Dad to dinner. Yes, again. That's the least we can do."

I start work two weeks after the end of spring quarter, a week before we move. Our new apartment is in Valencia, just across Lyons Avenue from Newhall.

Lockheed packs, moves, and unpacks us. That is part of Jim's deal—relocation. It's an amazing experience. We do nothing. Nothing but watch and point.

Our apartment building is full of young engineers and other aerospace professionals like Jim. Some are employed in Burbank but most work in Palmdale. Between work and the apartment, we become part of a five-couple social consortium. The nucleus is the guys. I'm the only wife employed by Lockheed, two others are teachers, one's a nurse, and one's a housewife. Jim and I are the youngest of the group; we are the only couple without children. Together we celebrate all holidays, birthdays, and births. We barbecue in the summer and ski in the winter. Most Friday nights we try the latest popular restaurant; we favor ones with live entertainment after ten. Saturday nights are saved for dinner parties; we enjoy showing off our cooking skills and wine selections. The guys play poker, we gals shop. We all drink a lot.

Our apartment is two bedrooms and two baths. We have my mom and grandmother over for weekends, and Jim's little sisters spend time with us. We are forced to give the Mustang up; the radiator literally blows up on Jim on his way to work. We buy a new Chevy coup. It's yellow with a black vinyl hardtop and black leather seats.

The only thing that would make our charmed life better would be a pet. We want a cat, but the building doesn't allow four-legged creatures. They okay a bird; we promise we will keep it in its cage.

Jim wants a yellow parakeet. He feels yellow makes perfect sense since I'm hell-bent on naming the bird after my favorite cartoon character—Tweety bird of "I thought I saw a putty cat" fame.

There's a local pet store in downtown Newhall. I'm captivated by a blue parakeet who is perched in between a lime green parakeet on the left and two pale yellow ones on the right. I am sure she is a girl; I am sure she is our bird. I nudge Jim.

"We'll take the blue one. Is it a girl or boy?"

The store clerk checks the invoice clipped to the cage. "It's a girl."

We pick a deluxe cage with a stand. It will be perfect in the corner of our bedroom. The cage has multiple perches and feeders for water and seeds that attach to the sides. We add a hanging ladder and a bell on a red rope. We buy kitty litter for the bottom of the cage; a friend has told us litter works better than gravel and keeps the cage smelling fresh.

Jim wonders if we should have two birds. He worries that Tweetie will be lonely while we are at work. We ask the clerk; he doesn't advise it. He says there is a chance that the two birds would bond with each other and not with us. He also tells us to wait on getting a mirror until Tweetie is familiar with her environment and recognizes us. He gives the same reason about bonding.

"Okay, Tweetie, it will just be us three." Jim steps close to the cage and engages Tweetie in a chat. "You, me, and Kathy. Great times ahead."

*****

The gate across from me opens. We all sidestep left as the hand that gives seeds and water pushes in from the right.

We flutter our wings, greenie squawks.

I try to climb up the side of the cage hoping to crawl over the hand and escape through the gate. Then I'll fly, fly, fly. At least that's my plan. I not sure I can, I never have.

The hand, all warm and squashy, opens and shuts around me. It's not hurtful, but my wings are pinned to my side. Flight plans cancelled.

My cage mates are hanging on the side of the cage away from the door. Toes curled tight around the cage rungs. I can see their nostrils turn bright red from the excitement. I wonder if mine are, how unbecoming.

I'm put in a box; it shuts to make a tented shelter. I hear someone say something about a handle. The space is dark and just big enough for me and my tail to fit. My toes try to grasp the bottom, but just slide instead.

*****

Jim picks up the bird carrier and hands it to me. Tweetie shifts inside. I can feel her slight weight work hard to find its balance.

"Sweet birdie, it's okay. We will go slow. Shhhh, it will be all right." I try to cushion the box by placing my hand under it.

Jim ushers us to the front seat of the car. He levels the box until it is flat in my lap. Again, the weight shifts. I catch my breath and pray we know what we are doing.

The bird stand slips together in three sections. A large ring slides into a clamp at the top of the stand's pole. The cage hangs from an S-hook at the top of the large ring. We move this apparatus toward the bedroom window. Tweetie will be able to see out to the tree-lined parking lot below. She can watch us go to our car or walk to the strip mall across the lot. We attach or hang all the cage accessories. We put in the water and seed cups. Now to get Tweetie in.

*****

I try to turn around, but my tail prevents it. I can hear them talking and fussing. They seem nice. They have been very careful with this box I'm in, and the one called Kathy speaks quietly; her voice is reassuring. There is a stripe of light in the corner of the box. I shuffle toward it, toe by toe I go. I stretch and turn my neck until my right eye can focus on the point of light and I see the scene beyond. They are hanging a cage from a circle that is on top of a pole. The cage is a much smaller version of the one I was in at the store with the other birds. I think that is where I'm going to live.

Tap, Tap.

"Sweet Tweetie, I'm going to put you in your new home." Kathy coos. "I'm going to open this box and pick you up and place you in your new home."

Jim says, "Kathy, I really don't think the bird understands all of that."

"Oh, yes I do, Jim. I do."

The box opens; a hand scoops me up from under my belly. My wings are held down by another hand. Up and over. The hands set me carefully on the bottom of the cage. I know what to do from here. I get a toehold and climb my way up to the first perch, then up to the next, and up one more to perch next to my seed dish. Jim and Kathy coach me, clapping when I reach the top rung.

"That's enough for one day. Kathy, I think we should let her get used to her new home. I'll turn the clock radio on. We can listen for her while we cook dinner. If she seems upset, we'll move the cage into the living room where she can see us."

I'm not scared. The lights are dim and the sounds soothing. It's nice to have a space just for me, my own toys, food, and water. I preen, fluff, and bury my beak deep into the seeds. Yum. I chirp to let them know I'm pleased.

*****

"Oh, listen. Tweetie's talking."

"I wonder how that will be at 5:00 a.m. on Saturday mornings."

"That's why we bought the cage cover. That is why we are going to use it. When a bird is covered, it goes to sleep, it feels safe, and I hear they don't get up until you uncover them."

"We'll see about that." Jim laughs.

The cover works as advertised. Tweetie wakes and sleeps managed by her cage "hat." We often cover her when we have people over; this makes Tweetie less agitated. It's like giving a person a sedative. She is a sweetheart. She likes to travel via finger from room to room; she nestles in the crook of our necks to watch television. We encourage her to fly; she is not interested. Jim thinks it is because her wings are clipped. I think it's because she needs another bird to show her how.

We join a carpool with three other men who live in the building and commute to Palmdale. This means four days a week we each get an extra fifty minutes of snooze time going and reading time coming home. The driver gets to pick the radio station and who rides shotgun. I want to take my turn; I love to drive. But the notion is vetoed. I'm disappointed; I guess they must think women are bad drivers. Jim praises my skills. He is a little irritated that he will be doing double duty.

Often, Jim has a headache or stomachache or… I insist on subbing, it is our car after all. Six months into the carpool, five friends share the drive.

Jim's work assignments are centered around events and schedules involving the rollout and certification of the L-1011. He uses Fortran, a computer language designed for scientific projects to automate, schedule, and track sessions of the plane's testing. (Fortran or FORTRAN is a general purpose and procedural programming language developed in the 1950s by International Business Machines

Corporation or IBM. It was intended for use in scientific and engineering-related applications.) Jim's group also deals with plant operations and "goodwill" between the public and the plant. I am not clear on all that he does; he seems a jack-of-all-trades.

I answer phones and type technical reports for a group of engineers that are responsible for the L-1011's S-duct. (S-duct, a type of jet engine intake duct used in trijet aircraft to improve performance and reduce total empty aircraft weight.) I sit at the head of a room of sixty engineers. I'm the only woman in the room.

The engineer's gray steel desks are in rows of ten split into fives by a wide center aisle. I look directly at the two sections of six-by-five desks. They are intermittently filled with white-shirted, pocket-protected, black-framed spectacled men between the ages of twenty-two and sixty. Our boss sits to my right in a glass office. There is another glass office to my left, the lead engineer's office. Behind me is the coffee station.

At any one time there are two to five men pouring, stirring, or yammering behind me. It's a distraction, but the gossip rivals any women's book club. I keep one ear open; every day is a soap opera.

"Welcome, Kathy. Boy are we glad to have you. It will be a relief to have someone who understands mathematical notation and how it *should* be typed out."

This is a repeated theme by all the engineers who come to my desk. I hope I live up to their expectations.

These men are stressed. They work in shifts. The bay is in constant commotion. Desks are piled with textbooks, pads of yellow paper, calculators, computer punch cards, and rolls of graph paper. They sit huddled over their desks with phones cradled in their necks or with feet planted on the desktop, chair tilted back, eyes to the ceiling waiting for the theoretical light to go on. Their wives call constantly. I patch them through. There is always a crisis: the baby's got a fever, what should we have for dinner, the drain is plugged, can you come home early I have a headache. I try to explain that their engineer is up against a testing deadline or is meeting with the boss. But they gush, "You don't understand. The dog has swallowed the baby's pacifier."

An engineer from the middle of the sea of gray desks approaches me.

"Hi, Kathy, I'm in charge of the coffee station. I take care of the supplies and money. Twenty-five cents a cup, we use the honor system. Now that you are here, I'd like you to be in charge of making the coffee."

"I don't drink coffee.

"Well…"

"What were you doing before I came?"

"I keep a schedule. Each participant takes a week at a time. Brewing, cleaning, stocking."

"That sounds like a great plan. So only the coffee drinkers are responsible for the coffee. Makes sense. If I ever become a coffee drinker, you can put me on that schedule."

"Okay, thanks."

I see my boss watching from his glass cage. He has a silly grin on his face.

I tell my carpool buddies about the coffee proposal. Jim is incredulous.

"Sweetheart, I can't believe you did that. I'm all for it, but wait until the other secretaries hear. Oh boy!"

"Well, I don't drink coffee."

*****

They have hung something on the side of my cage. Looks like a big bubble. I can see that there is water in it. Is it another drinking dish? I don't want to climb in it for a drink. I like the dish I have.

They are looking at me. They are waiting for me to do something.

Look, Tweetie, it's a birdbath. Come on over here and look. They speak in unison. They are so cute with their heads together, coaxing me, all smiles.

I'm frozen on my perch. I've never seen anything like this. What is it that they want me to do?

Kathy swishes her finger in the water. "Here, baby. It's nice and warm."

Jim offers his finger to escort me over.

I bite him.

124

They offer popcorn. I look the other way.
I back up on my perch to the top of my cage.
We repeat this scenario, several times.
They remove the bubble. I watch Kathy take it out of the room.
Again, with the popcorn.
I love popcorn. Jim feeds me a kernel at a time.

*****

Jim is holding a blue textbook. He is waving it at me.

"Kathy, if I can do this, you can. And you will love it. I know you will."

It's the Fortran textbook that Jim used to learn the computer language that supports his systems.

Jim talked to one of his supervisors and the engineering union rep; they agree there isn't any reason why I couldn't move to a technical position if I can meet the job criteria. Lockheed prefers to promote from within, women or men. They agree that learning Fortran coupled with my degree should qualify me for a tech spot.

Fortran is problem solving using prescribed symbols and syntax to render a solution using a computer. I'm lucky, my boss and engineers are supportive. They give me small assignments using the language. They take me to the key punch room where the operators turn my written code into punch cards the computer will read. I'm shown how to submit a "job." When my job is returned, my engineers huddle around my desk to see my results: simple reports, graphs, or mathematical progressions.

I love working for my guys, but I'm not the greatest secretary. I'm known as the girl who owns stock in white-out, liquid paper. The woman who orders supplies says she is going to check to see if it comes by the gallon. I am confident that my programming abilities will surpass my typing skills. Everyone is hopeful.

I watch the plant bulletin board postings for data technician openings. This is the position I'm best qualified for. It will be several grades up for me: more money, more responsibility.

L-1011 testing is nearing its final stages.

One morning our building and the adjacent hangar empties all personnel to the main runway to watch the L-1011 take its first flight.

My guys pace and smoke and run back and forth to check their charts and graphs.

The plane lifts from the tarmac and moves up in slow motion. An audible sigh sweeps over the facility and follows the plane skyward.

The plane is huge. It hangs in the air. Surreal. It seems caught like a hawk as it floats from current to current. Then it grabs the morning air and moves forward. It becomes a speck on the horizon. We suck our breath back in. Some adjust binoculars, most squint. The speck turns and goes from gnat to olive, sparrow to raven, plane to big beautiful jumbo jet. Wheels unfold. It settles toward the ground, wheels kiss the earth, and the plane taxies toward us.

Unabashed mayhem swallows the scene.

Now that the bird flies, testing moves to onboard systems. All plant employees can volunteer to participate in these tests. We board and deboard. We are served pretend beverages and meals. The favorite test is the evacuation drill. This involves the deployable ramps. The ramps that unfurl if the plane crashes or is otherwise disabled.

Everyone but me wants to volunteer to test the ramps. The volunteers board the plane, buckle up, and listen to the instructions given by stewardesses. Together they wait for the alarm, stand, and follow the lighted path to the side doors. They fling themselves, feet first, butt down, onto the ramp. One at a time they bump, slide, and tumble to their feet. Each volunteer receives a cheer from their fellow jumpers and a handshake from the "stews" manning the bottoms of the ramps. An FDA rep records time and "passenger" performance.

Jim becomes an expert ramp tester, sometimes jumping three or four times a day. He tries to get me to join him, but I'm chicken. At last, the escape ramps are FDA certified. I think Jim is disappointed. I'm sure this is an adventure he will not be repeating at least I hope not.

The Palmdale plant goes from L-1011 development to manufacturing. The teams of engineers and testing personnel are reassigned to Lockheed Burbank to support the myriad of follow-up tasks/tests needed for the planes as they roll out of production.

Jim and I are part of the move. We are thankful to have jobs and congratulate ourselves on not having moved to Palmdale. Our apartment in Valencia is just twenty minutes from Burbank. We will be a carpool of two. I transfer as a data reduction technician.

*****

When the sun is up, it is very quiet in my cage. I spend the day preening my feathers, digging through my seeds and singing to no one in particular. Once or twice K and J have forgotten to take my cover off before going to work or on errands. I don't mind, I just snooze until they come swish it off and make amends.

Kathy has moved my cage closer to the window, not too close to get a draught which is not good for me, but close enough that I can see over the treetops and across the roof of the car port. I watch people go in and out of the gate behind the carport. K says they are going to shop. There is a grocery and a hardware store in the strip mall just beyond the gate. Sometimes I watch K and J go through the gate. I squawk, they can't hear me. Sometimes I see them come back, arms full of bags. They most always bring me a treat.

I hear the door unlock and their bags go clunk on the counter. Rustle, Rustle. Rip. Tear.

"Here, Tweetie. See what we found for our best bird, a mullet branch. Let me hang it in your cage."

Kathy opens my cage door and clips the branch to the top with a paperclip. Lovely. I climb up rung by rung to sit on the top of my water dish. With a stretch of my neck, I can nibble the tiny seeds. One by one I crack them open with my beak and extract the tiniest of kernels with my tongue. The thin shells float to the bottom of my cage. Some land in my water. What a wonderful way to spend an afternoon. So much better than in a tub.

"Jim, listen to her. She almost sounds like she's purring."

*****

Burbank is very different than Palmdale.

127

Jim and I are not across the hall from each other. We are on different floors. I no longer clock in and out for lunch or when I run errands between buildings. I just clock in and out when I arrive and leave. I feel free, responsible, capable. I have no whiteout bottles in my desk.

I sit in a large room with a group of technicians. It reminds me of my engineers. Here there is a balance of men and women. We are analyzing and plotting flight data from the L-1011s as they roll off the production line and are tested one by one. We work in groups and are supervised by flight engineers. There is a day shift and a night shift. I work the day shift. We all share a desk with our night counterparts.

Jim and I add to our circle of work friends. We have lunch in the plant cafeteria most days. We gossip about the woman engineer who wears slacks to work, possible layoffs, the Mormon supervisor who only recruits techs from his church, the tech whose husband committed suicide while she was on maternity leave, the anorexic secretary on the second floor, the latest office affair, and where we can find authentic Mexican food to-go for our next potluck. We have pizza Fridays at Shakey's and weekend barbecues at whoever has a pool.

*****

Rumble. Loud. Louder. Loudest.
Pitching, every which way. Back and forth, over and under I go.
Falling. Bumping.
I wrap my toes around my perch. Tight, tighter, tightest.
On the floor, I flap my wings in hopes of becoming upright. No luck.
Help.

*****

I hear our alarm clock go off. I'm launched from bed by an indescribable groan. How can that be? I'm on my feet. I was laying down, now I'm on my feet.

The darkness is dense. I hear Tweetie squawking. Jim has my shoulders. We pitch forward and back. Rock left to right. Over and over. Has the bomb been dropped?

My questions can't be answered because I can't spit them out of my mouth.

Help.

Jim screams. "It's okay, it's okay, it's okay. Just an earthquake."

"Just an earthquake?"

The 1971 San Fernando earthquake, also known as the Sylmar earthquake, occurs in the early morning of Tuesday, February 9. It originates in the foothills of the San Gabriel Mountains. It has a magnitude of 6.5 and an intensity of extreme. The experts claim the duration as twelve seconds. That's wrong, I know it lasted hours.

We manage to get the bird cage upright. Tweetie seems paralyzed. We scoop her from the cage bottom. No blood, nothing seems broken. She rouses and insists on inching up my arm to the nape of my neck, burrowing her head in my hair.

We venture from the bedroom, creeping through the dressing room past the bathroom. It's still dark; we try a light switch, nothing. I stub my toe on the toilet tank top. What? It's at least five feet from the bathroom door. We make it to the living room.

Now just dawn, a pale light falls through the patio door revealing a heap in the middle of the floor. Random dishes, the TV, sofa pillows, turntable, stereo speakers, and a no-longer potted fern are mixed like tossed salad. Our wrought-iron bookcase is slumped, spilling its contents and stacking its shelves in a strange tepeelike configuration.

All the kitchen cabinet doors are open, wine glasses are hanging upside down by their bottoms.

We begin to rock. We cling together. Tweetie's now buried deep in my hair; my face is pressed into Jim's chest. Jim wraps his arms around us and whispers, "Here we go again."

Slam. All the cabinet doors shut. Glass breaks.

"Jim, is that creaking the apartment building?"

The complex has no structural damage. We manage to get Tweetie back in her cage and begin to clean up our mess. Keeping busy helps. We need to call our families; I am sure they are trying to get a hold of us. We speculate about when the electricity and phones will be back.

Too late we go to buy flashlights and water. We walk over to our little mall and join neighbors in front of the grocery. It's closed. The strong smell of bourbon and scotch permeates the air. We all welcome a good belly (hysterical) laugh as we peer into the windows and realize the liquor department is all over the floor.

Days later utilities are back, streets cleared, and stores opened. We've been in contact with our families via a public phone, which has been miraculously working. They are anxious to help.

"Mom, can we come for the weekend? Jim and I need to get out of here, the aftershocks are driving us crazy. The bird needs a break, we need a break."

"Of course."

*****

I love Mom's house. It's warm, and Grandma chatters to me nonstop. That makes Kathy laugh. She says, "Grandma doesn't chat to just anyone."

Grandma puts her face close to the cage. We are eye to eye. I chirp, she smiles and calls me "sweet little blue birdie." I shuffle closer to her, poke my beak through the wires in hopes she will offer me her finger. I can tell she wants to; she giggles and shies away. "Maybe next time, sweet Tweetie, next time."

I think Jim told her I bit him. I would never bite Grandma.

We sleep in the living room; my cage is on the coffee table. We forgot my cage hat. Mom has a scarf she gives Kathy to use. It's like being wrapped in a bouquet of flowers; underneath, it's all rosy in the lamplight, and when the sun spills through the shutters, I am convinced I'm outside. Maybe we can take it home.

There is no shaking or rolling. I like it here.

*****

We get back to our apartment and return to work. All seems normal unless a neighbor slams a door or a truck backfires, then I find myself hugging a doorjamb. Most of our broken stuff is replaced or repaired. Jim's turntable comes back from the manufacturer, no charge, a note is included regarding the stylus. "We've never seen anything like it. The needle was tied in a knot. We replaced it."

Three out of five of our couple consortium have purchased houses in Valencia. Valencia is a planned community, touted as the perfect place to bring up children. The planned neighborhoods are tied together with walkways called paseos. You can walk, skate, or ride a bike along these landscaped cement trails and never cross a street. There are parks and recreation centers anchoring each housing tract. Replicating these planned neighborhoods is part of the Newhall Land and Farm's masterplan. They own a vast amount of land from San Fernando to the fields approaching Santa Paula. They are replanting their orange groves and cow pastures with clusters of three- and four-bedroom homes.

Jim and I join the rush to homeownership. We want to paint our walls colors, crank up the stereo, get two kittens, and amass equity. We find a new development adjacent to Newhall/Valencia. These homes are not part of the Newhall plan. Their appeal is that they sit on a hillside with views of ancient oak trees, high desert scrub, and the always dry riverbed that runs from Canyon Country to Newhall. We cycle our families through our one-story house as it emerges from its cement slab, boosts walls, and dons its roof. We are financed, order furniture, give notice to our landlord, hire a pool architect, and become parents to kittens.

For now, the kittens are in our second bedroom. We plan to introduce them to Tweetie after the move. We start to pack; this time our friends will move us.

Jim's watching the local news while I mix kitty pablum and sauté hamburger for spaghetti sauce.

"Kathy, come take a look. They are talking about the housing development we are buying into."

"That's exciting, I'll be right there."

"No scary, not exciting. This is making me nervous. Look, a house slid down the hill just blocks from ours. Landfill, it was on land-fill. Wonder if ours is? Oh God, what if there's another earthquake?"

Our developer assures us our home is stable, there is no risk. We are not on landfill. The house that slid was a single situation. He says we still have time to change our minds.

Jim and I want out. Out we get. The bank agrees. There is no argument from the developer. All fees and deposits are returned. The furniture order cancelled. Pool plans filed.

Relieved and equally disappointed, we find another apartment just blocks from the old one. This time we are on the first floor. The master bedroom is huge. Off the living room is a fenced patio that runs the length of our apartment. The kitties have room to play, pee, and poop. Tweetie is happy in the guest room; she sits on a sturdy table by the window. We sign a year's lease.

Our plan is to match the next move with the end of our new lease. We restart our house search. We scour the flatlands of Valencia. Houses on hills have been crossed off our list. We only look at pre-owned homes. We like the idea of *established* landscape and a pool maintained by the homeowners' association. And an older home will have survived the great quake. There's comfort in that, and before we sign any closing papers, we will have a structural engineer certify the safety of the home.

*****

They are furry, little, and determined. I don't like them.

Kathy tries to keep the door to my room shut. She is having little success.

These miserable little cats, known as *the kitties*, lunge at the door until there is just enough of a crack that they can push their way in. They have no fear no matter how loud I squawk. They tumble over each other in a rush to get to me. Up they come, grabbing the bedspread of the guest bed and then sliding across the end table, slamming into my cage. They stop for just a moment, big eyes checking my position, then quicker than you can say "here kitty," they manage to attach all fours to my cage. Stuck, they begin to howl. You would think I hung them there on purpose.

"Hey, what's going on here? I'm going to get a lock for this door. Poor Tweetie. You've scared her to death," Kathy scolds. She pries them off my cage. Their pointy baby tails flick and their pin-pricky claws spread wide.

Jim's at the door. "Okay, hand them over, it's back to the bathroom. I'll move their stuff. So much for getting along."

Good God they are annoying. I'd rather have an earthquake.

Kathy finds my scarf, the one Mom gave me, and tucks it around my cage.

"There you go, that will make you feel better."

She shuts the door, and I hear her push something in front of it.

"You're safe now, sweet dreams," she whispers.

*****

We take the kitties to the park on Saturdays. There are trees and grass for them to play in. Much better than the potted plants on our cement patio. They assault the trees, climbing up about two feet before they fall backward. Just like the cliché, they land feet first. We get strange looks from dog walkers and a few "oh, how cute" from middle-aged couples. The fun lasts thirty minutes or so before the kitties sprawl tummy up in one of our laps.

Jim stands up. "Time to go. Now we can get some things done around the apartment while they snooze."

From the first, Jim and I shared household chores. Mom and Grandma spoiled me. I seldom made a bed or washed a dish. I never did a load of laundry or cooked a complete meal. My only household achievement was ironing learned from pressing my dad's handkerchiefs and perfected because of my sewing. I picked up a few *how-to's* in the dorm, but Jim took the lead with household tasks. There was only one task he wouldn't do—laundry. He was convinced that carrying a laundry basket back and forth to a public laundry room scarred his manhood. So he trained me on the finer points of front and top loading. In exchange he cleaned the toilets. Through this deal, we both maintained our dignity.

I'm worried about Tweetie; she has a growth on her beak. At first, I thought a seed was stuck in the corner of her bill. I check it daily; I think it's getting bigger. She doesn't seem bothered by it, but Jim and I take her to the vet to make sure she is alright.

I am not listening. The vet is talking, and Jim is nodding his head. I'm not listening. Jim tries to explain the problem to me, but I'm not listening.

"It's going to affect her eating." Blah, blah. "There's nothing to be done." Blah, blah. "The kindest thing…" Blah, blah.

I am not listening.

Jim takes care of Tweetie. All I do is weep. Weep and weep and weep. The apartment is so empty; there's no greeting when we come through the front door or chirp good night. I insist Jim remove her cage immediately: seeds, toys, scarf, all must go. I vacuum up her seed splatter, her only remains.

Now that Tweetie is gone, the kitties have no interest in the guest room. We leave the door open; they scamper right past it in search of Jim or me. They go where we go, they eat where we eat, and sleep where we sleep.

"Jim, how do you do it?"

"Do what?"

"Power through, keep a stiff upper lip, manage the hard stuff. The fish, Tweetie, the house, the earthquake."

"Well, I'd head for a doorjamb, but you always beat me." He laughs.

"I'm a jerk. From now on we should both head for the door-jamb when the shaking starts, we'll just huddle together."

"Deal."

CHAPTER 6

Prissy and Sooty

Description: After Jim and I sign the initial papers for the house on the hill, we go to the animal shelter and adopt two kittens.

Prissy: She is black-and-white, mostly white. She reminds me of Willie Whiskers, but her eyes are more yellow than green. She is regal where he was a rogue. She seems serene even though she is just six weeks old and sitting in a chain-link cage surrounded by bouncing meowing littermates. Her tail is all black. Her chest and tummy all white. Her white fur feels like I imagine Ermine would. I think she will be more longhaired than short. She seems petite; the officer at the shelter says she is the runt of the litter.

We make eye contact, and she is mine.

Jim wants to name her Princess. I can't stand that name; besides, it doesn't seem easy to call "Princess, Princess, Princess." We compromise on Prissy.

Her best quality: she's loves a lap.

Sooty: He is gray like the ashes at the bottom of a woodburning fireplace, the ones under the floaty white ones, the soot. His color is even, there is no variation. Ear to stomach to tail tip he is gray. Even his eyes are a shade of gray, green-gray. His fur is short, thick, lush. He is a whirlwind. He leaps from one perch to the next, batting at tails and knocking water, litter, and food here and there. He skids to a halt at the corner of the cage in front of Jim, plants his feet, and dares Jim to take him home.

There is no discussion about his name. Sooty.

His best quality: he's funny.

I'm on the pill. My period has been a mere nuisance since I started it. Before I was married, Mom took me to our family doctor. I had been a freshman in college when I saw him last. He had aged just as much as I had grown up. Mom and I were shocked when he explained he wouldn't prescribe the pill.

"Kathy, I would do anything for you or your Mom, but I can't do this. I'm Catholic. Prescribing the pill would be a violation of my personal ethics."

We were speechless. It never occurred to us Dr. Zell wouldn't prescribe the pill; he had seen me through measles, chicken pox, an almost-fractured kneecap and guided the family through the loss of my father and grandfather. His refusal left me at loose ends; I had the strange feeling of abandonment. What was I going to do?

"What I can do is refer you to a colleague of mine. He will be able to help. Excellent man, Protestant. I will have my nurse set up an appointment with him. Okay?"

An appointment was set. I sent Dr. Z a thank-you note. Thank you, thank you, thank you.

For the last two months, I have been spotting between periods. A friend says that often happens when you take the pill. Jim says I should go see my gynecologist.

"Sweetheart, we have insurance. You should see what's going on."

I make an appointment. I see the doctor.

"Well, that was interesting, No not interesting. Disturbing, irritating, worrisome."

"Wow, what's going on?"

"The doctor says I should stop the pill for now."

"What?"

I can see the panic I feel in my stomach in Jim's eyes. It's not just the chance of becoming pregnant but the need to make a change. A change to something we trust and consider our normal. Switching from the known to the unknown is risky business, especially in this case. I know he is thinking if not the pill what?

"What exactly does the doctor suggest?"

I paraphrase. "If you want to have a baby, do nothing, just let nature take its course. But know that after taking the pill as long as you have, it will probably take a little longer to get pregnant than if you hadn't. Count on a year. If you don't want to get pregnant, you can use traditional methods: abstinence, Catholic counting, condoms, or spermicides. Abstinence is the only method that's a 100 percent safe. The other methods are 80 percent to 95 percent safe. There are no guarantees. Luck always comes into play."

We choose condoms and spermicides. We are religious about this choice.

Six weeks later, I'm pregnant. My doctor reminds me, "I told you there were no guarantees."

*****

"Okay, kitties let's go," Kathy sweetheart calls.

"Sooty, it must be Saturday. The cardboard box is by the door and the blanket and car keys are on the table."

"I can't wait. I don't like the car ride, makes my eyes twirl and stomach icky, but I love the park. I hope we can climb another tree. I hope I get higher than last time. I hope the grass is long and full of bugs. I hope they bring the ping-pong balls and the string with the bell on the end. Oh, and a snack. A snack would be perfect."

"I want to eat a ladybug. I like the color. I wonder what they taste like."

"Grasshopper maybe. But like red not green."

"Sooty, can you clean my ears before we go? You didn't do a good job last night. Maybe if my ears are extra clean, we can find a bird before it sees us."

"Seriously, Prissy, now?"

"Please..."

*****

I don't like being pregnant. I don't know what women see in it. I certainly don't feel closer to God or Mother Nature. I'm seasick, bloated, and cranky. I don't glow, I growl. And now I'm stuck on the couch for three days. I'm spotting, so it's feet up.

"Sweetheart, everything will be okay. I read that in a few weeks you will be feeling better. Great in fact. Then we'll go out for your favorite, Mexican food. We'll have a celebration."

"Oh, hon, that sounds terrible. Can you hand me the saltines?"

Everyone is so thrilled. Family, friends, friends of friends. Everyone except for me and my mother-in-law. Her response to the news wasn't "congratulations" but "well, it's about time." My mother was speechless, I could hear her grinning ear to ear over the phone. My grandma hopes she can remember how to crochet, visions of blankets and booties dance in her head. Jim's dad has told him no less than ten times to be prepared to have morning sickness. He assures us he did with all four of his children. My Jim looks like a deer in headlights. He thinks we should focus on names (are you kidding me) and speed up the house search.

I hope I rally soon. My mom wants to take me shopping. I owe her a fantastic pregnancy; she's waited sixty-five years to be a grandmother. (My bother has no children. He had the mumps when he was ten. I think that may be one of the reasons Pam divorced him.)

Girlfriends stop by with bags of maternity clothes; they are disappointed when I don't put on a fashion show.

Jim did the laundry yesterday. I know he feels betrayed. Me too.

The kittens haven't been to the park in weeks. Prissy takes naps with me on the couch. She tolerates my constant turning from side to side. Sooty acts like I feel—he doesn't know if he wants in or out. He pouts at the patio door.

"Oh, please Lord help me find joy in this incredible, miserable condition."

*****

"Sooty, Honey told Sweetheart that we are not going to the park again, even though I am sure it is Saturday."

"Why?"

"Too much to do. Honey made an appointment to look at a house."

"Oh, did he say if the house had a tree?"

"No, but he said it has 'a lovely covered patio.'"

"We have a patio. But I don't think we have a *covered*."

*****

We find a house.

It sits at the crest of a slope, on a street that circles the housing track that it is a part of. We have confirmed there is no chance of slipping or sliding. The house is one story with an attached garage. Three bedrooms, two baths. It has a separate dining room and eat-in kitchen. There is a huge side yard with a covered patio. The star of the patio is a round picnic table. It's too large to move; we are betting the owners will leave it behind.

The backyard is mostly grass which spills over an incline that runs to the road below. There are several birch trees. But it's the front yard that sells us. It has a beautiful lawn outlined in trimmed bushes of various varieties. There are birds of paradise and yuccas. The owners had a cousin in the landscape business. The cousin did all the cement work. It's dark gray with a pebbled texture. It gives the house a dignified look. There are wide steps from the sidewalk to the covered entry. Planters full of seasonal flowers complete the picture. It is the perfect family residence. The street view suggests happily ever after.

Like my pregnancy, the house is surreal.

We make an offer. Accepted. Now financing.

Ten percent down. Our mortgage will be $31,500. The interest is in the teens, a hefty monthly commitment. Jim handles the paperwork, and our real estate agent suggests that we keep my pregnancy on the downlow. Approval hinges on the fact that we are both employed. Taking time off to have a baby is not a financial asset.

Friends and family move us in. We thank them with a barbecue. Jim Senior christens Jim's new grill with his famous Korean steaks. Everyone brings a favorite dish and their own moving-day story.

Fifteen adults squeeze around the picnic table. We put the kids on a quilt on the lawn: hot dogs and Ketchup. A very good mess.

A toast is made. "Here's to Jim and Kathy and family life."

*****

"Wow, they are having fun. Prissy just listen. I want out of here. Why are we in here?"

"Don't you remember Sweetheart explained that we were going to be in here for a few days."

"Where's the car? Don't they keep the car in here? Will they remember we're here? I don't want the car on top of me."

"Of course, they'll remember."

"So why are we here?"

"To learn the smell of our new home. So when we are out, we won't get lost. It will take a day or so. It's not so bad in here. See all the packing boxes, find one and take a nap. And look over there. A spider is doing a handy job with his web. Just look, Sooty, don't paw at it."

"Prissy, what about the stuff on our paws? It tastes like the same stuff Sweetheart puts on toast."

"It is. The more we lick at it, the more this will be our home."

"Well, that's weird."

"Sweetheart told me that her mom did this to her first cat when they moved. His name was Willy Whiskers. He was black-and-white, just like me."

*****

Four months pregnant. The fog lifts. I tell my boss and chat with HR. Saturday Mom and I are going shopping. Jim and I settle on furniture for the living and dining rooms. We finish painting those rooms just hours before the furniture is delivered. Jim is building a colored TV (from scratch) to go into the corner cabinet he built in the den (alias bedroom number 3). I have managed to peel the red velvet Victorian contact paper from the walls in the main bathroom and to remove the tacky turquoise café curtains from the din-

140

ing room windows. I will paint the bathroom cream on Sunday; that will be a relief. Jim and I put dining room drapes on our to-have list.

Jim takes responsibility for the outside. I take responsibility for the inside. Jim agrees to keep the toilets. I take back the laundry. For now, I will go to a Laundromat. Washer and dryer join the drapes on our to-have list.

The backyard has goffers. There are holes everywhere. Jim is literally ankle-deep in them.

"Kathy, don't come out here. You'll break your neck."

Prissy and Sooty sit on the edge of the patio waiting for furry little heads to pop up. They crouch and then leap to the edge of this hole and that. The only ones enjoying this game are the goffers.

Jim tries water, poison, and a smoke bomb. No luck.

The neighbor leans over the fence. "I have a guy."

Jim calls the guy. No more goffers.

Jim leans over the fence. "Thanks, I don't know what he did, but they are gone."

"Yep, he's magic. I'm afraid to ask him what it is he does to them. Not sure I want to know."

*****

Sooty darts out of the patio door, pushing Prissy into the doorjamb. He takes one jump to the picnic bench, one hop to the table. Then up onto the slump stone wall and one more leap to the crossbeam of the patio cover. Taking a moment to assess his distance from the birch tree, he squats low and pushes up through his back legs to his toes. He seems to fly. Front and back paws grab the birch's trunk. He positions himself on the first limb, haunches and stomach flush against the white bark, front paws reach out in front of him.

His gray-green eyes watch to see if Prissy notices his agility.

"Sooty, what are you doing? The goffers are gone. You are going to get stuck up there."

"I am waiting."

141

"For?"
"You."

*****

I ask my mom if she can come to Valencia and babysit. I ask her to change her life, uproot Grandma, leave her job, her church, her home, and everything familiar. I ask because I want the best for my baby. I want the best for me.

I blurt the question out over the phone.

"Mom, do you think you could come and take care of the baby when I go back to work? I don't want to leave the baby with just anyone. I don't know what to do. Jim and I know it's a lot to ask. Selfish really. Mom?"

"Kathy, stop crying. Of course, I will come. I have been looking for an excuse to retire. I would love to take care of my grandchild, to be closer to you, to be part of your lives. Grandma won't be upset. We'll all be together. Next time we come out, we will make a grand plan."

"Oh, Mom, thank you."

*****

"Sooty come here, look."

The door to the baby's room (alias bedroom number 2) is cracked open.

Sooty pushes past me and pads into the middle of the room. The room is no longer white with miscellaneous boxes in the corners. The walls are filled with one-dimensional images resembling trees; they are the colors of swimming pool water, sunshine, and spring grass. They float randomly over the walls. Big, little, and in-between.

"Prissy, what are these, what's on the walls?"

"That's called wallpaper. Bruce put it there."

"Oh, the man that came with 'my mom' and 'the grandma' the other day?"

"Yes, Sweetheart told me he is her brother. Like you are mine." Prissy fills Sooty in. "He's a house painter and wallpaper hanger. He and his wife have their own business. Guess he used to play the trumpet. The wallpaper is his gift to the baby. The floating pictures are called lollipop trees."

"Oh, I like Bruce. What's a trumpet? What's a lollipop? No matter, he let me hide under the giant white sheet he laid in the hall. I like 'my mom' and 'the grandma' too. So many comings and goings. Hey, what's this? It looks like a giant cage. Can we climb inside?"

"No, no, we can't do that. Remember Sweetheart said when the baby comes, we aren't to go in this room. We shouldn't be here now, but I had to show you."

"Why can't we be here?"

"Too much fur, our claws are sharp, and our tongues are rough."

"Oh."

"I love the wallpaper. You can't climb the trees, but I think they will bring sweet dreams."

"Do you think they will put the baby in the garage for the first three days it's here?"

*****

Kimberly's born six days before Christmas. She's a painted porcelain doll. Warm rose cheeks with tea and cream undertones. Six pounds five ounces. Her countenance is serious. She has a swath of fine dark hair and Jim's almond eyes. Her nose is mine. She is the most beautiful thing I have ever seen. That the world has ever seen.

Jim takes us home from the hospital in his Z. I hold our sleeping bundle in my arms. We promise her that her birthday will always be celebrated before we do anything Christmassy: shopping, the tree, decorations, cookies. We promise she will be first, always.

Jim and I announce that we will spend the first week alone with our baby. Just us and Soot and Priss.

Time flies.

Jim returns to work.

Now it's just us two. We are alone. Just me and baby. The kitties are watching my every move. To this moment, I've been confident

I was and will be the best mom ever. Until this moment. Now I am not sure, not sure at all.

"Dear God in heaven, have you lost your mind? How can you leave this innocent soul to my care? I don't know what I'm doing. I don't think you know what you're doing. Help."

The phone rings.

"How are things going?" It's my mom.

"Well, I'm, I think… I'm, well, overwhelmed and…"

"Kathy?"

"Yes?"

"Put on the kettle and make some tea."

"Okay…"

"I'll be there in just a little bit."

"Okay."

I hear her knocking. I find her at the front door holding a square pink box.

"Tea ready?"

"Yes."

"Let's get to it. Sit down."

She places the box on the counter and carefully extracts a three-layer chocolate cake. She places it between us on the kitchen table. Kimmie sleeps nearby in her rolling bassinette, the kitties are close at our feet.

"Forks?"

"Here."

We spend the next half hour sipping tea and eating chocolate cake. We eat it right off the platter.

Mom's smiling at me; I sigh and smile back. Memories flood: Mom has two trusted remedies for physical and emotional ailments. Prunes for the physical and chocolate cake for the emotional. She never hesitates to dispense either as needed.

Kimberly stirs. Mom picks her up, gives her a pat, and hands her to me.

"Kathy, she's perfect and so are you."

*****

Sweetheart opens the door. We are at her heels. She points to the space where the door has been.

"Remember our deal?"

Prissy confirms with a soft meow.

We lay down; paws in, hunches out, tails wrapped, and under chins.

Sweetheart crosses the room to the big cage they call the crib, and she looks in.

"She's still sleeping. Let's leave her be."

I nudge Prissy. We move just enough so Sweetheart won't trip on her way out.

"Okay, guys, let's find you a treat. You were so good, staying in the doorway. Smartest kitties ever."

*****

In March 1994, my mom and Grandma move to the apartments where Jim and I first lived in Valencia. We manage to get all of Mom's furniture into the two-bedroom unit. Grandma is thrilled; she has her very own bathroom and a dressing room. Mom has bought her new towels, peachy pink. We install Mom's washer and dryer in our garage. No more Laundromat.

I go back to Lockheed for a day. My maternity leave is over. I start a new job in two weeks.

While I was on leave, a woman in Jim's group told him about a training program at Security Pacific Bank. It's where she trained to be a programmer. She thinks it would be a great opportunity for me, and she emphasizes you get paid to train. She gives Jim the phone number.

I call. Interview. Cross my fingers. I'm accepted.

The program is in Glendale at the bank's headquarters. Just an extra fifteen minutes south on the freeway from Lockheed. Participants work at their own pace through a set of training modules. My interviewer says it should take about six months to complete. Once you pass your final coding project, you are assigned to one of the bank's automation systems.

Before taking on the new I must process out of the old. Lockheed needs paperwork of course, but they insist I be medically discharged. Like a stuffy nose, I must be discharged. My doctor's release is not enough; I need to return for medical exam. I'm asked to touch my toes, stand with my arms out, and touch my nose. I'm stunned. A thirty-minute commute for a five-minute exit. What a waste of time. Glad I'm going, not coming.

I have two weeks to get myself in order.

I'm nervous about leaving Kimmie, my sweet pea. Between loads of laundry, bottles, and diapers, I spend my time watching her sleep, breathe... I'm lost in her spell. She coos, kicks, and smiles at Jim and me. Her serious eyes tell us she is concerned that she has been left with inept caregivers. She may be right. Unlike our friends we don't have all the answers.

The cats continue to respect the *no kitties in baby's room* rules. They know they will get a turn with Sweet Pea when we put her in her playpen. There they will be eye level with her. They don't seem to mind the occasional jab to the nose from a waving fist or foot as she rolls side to side in the soft-sided mesh square.

I pour through my closet assessing appropriate business attire. The bank has strict rules. I'm going to need dresses. I have a few that qualify, and they fit, but I am going to need more. I would love to make them; I miss leafing through pattern books and roaming aisles of fabrics. But I can't find the time. Mom and I will shop this Saturday. Jim will babysit.

With a week to go, I pen a booklet for my mom, *The Care and Feeding of Kimberly*. It contains all needed phone numbers, baby's food preferences and daily requirements. It documents Kim's known quirks and favorites to date. I'm sure Mom won't need this other than the phone numbers. She has been a quick study. But it's a relief to me to write out, to affirm I do know something about Sweet Pea.

First day. Up. Dressed. Headed to the garage.

You know that old line "parting is such sweet sorrow." I don't think I could get out the door if it wasn't my mom holding Kim. Mom has her in the crook of her right arm. Kim is in her pale yellow jammies covered by a too-large plastic bib, waiting for her banana

146

mush. They both grin at me. I wipe the tears from the corners of my eyes. My hand is on the doorknob, I can't turn it, I need one more hug.

"Go, Kathy, you'll be late. We're fine. You will be too."

*****

"Jim Honey doesn't do that. He just goes. Prissy, are you listening to me?"

"Men."

*****

I thought I knew how to count. I'm embarrassed to learn that it's zero through nine, not one through ten. At twenty-five this comes as a shock, just as shocking as recognizing that our base-10 system, decimal, is just one of many numbering systems. Binary, base 2, is what the computer uses. Ones and zeros in combinations, simple patterns of on and off. Combinations dictated by code; code determined by programmers. I am fascinated.

The bank's program is engaging; I often forget myself attempting to find the perfect solution. I look forward to arriving in the morning, to seeing if the previous night's submission is successful, to discussing *what-ifs* and *how-to's* with peers. What kind of mother am I? Shouldn't I prefer being home?

I complete the program and break out in a rash from neck to knee.

Stress the doctor says.

"But it's over. I made it."

"Think of it as a delayed reaction." The doctor dismisses me with a prescription for Benadryl.

I'm assigned to a group that supports the bank's payroll system. It's what they call a back-office application. Most of my team and our floormates are my age, but few are married, fewer have children. We sit in two-men cubicles. Rows and rows of cubes fill the floors of the bank's headquarters. Managers and managers' managers surround the floor in doored offices. I don't punch a clock. I am a timekeeper. I come and go as I please. The badge I wear around my neck is for floor access; it does not denote my job status.

"Hey welcome. You married? Well, we'll give that a year. Divorce, it runs rampant here. Don't know why, just saying." This declaration comes from a head perched on top of my cube's wall. It continues with its less-than-welcoming diatribe. Blah. Blah. I stare and turn to my cube mate.

"Don't pay any attention to him. He's just sore because his wife left him for one of our IBM reps. It happens, doesn't mean it will happen to you."

Incredulous, I concentrate on the program listing in front of me.

Jim makes a career move too. He follows a Lockheed peer to TRW. More responsibility, more money, more prestige. We trade in our Z for Datsun's latest model; this one is a dignified blue, not cool lime. I drive a ginormous Chevy station wagon with wood paneling. We buy a ski condo in Mammoth at the base of lift 7. We give Mom a raise, hire a cleaning service, and purchase season tickets to UCLA football. The dining room drapes go in. Jim hints it may be time for a bigger, better house. Real estate is hot; we don't want to miss out.

Kim continues to captivate. She doesn't crawl but rolls from room to room. The cats follow her every move, leaping over her and sometimes getting caught under her. The three are delighted with themselves; they put on quite a show. I read about the need to crawl, I show her how, over and over. She's having none of it. I call the pediatrician; I hear a laugh in his "don't worry" response. Kim is not only mobile but also verbal. She has three words she uses reliably and with intention: Mama, Dada, and what sounds like *Nonie*. We expected the first two. The third is a surprise and obviously meant for my mom.

*****

"Watch out, Priss, here she comes."

Prissy jumps onto the coffee table as Kimmie rolls into its side. Priss gives her a pat on the top of her head. No claws, just a poke

148

to say, "Hey be careful." Kim pushes up on her left hand, her right elbow remains on the carpet. She stretches her chin up until she is almost eye level with Priss.

"Is she stuck?" Sooty belly crawls under the coffee table so he can examine the situation.

Nonie sits down on the couch. "What's she up to, kitties?"

Sooty moves to Nonie's side. Prissy remains on the coffee table. Wide eyed she watches as Kim pushes up with her right arm. Her left hand smacks the flat surface. The sound sends Prissy scooting to the table's edge; Kim grins at Nonie.

"Wow, baby girl, what are you doing? Sooty, Prissy, what's our girl doing?" Nonie leans forward in case Kim slips.

Kim gets her feet under her, and her tiny toes dig into the plush carpet. She's up. With both hands on the table, she leans forward. She rocks and steps, rocks and steps, hands follow, smack, smack. And she's down. Flat on her diapered bottom.

Nonie applauds. Prissy scurries to meet Kim on the floor. Kim reaches for Soot's tail on his way to join them.

Nonie cautions. "Okay, guys, mums the word. Baby's first steps are meant for mommies and daddies, not for grandmas and kitties."

"Like we could tell if we wanted to. Priss, do you think she can climb trees too?"

"Oh, Sooty, I think she has to learn to walk without the table first. And I don't think Sweetheart and Honey will be letting her climb anything for quite a while. Remember she's a baby not a kitten."

"Okay…wish she were mine. If she were mine, I'd teach her to climb."

*****

Kim walks at eight months. She just rolls to a stop. Grabs the edge of a chair. Stands and walks. How magnificent is that?

Magnificent and scary. She's so tiny. She is easy to trip over. Between her and the cats, someone is going to be howling. I'm convinced that she needs to learn to crawl, even if she learns it out of order.

She stands up. I sit her down. I demonstrate crawling. She stands up. I sit her down. I demonstrate crawling. Over and over and over.

"Kathy, this is nuts. It's only frustrating her."

"I know, Jim. But the experts and even some of our friends are adamant about it. They say if she doesn't crawl, she'll never learn to read, her speech will be delayed, her coordination will suffer, she won't be socially adept."

"But her doctor doesn't say that or Nonie. Relax. Give her a break."

I suspend the torture sessions.

Kim's first birthday and second Christmas are here. As promised, we celebrate her birthday with no hint of Christmas. A huge party of pink and white everything. Friends, family, and their children pack our house. Kim holds court from her high chair. We present her with a small cake and encourage demolition. She places her finger in the icing, examines it, pops in her mouth. She repeats this several times. Her eyes smile despite her thoughtful countenance. Still almost bald, she reminds me of a too-serious baby Buddha. I should knot a red ribbon on the tuff of hair that sprouts from her crown. She's the baby of the group, but her demeanor is that of a tiny, worried queen. Does she feel responsible for us? I don't think she is pleased with our antics. I pray she relaxes into toddlerdom. I whisper in her ear, "Baby, baby, let me do the worrying, that's what mommies are for." I can tell she's skeptical.

Christmas is a big success. We opt for an eight-foot tree. Jim grumbles through the lights. Nonie and I frost it in Lux snow and stuff ornaments from branch tip to trunk. Kim and cats are mesmerized, content to sit side by side watching the twinkling and shimmering. Jim admits it's a wonder. We celebrate with coco and cookies. A Hallmark moment.

Happy New Year. It's our year to host the party. We fill our bedrooms with friends' children. Blankets and teddies and binkies and bottles. We wait until no sounds reach the hall. Then ten couples drink too many Brandi Alexanders, eat too many crab puffs, and watch amazed as our eight-foot wonder crashes through the patio door. The door thank God is open. We needed air. We dance, laugh, and flirt like the college kids we are no more. The neighbors are setting off fireworks. We dispense confetti eggs, pots and pans, and wooden spoons.

"To the front porch everyone. Beat those pans like there's no tomorrow." This is Jim's favorite part of the New Year hoopla.

I check on the children. I stop to listen; no sound from either of the closed rooms. I crack each door and peek. All accounted for, blankets no longer tucked, and Kim has a crib buddy. Each tiny person sleeps content. I cross my fingers and pray that no one wakes until at least 8:00 a.m.

We serve coffee. Useless but expected. Couples with kids at home leave to relieve sitters. The remainder drape themselves over chairs and couches; some find spots on the carpet. I toss pillows and quilts. I right the tree and shut the patio door.

"Jim, I can't remember who said waffles tomorrow at eleven."

"We'll check in the morning. I sure hope it's not us. Come, kitties, it's safe. Come keep our feet warm."

*****

"All clear, Priss."

"Are you sure?" Priss creeps to the edge of the bed skirt. Lifts it with her nose just enough so she can see that the bedroom door is shut. She can feel Sweetheart and Honey settle into the bed above. Feeling Honey's invitation is safe; she emerges from the dark under bed and joins Soot who is posed to leap to the foot of the bed.

"Sooty, I thought our tree was going to kill you!"

"Me too. One minute I was enjoying the music wedged between the tree stand and the box with the new rice maker and the next it was raining green needles, soap snowflakes, flashing lights, glass balls, and cranberry popcorn strings. Everything went tilt, no way out. Something had my tail, maybe a foot. I managed to make it under the dining table and then to the kitchen. I skittered under the kitchen table just missing someone with a tray of God knows what and made them scream. I slid over the entrance tile, flew down the hall, and body-slammed into the bedroom door. Must have hit my head, next

I knew I was under the bed next to you. I think we should start and end all future parties under the bed. I'm too old for this nonsense."

"Good idea. I need some sleep."

Back to back they curl up at the foot of the bed, noses buried in tails, not minding that Sweetheart slides her foot under their warmth. Welcome 1975.

*****

"Jim, have you seen Priss? I've been calling her all morning."

"Last I saw her she was sitting on the picnic table gazing at something on the hill across the street. Probably had her eye on one of those big black birds."

"Prissy, Prissy." I call out the kitchen and the front doors. No response. "Jim, I'm going to take a walk and look for her. Listen for Kimmie, she's napping. I won't be long."

"Okay."

It's dreary out. Overcast. I get a sweater, probably need a jacket. Soot is stationed at the back-patio door.

"Sooty, I'll find her. Go get Jim if she comes while I'm gone."

Sooty continues to stare out the glass, ignoring my chatter.

I find her. Up against the curb behind the house. I call her, no response. She just lies there on her side. I tell myself she is just sleeping. I can't force myself close enough to see... I run back to the house.

"Jim."

"Stay here, Kathy. I'll go."

We call animal control; they come in a van and remove her from the street. Jim makes the arrangements. The animal control officers are very kind. I check on Kimmie, still deep in sleep. The officers say it looks like a car must have hit her, and she made it to the curb. Because she is right below the yard, they feel she was trying to get home. Sooty knew where she was, I should have followed his gaze. I should have never let her out of the house, ever. I hate that street. Jim scoops Sooty up; we threefold ourselves into the corner of the couch.

CHAPTER 7

Just Sooty

Description: Still the color of soot. He's not quite three and more cat than kitten. He's sleek and savvy, a master of the hunt; blue jays and mice are his forte. His eyes are a deeper green now. His fur is even thicker. He is well-groomed, spending hours bathing at the foot of our bed. His sweet spot is Kim. Since Prissy's abrupt departure, he has made Kim his charge, following her from room to room, guarding her high chair, posting himself as sentry at her bedroom door while she naps, and hovering from the toilet top at bath time.

He maintains many kittenlike antics: tackling himself in the mirrored closet doors, swatting at the bubbles as the bathwater fills, or diving into empty grocery bags. I think of him as perpetual motion.

He never misses a night at the bottom of our bed or a chance to slip out the front door to chase Mr. Jay from the garden hose bib. He's mostly happy I think, but sometimes I catch him sitting, staring out the patio door. I suspect he's waiting for Priss to run across the lawn to taunt him through the glass.

"Hey, Soot, what are you doing? You're breaking my heart. I miss her too. Come into the kitchen with me. I'll find you some people tuna."

I know I'm not supposed to feed cats people food. Just like I know I shouldn't eat sugary or salty foods—no bacon, no chocolate chip cookies. I know a lot, I do. I know that feelings are not fixed by knowing. Sooty likes people tuna; it makes his motor go and push hard against my leg. He makes his front paws go up and down. I know he feels better, and so do I.

Real estate continues to soar. Jim and I are swept up in the buy-sell profit wave. Jim discovers that when you are going through escrow, no one seems to care if you are going through escrow. By Thanksgiving we are closing on a two-story house under construction, a one-bedroom condo in Mammoth, and a two-bedroom duplex in Saugus.

"Are you sure we can do this?"

"Yes, Kathy, I'm sure. We have plenty of equity in this house for the downs. In Mammoth we will be on a rental service. When we aren't there skiing, renters will cover the mortgage. Nonie will love having a yard again. The duplex is perfect for her and Grandma. We won't charge rent, we will stop paying her for babysitting. I think that's fair, and the duplex will sit and gather equity. At our new house, we will be able to put in a swimming pool, we'll have money to decorate, and I will have a regulation pool table in the family room. I've checked the room's dimensions. They are perfect. TRW says they will pay for me to get my MBA and give me a raise once I finish. Pepperdine has a program they want me to enter. With all the tax deductions, we should be in great shape."

"A swimming pool? I've always wanted a pool." I remember how I almost had one on Bilton Way, how all the kids on the block were so envious.

*****

I'm back in the garage. Kathy took me on a tour of our new house. She tucked me under her arm so I wouldn't get lost then she put me in here.

This is some place. Priss would have loved the stairs; the landing in the middle of them would have been her spot. It will be fun to explore the rooms and closets, I love closets. They have been talking about the backyard, guess it's all dirt—no grass, no trees, nothing.

Jim has big plans, knowing him I'm sure there will be a tree or two. Wonder what there is to chase here.

*****

Our new neighborhood, just a mile from our old one, is all new construction. It is occupied by all twenty to thirtysomethings. The majority have one to two kids, a dog or a cat, and some have one of each. A pool goes in just about every other yard. Slump stone walls divide the yards one from another, chain-link and wood fencing are a no-no in Valencia. Front lawns go in before the back ones. Brick and cement hardscaping appear dividing swaths of green into neat rectangles. The city insists on giving each new homeowner a tree for the front yard. The sycamore we receive is not part of our vision. Jim moves it to the backyard; we replace it with an ornamental plum. The dark burgundy leaves of the plum tree are stunning against the deep green of our lawn.

The Vietnam war is ending. Blurry images flash across the television screen documenting protests, battles, and deaths. Shots of flaming palm trees and exploding napalm haunt the news.

Jim had a high school friend stationed in Vietnam. They had a "business" arrangement. Jim sent him a cashier's check to purchase stereo equipment from a local black market. Jim waited and waited; he never received the stereo. His friend returned to the States; his dad gave Jim a call and suggested Jim get together with him. He learns his friend is in or has been in a program for drug dependence. Jim contacts him and plans a dinner to catch up. The stereo equipment is not mentioned. His friend promises to keep in touch. He doesn't. Jim lets it go.

Two new programmers join my work unit. Two young handsomely opposite young men. Both over six feet. The blond is a college boy, a fraternity brother, cocky, charming, unaware of his galling innocence. The dark-haired man is a young veteran, sullen, distant, just back, coping. I'm the senior programmer; my job is to bring them up to speed on the banking systems they will be supporting.

Both men are sharp. Both anxious to succeed. I imagine that each looks at this job as a stepping-stone to a bigger and better one. At first it appears they can't stand one another. But they feign tolerance. Blondie likes me. He is amused that I'm married, working, and have a child. "Not at all like my mother," he says. Tall, dark, and handsome (TDH) is courteous and civil to me, but I sense I rub him the wrong way.

We code, decode, test, and implement new and fixed financial routines for the bank's general ledger. We have lunch together most days and occasionally we have drinks afterwork.

"I have a new girl, maybe we could do something as couples," Blondie suggests.

"Okay, that sounds fun. I would love you guys to meet Jim."

TDH gives an affirmative nod.

I offer to host a barbecue, something low-key, casual. We pick a Saturday.

The Monday after the barbecue, TDH enters my office. "Can we talk?"

"Sure, what's up?"

"My wife and I had a great time at your house. It's been a while since we have relaxed with friends. I'd forgotten. I wanted to apologize."

"For?" I can't imagine.

"Well, I couldn't understand how you could marry an Oriental. The thought of it made me so angry. I couldn't separate what I'd seen in Nam from what life is here. I was afraid to come to your house. I imagined your husband lobbing grenades. Sneaking up on me behind the bushes while you served beer and ribs. Crazy right? It's all crazy. My wife made me come. She was so pleased with the invitation. We don't get many. She insisted. I'm glad. You and Jim are great. I'm so glad we had a chance to get together. Blondie and his girl are great too. Maybe we can all get together again. I've been wrong about a lot. Thank you for giving me a chance to see things differently."

He turns and leaves.

I have a favorite photo; it's a black-and-white. Someone took it at a programming seminar. It's of me and *my boys*. They flank me. My arms are around their waists, their ties are loose at their necks. We are outside. We are squinting; the sun must be high. Our smiles are almost laughs as we clown for the camera.

*****

Now I'm locked in the house. First the garage and now the house. Kimmie's playpen is against the sliding glass door. She holds on tight to the side and peers out the window. Pooh-be is tucked under her arm, and her middle and ring finger are plugged into her mouth. I sit close by under the pool table. A big machine is digging a big hole. It goes in and out, up and down the slope it's making.

"Nonie, Nonie, Nonie," Kim squeals as the digger dumps more dirt onto the growing mound under the sycamore tree. "Out, out, out."

Nonie answers from the kitchen. "No, you stay safe in the pen for a few more minutes. I think they are digging to China. Spaghetti-O's in a minute. Where's Soot? Oh, I see you, sweet boy, stinky cat food for you."

*****

Jim starts his MBA program. He's home late most nights either commuting to the Pepperdine Malibu campus or putting in extra hours at his office in Westwood. My schedule is more dependable. I rarely have a night trouble call. When we are both absent, Nonie sleeps over. Like the old cliché, Jim and I are *ships passing in the night*: missed dinners, quick conversations, early mornings, hugs and kisses on the go.

Pool's in. Safety fence up. Swimming lessons.

Kimmie is an expert at the backstroke. Two and a half, stick-straight cropped hair, not yet three feet tall, dazzling in her sleek red bathing suit, she jumps in the deep end flips to her back and strokes her way back and forth, up and down the pool. Her instructor is as proud as we are. Olympics?

It's our first back-to-school night. Jim and I sit with our knees close to our chins. There are three other couples and four women in the room with us. The single women seem to have older children either in other classes in the preschool or already in elementary school. Some of the parents know each other.

Mother 1: "Oh hi, how are you? What did your family do this summer? We took the boat to Catalina and then rented a condo in Hawaii for two weeks. They made Bob a manager, and…"

Mother 2: "Hawaii oh yes we do that every summer. Joe's been in management for years. Christopher knows all his colors, does Josh know his? Meagan's first-grade teacher wanted to move her up a grade. We decided that she wasn't mature enough yet. Maybe next year. I hope we made the right decision, she's so smart."

Jim leans close. "Does Kimmie know her colors?"

"Well, she knows yellow and blue and that the grass is green. And that apples are red. And her favorite jammies are pink. Hey when are we going to Hawaii?"

"When you get into management and after I get a boat."

"I won't hold my breath."

The preschool is affiliated with a neighborhood church. Our Valencia crowd swears by it. Last count five toddlers from the group have graduated and are now accomplished grade schoolers. We put Kim on the waiting list the day after her second birthday. She started at two years seven months; meeting the potty training requirement and sufficiently knowledgeable in the preschool basics of sharing and handwashing.

I'm the only working mother in the room, maybe in the school. Jim thinks that's something to be proud of. All I can think is "does she know purple and orange and what about brown?"

Miss Jeanne enters the room; she will be Kimmie's teacher. The chatter stops. Her demeanor is calming, soothing, grounding. I take a deep cleansing breath. Our friends were right; this is the best school.

*****

I wonder what's over that wall.

Last week the swim lady threw me into the pool. She told Kathy I needed to know how to get out. What? I got out alright, I hate water. She kept shouting, "The step is over here, over here." The step, who cares about a step. I clawed myself right up the side I was next too, shook the water from my fur, and scrambled up the sycamore tree. Problem solved, I don't have to know how to get out if I never get in, and I will never get in again.

I wonder if there are more pools over the wall or trees or goffers or Prissy; maybe Prissy is over the wall, maybe that's where she went.

*****

I love my job. I love escaping daily from the push-pull of marriage, motherhood, friendships, and family contingencies. For eight hours real problems are suspended, replaced by concrete ones solvable by simple deduction and tenacity. The only thing I don't like is the sour feeling at the pit of my stomach, the feeling that bubbles up in the dark of night and asks, "Kathy, why you don't want to be a stay-at-home mom?" I can't help but wonder, "Am I a good mom? I want to be a good mom."

Kim has been in preschool three months. Amazing. We schedule our first parent-teacher conference. Nonie will come with us; after all she's the one that takes Kimmie to school and picks her up. She knows the teachers and other mothers better than we do; she makes sure Kim's cubby is cleaned at day's end and her sweater and lunch bag not forgotten.

Kimmie is trying to hold everyone's hands as she pulls us to Miss Jeanne's classroom. Miss Jeanne invites her to explore the nature table while we chat. Kim makes her way toward Harry the hamster. Nonie and Jeanne greet each other with a hug; they know each other from mutual church activities. Miss Jeanne is equally warm with Jim and me.

"Kimberly is bright and curious, often serious and a good sharer. She's made many friends and is very fond of paint, any kind of paint especially if you can put your hands or feet in it. My favorite Kim quality is that she is thoughtful about any new activity; she often stands back and watches before engaging. That's a very "smart" quality for an almost three-year-old. We are so pleased to have her here, and of course Nonie is a bonus."

On that happy note, the meeting ends.

"Miss Jeanne, could I have a moment with you?"

"Of course."

I ask Jim and Nonie to get Kim. "I'll be just a moment, meet you guys at the car."

"Miss Jeanne, I'm concerned about being a working mom. Is that bad for Kim? Would it be better if I were a stay-at-home mom? I feel so guilty. I confess I like working; it makes me feel good."

"Kathy, truth is it's more of a plus than minus. Children with working mothers know how to say goodbye at the door, they aren't clingy, they are more mature and often are our classroom leaders. They have other problems of course, but not caused because mom works."

"That's good news, I've been so worried."

"I love my job too. Work fulfills us, makes us better not worse. Kimmie's a lucky girl and so are we."

I feel lighter, yes lighter. "Thank you so much."

"Hey, sweetie, everything okay?"

I fill Jim and Nonie in.

Kimmie says, "I love Miss Jeanne."

"Me too, baby, me too."

*****

Kimmie is tugging on her ear.

Jim's not here, a business trip, I think.

Kathy says she and Nonie are going to take Kim to Kaiser. I think that's where they keep the doctor.

Kimmie rocks her head this way and that. Kathy gets the car keys.

I decide to guard the bedroom door until they return. Maybe Kimmie will want to play when she gets back.

Kathy says, "Don't worry, Soot, our girl will be okay. The doctor will have medicine to fix her up."

I hope so. I think the best thing would be a mouse to chase or spoonful of people tuna.

*****

Jim is receiving his MBA this Saturday. It will be a formal graduation with cap and gown. We are excited. Halfway through the MBA program, Jim discovered that our next-door neighbor was also getting his MBA from Pepperdine. They sometimes discuss assignments. His wife and I have become friends and have planned a combined celebration Saturday night. We are inviting friends and family; there will be champagne and a giant cake.

Kim is excited; we decide to take her to see Daddy graduate. Jim has explained the entire event to her. He's modeled his robe and mortarboard for her. The "hat" made her giggle.

The five of us will drive together taking the wood-paneled station wagon. Morgan and Shari have no kids, so there's been a lot of teasing about our mode of transportation.

On time, Shari and I head to the auditorium, and Jim and Morgan find their way to the location of the processional lineup. We find our seats and settle Kim between us. Shari tucks our sweaters and coats under Kim to bolster her high enough to see where Jim will walk across the stage. We marvel at the number of graduates and the size of the arena.

The music begins.

"Kimmie, look do you see Daddy? He's right over there. And there's Morgan. Wave."

"Mama, I got to go."

"What? Now? Can't you wait? It's almost time for Daddy to go on the stage." I swore I would never hesitate to take her if she asked, after all that's what potty training is all about taking them when they ask. It's a commitment. A promise a mom makes to her child. If you ask, I will take you. If I take you, then you will trust me; and best of all you won't pee your pants. Simple give-and-take. But I am so tempted to make her wait, to take a chance. I want to see Jim get his degree, to shake the dean's hand, to snap a picture. We didn't go through graduation at UCLA; it wasn't a cool thing to do at that time, but it is now. I want us to have this as a family memory.

Mothering wins out…

"Okay, baby. We'll hurry, we'll make it back in time to see Daddy. Come on let's go."

We shimmy across half a row. "Excuse us. Excuse us." Trip into the aisle and head toward double doors marked Exit. I am sure there are restrooms on the other side of those doors. Kimmie is keeping her end of the bargain; she is pumping her legs as fast as they will go. Thankfully, the restrooms are as expected right outside the exit doors. We storm in. We are alone. Terrific, no wait. We pick the first stall, paper the toilet seat, tug her panties to her ankles, and I place her on the throne. I hold her safe and she declares, "Oh, a big girl's seat."

"Okay, my love, go."

"I can't."

"You have to try. We have time, relax."

There is an intercom in the bathroom, and you can hear the proceedings. Guess Kim and I aren't the only ladies that have been called by Mother Nature at an inopportune time. The sound is not clear, but I can make out they are on the *M*'s,

Kim is swinging her feet. She looks up at me. "Mommy, I don't have to go."

"Oh, sweetie, we don't want to go back and then make a mistake. Just sit a minute more."

She sets her jaw and squints her eyes. We wait. Nothing. They are on the *O*'s.

"Okay, sweetie, let's get down and wash our hands."

"But I have to go."

"Okay." We wait. Nothing. She spins the toilet paper roll. We wait. Nothing. They are on the *R*'s. Nothing.

"Kimmie, sweetie…"

"There, Mommy, there."

"Fantastic!" They are on the *U*'s, and my mind asks, "How many *U*'s can there possibly be?"

"I did it."

"Yes, you did. Now we must hurry. Come on, quick like a bunny."

They start the *W*'s as we finish washing our hands. We opt to let them drip-dry. I push Kimmie out the door and down the aisle just as they call somebody with a *Y* last name.

Shari waves us to ours seats and says, "I got a picture of Jim shaking hands and receiving his diploma. Oh, Kathy, I'm so sorry."

Kim is incredulous. "Mommy, when is Daddy going on the stage?"

*****

I'm sitting on the stairs. Because they are open between each step, you can see what's happening everywhere downstairs. Sometimes Kimmie sits with me. She dangles her feet through the holes between the steps and likes to toss Weebles on the carpet below. *Thud.* She can't fall through, but I could and did. *Shhhhh.* Cats don't fall, we are too smart for that…

*****

MBA in hand, Jim launches into management: more meetings, more late nights, more travel. He loves traveling; he wears it like a badge of honor. It's as if he's joined a secret club. He's gone two to three days a week. Weekends are stacked with family and social commitments: dinner parties, kid parties, barbecues, UCLA football games, concerts… We are living the good life—the good and tired life.

I'm considering a job change. I've been with the bank over two years, and headhunters call me weekly. Programmers are a hot commodity, and job hopping is an accepted way to fast-track salaries and responsibilities.

I take a job close to home in our local business park. It's with UNIVAC a small company supporting major aerospace industries. The Valencia group is working with Lockheed in testing the aeronautical systems of the SR3 surveillance plane, an iteration of the

Blackbird. I'm excited to learn another programming language and to receive a 20 percent salary increase. In addition, I will be able to run home for lunch with Kim and Nonie. I am thrilled to be involved with the testing of this mysterious plane; I feel very *Man from U.N.C.L.E.* The government vets me, as well as my family and neighbors. I am given a security classification, a UNIVAC orientation, and assigned to a group of programmers housed in individual cubicles in a windowless building.

My group is comprised of men and women close to my age and technical background. We are new to UNIVAC and aerospace programming. We have been recruited because the SR3 is nearing a production deadline. Several of us have had general experience with Lockheed, McDonnel Douglas, or Hughes. Our team manager and the team's senior programmer are experienced UNIVAC techies and know the SR3 flight systems inside and out.

The new code isn't hard to learn; although its language's acronym, YUK, would suggest different. The problem is that the code sequences are parceled out, so each programmer has limited insight into the problem to be solved or the object to be tested. I assume this is part of the security protocol, but it exacerbates the ability to understand testing parameters and makes me worry about how comprehensive testing can be. I find it hard to jump into the middle of a routine with no background info and no hint on how your piece of the puzzle fits into the whole. This feeling of apprehension is magnified each time I draw midnight test time at Rye Canyon's "mini skunk works." I hate the dark drive up the canyon to the unmanned security hut guarding the semiopen gate. I hate parking in the almost-empty lot and finding my way to the simulated cockpit. Where is everybody? I climb up into the cockpit and wiggle my way into a small seat with just enough room for me, my test manuals, and a flashlight. I'm not impressed with all the blinking lights, I'm scared. I take a deep breath and ask, "What am I doing here?"

*****

"Sooty, Sooty, where are you? Time to come in. Hurry before a skunk gets you."

I hear Kathy; she's home late. Jim lets me out most nights; he knows a guy has to do what a guy has to do.

I love prowling around when everyone is asleep. Tippy toe, tippy toe.

I hide behind the pool equipment and wait. I'm so quiet, so still. I see them sneak along the wall. They scurry along the top. First one, then another, then whoosh, got you. Wish Priss could see these chubby little mousers. I pull their tails off and sometimes their heads. I like to leave what's left at the patio door. That's okay with Jim, but not with Nonie or Kathy. Someone always makes sure Kimmie doesn't see.

"Do you hear me, get in here it's late. And don't bring any rodents with you!"

*****

Nonie's a godsend. Our beds are always made. Laundry done. She shows Jim how to pack, unpack, and stay packed (my dad was a traveling salesman, the woman knows how to pack). She's happy to prepare dinner asking only that I provide food and a menu. She shares dinner with us most weekday nights ever since Grandma went to the nursing home. Nonie has Kim in little tots' gym, Sunday school, and buys us a piano so Kim can take lessons. She is sure Kim is musical like Bruce. Nonie dusts every day, every room. I get a housekeeper and tell her to stop. She doesn't. She tells me she gets bored in the afternoons. I suggest a book.

Grandma Patrick turns one hundred and one. Kim calls her Pakie. They share December as their birthday month. We take cake, candles, and flowers to the nursing home. Grandma has been there almost two years. It's a good place, we are lucky; Grandma calls it home. Kim sits on Grandma's lap as Pakie presides over the festivities in the dining hall. The residents and staff cheer as Grandma blows the candles out, all of them. Nonie and Aunt Ruth slice the cake. Kimberly looks like a storybook doll as she passes out pink pieces of frosted cake. She is wearing a bonnet and pinafore of white linen, so girly. She squeezes between wheelchairs, dining tables, and walkers. You can barely see her bonnet among the white and pink heads bobbing to greet her. Her new Mary Janes are a hit. Her cheeks are pink from kisses. She makes her way back to Pakie and points to a man; he waves.

"Pakie, he wants to know why cakes only have four corners."

"Oh my, that's a good question. I don't know. But there are never enough corners when it comes to icing."

"Jim, get that picture," Aunt Ruth directs as she cuts the final piece of cake.

Jim pushes through the crowd. Kimmie, just days from three, has climbed back into Pakie's lap. Her brown eyes gaze into Pakie's blue. One old one new, their faces mirror the almost one-hundred years between them.

*****

Tonight, I am going to follow that mouse, the one with the long, long tail that I can't quite catch. I'll creep and creep. I'm going to see where he goes when he whooshes down the back wall and onto the field. Where is he headed? That's what I want to know. Tonight, I won't chase. I'll follow. Tonight, we will share an adventure.

"I'll get the backlights and let Soot out." Jim switches off the late news.

"I'll let him back in when I check on Kim," Kathy calls from bedroom.

I sprint out the back door straight to the sycamore. Its first branch is flush with the slump stone wall that separates our yard from the empty dirt below. I will wait here, right here for Mr. Tail. There is rustling at the other end of the wall from the bush that shades the pool equipment in the day's heat. I wait, I am still like a rock. I crouch low, very low. I become one with the wall.

His beady black eyes reflect the moon as he begins his trek atop the wall toward me. A hundred feet from me, then eighty, sixty… I hold tight, thankful that sycamores have large leaves and that I am the color of night. I swallow the urge to leap, to chase. I hold my claws tight and watch. Here he comes. Now in the middle of the wall he stops, lifts his head and sniffs, his whiskers all a quiver. I wonder if he will smell the chicken I had for dinner. Then he's gone. I hear the quiet thud as he lands in the dirt on the other side of the wall. I stand and watch as he scurries up and over dirt piles.

I must be quick to follow, quick and quiet. I slide my front feet down the wall reaching as far as possible so my jump to the ground will be like spilled milk rolling over the edge of a table. I never lose sight of Mr. Tail. He's moving fast, so am I.

At first the dirt is flat and hard, then turns to soft piles and deep pits. Up and down we go. I see him and then I don't. I try to keep my eye on the tip of his tail. Does he know I'm following? Or is this his moonlight routine? I think he knows and is having fun with me.

Out of nowhere we are smack against a pile of wood. Mr. Tail leaps from shaft to shaft. I follow at a distance. I think this pile must be the wood Jim was talking about for the new school. I heard him tell Kathy about it; it will be where Kimmie goes when she is old enough for kindergarten. Mr. Tail climbs higher and higher; at the top he stops and looks right at me. He's smiling. With a whoosh he disappears between cracks where only my paws will fit.

Game over. I move a few beams up and look around. Where am I?

The moon seems to have a bite out of it, but its light is still bright enough to show piles of dirt to the left and right. I see trees ahead. I look over my shoulder, relief, there's my wall, my sycamore, my home.

"Kitty, kitty, Soot, Sooty. Time to come in. Sweet Soot, come."

The words come on waves through the night air. Tired, I trot toward Kathy's voice. She repeats her call. I move closer, faster, anxious to get home. With a giant leap I land back where I started, on top of the wall. I meow loudly hoping Kathy will hear and not shut the door.

"Oh, Soot, there you are. Hurry. Get in here, it's late. I was worried. Come on, kitty. The foot of our bed is waiting for you."

I hurry between Kathy's legs, fall to the floor, and roll over on my back. She almost trips. I wait for belly rubs. She obliges. I purr as loud as I can, Mr. Tail forgotten.

*****

Jim is out of town, Texas somewhere, computer installation of some kind. Nonie has taken a trip back to her childhood home, Rochester, New York. It seems an old flame has gotten the "gang" back together for a reunion. I'm surprised, it's not like my mom to reminisce; but I learn she is a faithful letter writer, and her circle of friends is wide. Good for Mom! I'm taking advantage of Jim and Mom's absence for some alone time with Kim. Most days Kim will be with the wife of my carpool buddy; they have two boys. Kim loves staying at their house. I will take a few days off of work so I can take Kim to preschool, watch her gym class, have a McDonald's date, take her to Placerita Canyon's nature museum, and bake cupcakes for her dad's return. We've even planned an overnight; Soot and I are going to let her sleep in the big bed with us.

Just home from the museum, Kim and I are planning pizza for dinner. The phone is ringing. Kim is busy sorting spoons and forks from the dishwasher.

"Hello."

"Is this Kathy Whang?"

"Yes."

"I'm calling regarding Amanda Patrick. That is your grand-mother correct?"

"Yes, is something wrong?"

"I see that your mother is out of town. You name is next on the list. Can you please come to the convalescent home?"

"I was planning to see Grandma tomorrow. Can I take care of whatever you need then?"

"We really need you to come this evening."

Grandma has been under the weather, a touch of pneumonia. Her doctor said its nothing to worry about. He gave my mom the okay to take her trip. Mom is more than halfway through her two-week reunion.

"Is there something wrong with my grandmother? Has her pneumonia gotten worse?"

"We need you to come over so we can discuss."

"Look I have a three-year-old, and no one to watch her at this time. Are you sure this can't wait until tomorrow? I can come early in the morning."

"I'm sorry we need you to come this evening."

"Has my grandmother passed away? Please tell me what's going on."

"Please come as soon as possible?"

"Okay." (I have no other choice.)

Kimberly is sitting cross-legged on the kitchen floor. Spoons and forks separated in piles in front of her. She looks up and smiles. I guess I could take her with me, but I don't know how long I'll be, and she needs dinner. I slap together a PB&J sandwich and give her a glass of milk.

"Pizza?" Kim wrinkles her nose at her PB&J.

"Not tonight, sweetie."

"Want some?" She offers me a bite of sandwich from the half she's just licked jam from.

I call my neighbor. Nonie often watches their little boy; maybe they can watch Kim. I explain the situation. I sense they are less than pleased. I am sure it's their son's bath time. They rally, "Sure, bring her over we can put on cartoons."

I call Aunt Ruth. I hate to, but I really don't want to do this alone. I explain what I think is going on.

"I don't want to go over there. I am sure she has passed. The words are hard to push out. I'm afraid, I don't know how to do this. What will I do about Mom? And, Kim, I can't leave her too long."

"Kathy, Uncle Les and I will meet you at the home. Give us an hour and then head over there. I am sure your assumption is right. I'm guessing there is some law about what they can say and can't say over the phone. Which is ridiculous, but what can you do? Take Kimmie to your neighbors. We'll be there soon."

The convalescent home sits on a small hill just minutes from my house. The facility sits at the top of a driveway lined with oleanders which seem forever in bloom. Grandma's room looks at the hill behind the building; it too is full of oleanders. She likes the view, says it reminds her of a park. I have been slow to arrive giving my aunt and uncle more than enough time to get there. It's about 8:00 p.m. I push open the entrance doors. As spotless as they keep the place, the smell of urine and disinfectant linger. I head down the hall to my grandmother's room. I hear voices mumbling ahead of me; my aunt steps into the hall and wraps her arms around me.

"Well, Muth and Fath are back where they belong, together." My uncle puts his arms around the both of us. Aunt Ruth continues, "We've called Dottie. She was still up, and I know she wouldn't have wanted us to wait until tomorrow. Les and I told her to finish her trip. Cutting it short by a few days doesn't make a lot of sense, and this way no flight changes need to be made. Muth wouldn't have wanted her to miss out on any fun. Les and I know what to do; the plans have all been made. There's nothing for you to do here. Best you get back to Kim. We are headed home. We can regroup tomorrow."

We walk to our cars. My aunt and uncle are both close to eighty. My aunt is short and stout, my uncle thin and of average height. They are sure-footed and clearheaded. I marvel at their strength, their seamless acceptance of death as an extension of life. I am horrified at my ineptitude. I should have been there for my aunt and mom. I am embarrassed. Such a coward.

I retrieve Kim; she is bleary-eyed from TV. I put her in bed in her clothes. She needs a good scrub, but that will have to wait. I wash her hands and face with a warm washcloth. Kisses. Lights out. Sooty rubs his face against the doorjamb, eying the afghan on her toy chest.

"Go ahead, stay in tonight, Soot. The mice will wait."

I call Jim, looking for comfort I don't deserve. Looking for a "poor, poor you." Looking for a "I'll catch the first flight home."

"Jim."

"Kathy? It's late. Why are you calling?"

I tell him about Grandma, the evening, my aunt and uncle, Kimmie. I wonder if he is paying attention.

"I'll call you tomorrow. I'm sorry about your grandmother. I need to get to sleep."

Unsatisfied, I hang up.

In the kitchen I turn off the ceiling lights; their fluorescence is blatant, more than annoying. I choose dark. I peer into the refrigerator hoping for an answer but not sure of the question. There are stacks of leftover this and that. Nothing appeals. I give the freezer door a tug, locate the mint chocolate chip ice cream, its usual seduction now lost on me. I push the door shut, fumble into the family room, and feel my way to the stairs. Moonlight streams through the front windows making long shadows slide through the open steps. I feel displaced, severed. I pass Kim's room, hear her sleep breathing. Comforted, I leave her bedroom door open. I find my bed, crawl in, and pull the blankets over my head.

I drive to LAX for Jim on Friday, and the following Friday I pick up Mom.

The family gathers, and Grandma and Grandpa are together at last, happily ever after.

Jim is distant. I'm…

Something is wrong. What?

Jim and I adopt a picture-perfect couple pose. We are very convincing. We surround ourselves with group and family activities careful to avoid any "just us" encounters. The illusion is cast. All agree we are the couple extraordinaire; sometimes we even convince ourselves all is well and have the perfect week or weekend. Sometimes the distance is just a passing sigh. Sometimes it's painful.

We each develop our own circle of friends. Friends outside of our couples' network. I think of them as Team Jim and Team Kathy. I like the feeling of just being Kathy; Kathy has a husband, Kathy has a child, but Kathy is mostly Kathy.

Jim and I have long, intellectual talks about us. We are worried about us. We try counselling but are dismissed because we are so mature. Meaning I guess we don't yell or scream or stomp off. What? What did the guy say? "Oh, you both are intelligent and mature, I

am sure you will work this out. I don't see what value I would be."
His receptionist says, "Seventy-five dollars, please."

I think Jim and I are special; well, were special. Probably married too young, naive to the consequences of commitment. Victims of innocence and love rusted away by expectation and secular needs. I'm hoping this vacancy between us is a phase, a glitch, a bump in the road. I work hard to convince myself it will pass. Jim is trying too, very trying.

*****

I like the shade of the sycamore. Its large leaves filter the sunlight and hide me. I am a good climber, not afraid of the tallest of heights or squirrels chattering or blue jays diving. On a branch or on the wall beneath the swaying leaves I can see the school growing out of the field. Men are moving lumber and pouring heaving gray goo out of a truck with a churning back. Cement. That's its name. The men holler, "Bring in the cement."

Sometimes I wish I were a man with a belt of clanging tools and heavy boots that go clump, clump, clump as they stride across the ground.

Tonight, when they have gone and its dark, maybe Mr. Tail and I will have another romp. If the cement is still wet, we will make prints to tell them we were there. Will they see? Will they care? Maybe I'll catch Mr. Tail put my teeth around his neck and then let him go just to show him I can. I don't know, I'll wait to see what the night brings.

*****

Jim, I'm going to take a walk around the block. I can't find Soot. He didn't come in last night, and he doesn't answer my call."

"Okay, make sure you check in the construction behind us. I know he thinks that's his private hunting grounds. Maybe he's hiding in a lumber pile waiting for God knows what. Do you want Kim and I to go with you?"

"No, you guys stay here in case he comes home."

I walk around the cul-de-sac and take the paseo along the wash just in case Sooty has taken his hunting over that fence and he can't find his way back.

"Here, kitty. Here, kitty."

I go down the street that will take me to the almost-built school.

"Here, kitty. Here, kitty."

It's early Saturday morning, too early for lawn mowing but not for the smells of frying bacon and syrupy pancakes. And coffee. That's what I need, coffee.

"Here, kitty. Here, kitty."

I jiggle the chain-link fencing guarding the construction and squeeze through the loosely locked gate. I'm careful to avoid piles of dirt, broken lumps of concrete, and various lengths pipe.

"Here, kitty. Here, kitty." No answer.

I call and call. I look toward our house. Jim's is peering over the wall. He must be standing on a picnic bench. He's waving. Oh, maybe Sooty is home!

"Any luck?"

"No." I continue around the block.

"Here, kitty. Here, kitty. Oh, kitty, where are you? Sooty kitty, please come home."

CHAPTER 8

George Washington

Description: Gorgeous. Unique. That's George. Born on George Washington's birthday he couldn't escape his name. He lives up to it with his regal stance and serious gaze. He's a beautiful kitten, a beautiful cat.

He is neither black nor white; he is not gray. Each hair in his fur coat starts white and ends with a black tip. Each and every one. Except for the tip of his tail, the fine fuzz inside his ears, and his paws which are white. There are definite rings running up his legs and around his tail. They seem to be made from the black tips starting closer to his undercoat. His whiskers are white. The features of his face are outlined in black: the washed-out pink of his nose is etched in black making a tiny heart in the middle of his face, someone has taken eyeliner to his round yellow-green eyes, and the soft skin of his mouth is sketched in black.

People ask, "Just what color is he?"

"He's not gray."

"So I have a friend that has a kitten that she can't find a home for. I thought…"

"Oh no, I'm not ready for that. Not yet maybe never."

"I was going to take him, but my boyfriend won't let me, he's allergic."

"We're not over Sooty yet. Jim says we go through cats too fast. No, can't do it, not now."

"But, Kathy, he's so beautiful and sweet, and he was born on George Washington's birthday, obviously has a great name already. Come on. You don't want him to end up in the pound, do you?"

My coworker digs into her purse and produces a picture of George.

I show the picture to Jim.

"Okay, but just one. I don't care if there are others in the litter. I can't do two cats again. This way if Sooty finds his way home he won't feel totally displaced."

George peeks out of his box. Paws first and then nose, whiskers, eyes, and ears. My friend has brought him to the office. Everyone is enthralled by his good looks. He is passed around, held high, and examined nose to tail. He is all about the admiration. He sits straight up and meets our stares, big round eyes glistening. We let him leap across the piles of computer printouts and manuals. At lunchtime I take him home to meet Nonie and Kim.

George is a big hit. He's Kim's Georgie and Nonie's Georgie Boy. Jim escorts him around the yard pointing out Sooty's favorite haunts, mice holes, and squirrel branches. Jim and I are overprotective when it comes to letting George roam at night. We let him out to hunt at dusk and call him in at our bedtime. He doesn't question this routine; it's all he knows, and for a cat he is very compliant.

Like Georgie, Jim and I are compliant. We continue with our marriage motions. A couple suspended. Best friends, still, not knowing how to help each other or us.

*****

I like it here. There's a couch by a big window. I lay on the back and watch the birds and butterflies skim the grass. I know the birds are looking for worms, but what are the butterflies looking for?

I'm the only cat here. Although they keep talking about a Sooty. They seem to have lost him. I hope they don't lose me.

There is Nonie, Jim, Kathy, and Kimmie. Kimmie is mostly mine; she is little, they call her kid, not kitten. We take our afternoon naps together on the family room floor by the big glass door, sort of under Jim's table. Nonie lays a blanket down; Kimmie has a teddy to hold, and I snuggle into her back. We like the floor it's cooler down here. It's summer outside, it's hot. Nonie tiptoes to the living room to read while we snooze. She says, "You two have a good sleep. I'll just be here putting my feet up. Sometimes I hear her snore."

*****

"Kathy, I'm not sure I love you."

"Okay, then stop giving me mushy cards on holidays and my birthday signed 'I love you.' Okay?"

"Okay."

"Do you want to take a break, a separation, a divorce?"

"No."

"Any ideas, this limbo is getting to me. I'm always waiting for the other shoe to drop. And I don't know how to stop it."

"Well, my friend and his wife have an open marriage. He does his thing, and she does hers. They get together for kid activities."

"That's not happening."

"Okay. Let's wait it out."

I make another job change. More money, back to a computer language I know and a chance to code interactive screens. It's a small insurance operation in the valley just a twenty-minute drive, no night calls, not even long hours.

Jim wants a boat and a matching van to tow it.

He argues, "We can do family things. Kimmie will love it. You can learn to water ski. We can take it to Catalina and Tahoe and do boat camping. Our friends will love it."

"Okay, I want something too."

I'm thirty, and like most females my age, my clock is ticking. It doesn't matter that I have Kimmie nor that she's perfect. What did my friend say? "Babies are like potato chips you can't have just one." I am a textbook case: thirty *equals* gotta have a baby, *now*. How upsetting to realize I'm just like everyone else. A victim of my hormones.

"I want a baby. I'm having my IUD removed. I didn't want to blindside you; I know it's selfish and the timing is not the best, but I really want this. What do you think? A boat, a baby, a new start. Deal?"

We haven't discussed more children; we never discussed children at all. We never had a grand plan. Maybe we should have.

"Kimmie would love that. She's been asking for a brother or sister ever since she started Miss Jeanne's. She should have an ally. That's fair, Kathy. Deal!"

Motivated by our distinct agendas, Jim and I fall back into or would it be forward into love. "I love you" is written, said, and meant. Mushy cards are back; weekends and dinners without friends reinstituted.

The IUD is out. My doctor cautions (again) that it may take a while before I'm pregnant. Does he not hear the ticking?

We go to boat shows, take SABOT (a one-person sailboat) lessons to get our water safety certificates, talk with custom van dealers, decide on color schemes, and become owners of a 26' Sea Ray and decked-out Ford van to tow it: cream, beige, and brown.

Nonie is a neighborhood favorite. I often find her entertaining Kim and friends in the living room. Picnics and story times are her forte. She spreads her red-checked tablecloth on the carpet and serves PB&J and story after story. Kim and her pals are enthralled. Nonie sits on a stool, and Georgie perches on the coffee table; the children edge the tablecloth cross-legged. I often catch this gathering when just home from work. I sometimes hide behind the door and enjoy flashes of my childhood, and thank God for Kim's good fortune.

"Marriage encounter, I want you to go to marriage encounter."

"Marriage what?"

"Encounter." Fran and Tom are sponsoring us. All our other couple friends have been. Tom says it's like a recommitment, says it's made a real difference in their relationship."

"How did that not come up at the last dinner party? Sounds gimmicky."

"It's sponsored by the Catholic Church. I think they're pretty legit."

"Oh yea, I have my doubts."

"Kathy, come on how bad can it be?"

"Well…"

"It's this weekend, Friday night through Sunday afternoon."

"Wow, am I being set up?"

"Kind of, Tom set it up. I couldn't get out of it. I've already talked with Nonie, she's on board. She has a great weekend planned for Kim. I'm not thrilled either, but I just couldn't say no."

"Are you sure they are going to let us out on Sunday? I'm concerned. Okay, but I draw the line if it comes to walking on hot coals or eating spiders, I don't need to explore me or you that badly."

"I'll take you out to the Backwoods Inn for prime rib once we escape."

"Ha, okay. God I can't believe we're doing this."

Kimmie is not pleased. She refuses to wave goodbye. George peeks between her legs, Nonie holds her hand. We would be upset except we know once we leave the driveway the tears will stop and the Nonie party will begin.

*****

"Nonie!" Kim screams and slides down the stairs on her tummy. I follow leaping from top to landing to bottom stair.

"Nonie, what are you doing?"

"I'm making a tent."

"But that's Daddy's pool table. We mustn't touch."

"We aren't going to touch. We are going to camp underneath."

"Oh. Georgie too?"

"Of course. Baked beans and hot dogs for dinner, we'll eat in the dining room like ladies. George will have people tuna in his bowl. Then we'll have coloring books and stories in our tent. Then watch TV if you like, a bath and bed. Oh, ice cream between bath and bed. I have whip cream for Georgie Boy."

"Me too, I want whip cream. Where will you sleep?"

"In Mom's and Dad's bed so I can hear you if you need me."

"Okay, come on, Georgie, get in the tent. Look here's a flashlight and animal crackers, not too many we want whip cream later, right?"

I love it when Nonie stays over. If we are lucky there will be bacon for breakfast or donuts or pancakes or even sausage. I love syrup and butter. Nonie puts butter on everything.

"Nonie, what will we do tomorrow? Can Georgie and I have breakfast in the tent?"

"I think that can be arranged. Now come on you two, dinner is served."

*****

I'm pregnant. We haven't shared this with many. Being older I want to wait until the fourth month to go public. Nonie knows, but no one in Jim's family does and none of our friends. I'm not as seasick as I was with Kim, but I've packed crackers in my "encounter" bag just in case. I am sure I will have indigestion.

Marriage encounter is a weekend away for couples who want to take their marriage from good to great. Versions are sponsored by several faiths. The program usually runs from Friday evening at 8:00 p.m. to 4:00 p.m. on Sunday afternoon. Couples experience unique presentations and dynamic discussions in the comfort of a secluded environment. There are group events as well as individual couple exercises. These "encounters" are designed to enhance communication between and appreciation of one another within the couple.

We are in the hills of Glendale somewhere. We arrive in the semidark of summer. The facility reminds me of campuses I've stayed at when attending Methodist youth retreats. Maybe I've been here? It's park like with dorms surrounding central meeting rooms and the dining hall. The buildings are connected by dirt paths lined in shrubs and covered by far-reaching oaks.

We attend a brief introduction, are given the weekend's agenda, and escorted to our rooms. We are asked not to "mingle" with other couples.

The rooms are basic—twin beds, bureaus, desks, closets. A group bathroom is down the hall. I thank God I'm not at the need-to-pee-all-the-time phase of my pregnancy. Jim rolls his eyes, and we shove the beds together. We hear the couple next door shuffling around.

"We should go and introduce ourselves." Jim laughs.

"And get in trouble on the first night? Behave."

"There's no phone."

"What if Nonie should need us?"

"I gave her their general number. Someone answers the phone twenty-four hours. They will come get us in an emergency."

"Jim, have I said *creepy?*"

"Shhhh, at least we are together. Don't fall through the crack."

There are group exercises and couple assignments. We are given questions to ask ourselves and each other. We are asked to write deep and meaningful love letters to one another on topics designed to expose our real feelings, hopes, and needs. Share, be open, show empathy. Repeat.

Each group session is followed by a personal encounter in our room.

"Remember, do not discuss your assignments with other couples," the director implores as we all follow the path back to our rooms.

"What is he afraid of? That we will plan a coup or hike through the oaks to the freeway?" I can't help but giggle.

By Saturday afternoon, Jim and I have decided to cheat. It's not that we don't see the value in this touchy-feely approach, we do. But we have talked and shared. There's nothing more to say to one another on this particular subject. Our questions have been answered. We respect one another, we want to rekindle. But knowing each other's deepest feelings does not change them. As hard as we try our feelings are our feelings. You *can't force a square peg in a round hole*. We choose naps, not letters.

"Well, we are almost done. This is the last session." Jim smiles. "We get through this, and Backwoods here we come."

"Thank goodness, maybe I'll treat myself to a glass of wine."

Jim and I are surprised to learn that we are expected to go to a celebration dinner this evening. We are even more surprised to pass through a line of well-wishers as we exit toward the parking lot. Tom and Fran and two other couples we know are waving and offering hugs, all smiles and encouragement.

"Have we joined a cult? I'm exhausted. I can't do dinner. Can we just go home and order a pizza?"

"Yes, let's get home and see our girl. Any more of this kumbaya will be the end of me."

"Thanks, Jim, Backwoods next Saturday?"

"Promise."

Kim hardly acknowledges our return. She is busy with Play-Doh in the kitchen. Nonie is anxious to hear all about it. We give her a five-minute overview and promise all the details over pizza if she will stay and join us.

She has a funny look on her face. "Fran called. She and Tom will be here at six to pick you up for the group dinner."

We acquiesce. They're friends; they care, we care. We order pizza for Nonie and Kim, put on smiles, and go to dinner—two square pegs.

*****

I'm going to have my picture taken. Kathy says her friend is entering a photo contest, and she wants to take a picture of me. She says her friend thinks I'm unique. All I have to do is sit on the back of the couch on my spot and look regal.

Her friend gives me bites of cheese and wags a feather over my head.

"That's it, Georgie. Let's see those big almost-yellow eyes. Wrap your tail around your feet. Here's another bite of cheese. Let me scratch behind your ear. You're doing great"

It pays to be beautiful.

*****

This time pregnant I make a plan, a pact. I won't whine. I won't weep. I won't demand. I will keep to a minimal wardrobe knowing it's only nine months. I will weigh daily. I will help Kim understand that love multiplies.

Five months in. I haven't gained a pound. I look and feel great. I'm enjoying my condition, pleased, content. I've renewed my love of sewing, and my maternity wardrobe exemplifies the practicality of mix and match. Jim and I have begun to talk to Kim about the baby; she has already told Miss Jeanne. I will talk to my manager about my leave next month. Jim praises my cheery disposition. We discuss the pros and cons of having a boy or girl. We ask Kim if she has a preference. She ponders, "A boy, is that a brother? My friend has a brother. I want a brother."

Jim calls me at work. He wants to take me to lunch.

"Okay, what's up?"

"I'm in your area, thought we could have lunch. Is there some place nice you'd like to go? I'll call and make a reservation."

I give him the name of the restaurant that we use for work celebrations. It's close.

"I'll pick you up at noon by your main entrance.

"Okay, see you."

Jim is always on time. It's bright and warm outside. He is standing by the car and opens my door as I come out. The restaurant is cool and dark. Busy but not loud. This is a welcome break; it's been a crazy day.

"This is a nice surprise."

We order.

"Kathy, I need to talk to you. You know the therapist I've been seeing."

"Yes." I do know the therapist. I've met him. He explained to me that he and Jim are working on *Jim issues* and that I shouldn't feel excluded. It's not about me. It's about Jim. He said, "Don't take it personally. We will keep you in the loop."

Jim hurries on. "He… I think the best thing for our marriage is a break."

"A break? Now? With the baby coming?"

"I will stay until the baby is born. Then I'll move to an apartment. I'll rent one near work, Inglewood or somewhere nearer Westwood."

Lunch comes. We don't eat.

Dumbfounded and devoid of emotions, I ask to go back to work.

A week later I tell my mom about my lunch. Kim is watching TV in the den, George is eavesdropping from under the pool table, Jim is out of town.

"So you know Jim's been seeing a therapist, and they think a marriage break is in order. I don't have a lot of details. For now, the plan is that Jim will stay until the baby is born. Once I'm comfortable managing both the baby and Kim, he will leave. I don't know nor does he for how long that means. We will be separated, not officially just personally. Finances will remain the same. Jim is planning on being home most weekends to be with Kim and the baby."

Mom's scrubbing a pan harboring burnt mac and cheese. She holds her brush midair. "Oh, Kathy. What will you tell Kim?"

"We haven't decided yet. We'll wait until after the baby comes to talk to her."

Mom is silent. If she has more questions she doesn't ask.

Jim and I continue our charade. Sometimes I wonder if the *lunch* actually happened or maybe it was a figment of my pregnancy brain.

*****

"Georgie, come look."

I'm in the middle of cleaning my toes. My left back leg is stretched straight out, my right leg reaches to the ceiling, toes spread, I am mid tongue. I'm the contortionist extraordinaire. (That's what Kathy calls me.) I dive my tongue in out of each space between each toe. I am doing a superb job. I'm persnickety about my toes. Kathy says I should have a manicurist; she's afraid I'm going to dislocate something.

"Georgie!"

Oh, okay. I stand and stretch, maybe something's wrong. I take the stairs three at a time.

"Look. I have a new bed. See. Mom says the baby needs my crib. Mom and Dad are going to move it to the other room. I have to sleep in this bed. We are going to pick sheets. She says you can sleep with me in my new bed. She says I am too big for the crib."

Well, I think the baby will be too small.

✶✶✶✶✶

"How was your day?" Jim asks. He's just home from work; he grabs Kim and swings her into his arms.

I'm stir-frying bell peppers, cauliflower, and hamburger. The rice pot is bubbling.

"Oh my god. Always some dirty old man lurking around. That programmer who's on the systems team grabbed me and tried to kiss me in the copy room. Nasty. Wanted to know if he could have a hug."

"Really? You're kidding. What did you do? Did you tell someone?"

"I shoved him into the corner. I told him to knock it off. What an idiot. Wonder if he would have wanted a hug if he knew I was pregnant."

"Kathy, you need to do something."

"I'm going to watch him like a hawk. There's nothing to do, no one else saw. I took care of it. I gave him a good shove. He said, "Sorry.""

"I'm sorry, I'm really sorry this happened to you." He puts Kimmie down and drapes his arm around my shoulders. I stir unsolicited tears into sizzling hamburger.

Christmas 1978. Jim and I love Christmas; it is easy for us to make the season our reality. We feel safe in our traditions—cutout cookies, finding the perfect tree the day after Kim's birthday, gift shopping, deciding to soap or not soap the tree, placing Kim's pink bow from her baby bouquet on the treetop, Christmas Eve at Jim's family, midnight candlelight service at Nonie's church, stuffing stockings, leaving cookies for Santa and carrots for Rudolph, having Nonie sleep over, waiting for Kimmie to discover what Santa has left, staying in our PJs all Christmas Day, ending with spaghetti dinner and Nonie's raspberry-and-cream-cheese Jell-O surprise.

Jim's work Christmas is typical for aerospace companies in Westwood high-rises. TRW spares no expense; there is always a lunch at a five-star restaurant, open bar, employees only. Kim and I meet Jim afterward. Everyone loves to see Kim; they remark on her growth and her serious demeanor. We walk to Bullock's Westwood to see Santa. Kim obliges us and sits on his lap, no tears, click another perfect picture. On the way home we drive through the UCLA campus, sometimes we stop at the student store; we show Kimmie where we met, where we lived. She loves Janss Steps; we hike up and down. We tell her, "This is where you will go to college." On the way to the freeway, we show her our first apartment. It looks the same; it is well-kept.

Christmas at my work is low-key. We have lunch brought in and have a gift exchange. The gifts are anonymous. Some silly, some cool, mine…

The ritual is to open each gift in front of the group; they want to see if you laugh, cry, or cheer. We stand in a circle. One of the women reads the tags and distributes each gift. Mine is in a small box. Plain green paper, white ribbon. I pull the bow, tear at the paper, lift the lid, and fold back the tissue layers.

"What is it, Kathy? Hold it up." The group encourages.

I remove the first piece. A hot orange lace bedecked bikini bottom—lingerie. I don't bother with the second piece, a bra no doubt. I'm mortified. The crowd is silent.

"Okay, guys, next victim." I force a nonchalant tone.

They move on.

My carpool buddy steps behind me and takes the box. He's older, fatherly, embarrassed for me. "I'll just get rid of this. We leave early."

Just a few more months, I console myself. I'll take care of this nonsense when I return from my leave. I push it out of my mind. It's hard to shove the orange out, harder not to go punch my secret Santa in his nose.

It's April. In February, my OB-GYN said, "Start gaining weight." I have managed to do a fine job of that. Weight and water. My blood pressure is high. My doctor insists on an ultrasound thinking my size indicates twins. I toddle in; the nurse is kind, smears me with jelly. Not twins, just a big baby. The doctor asks if I want to know the baby's sex. I do, I hate green and yellow. I've gone mostly white. I would love to know if I should add blue or pink, lace or denim.

"It's a boy." I report to Jim. "It's a boy, and I'm officially on bed rest."

"Not twins then." I hear the relief in his voice. I'm saddened.

I'm bloated, bigger than big. Jim suggests time in the pool.

"Don't you think that will be soothing? Maybe floating would feel good, no weight on your feet."

It's chilly outside. Jim heats the pool to ninety. "Damn the gas bill," he declares. He finds me a huge T-shirt, huge, and convinces me it's the perfect maternity bathing suit. He escorts me down the steps. I go carefully down one puffed foot at a time. The water is warm, like a bath. With each step I'm lighter. Jim lets go of my hand; I'm launched. Nonie, Kim, and George stare through the patio door, incredulous. Oh, the relief. I'm a giant soap bubble, no, a beach ball caught by the wind. I glide from side to side, featherlike.

Bed rest is so boring, so uncomfortable. I can hear life going on downstairs. They are having a wonderful time. I'm not. TV stinks. I'm forced to face all those thoughts I have been holding at bay. Most of my life I've been surrounded by women, what will I do with a boy? Will I love him as much as I love Kim? How will I help Kim understand that babies get all the attention? It doesn't mean anyone loves her less. Will Nonie be able at seventy to handle two small children? Is Jim really going to leave? And if he does, how long will it last? What will we tell Kim? What? What? What?

On sharing day, Kim tells her classmates she is going to have a brother. Nonie buys blue sleep sacks, bath wraps, and boy socks. I cheat and sneak out to our local children's store; I purchase a dinosaur of plush sapphire blue and red tennis shoes size 0.

I need to cheat one more time. In the fall, Kim will start kindergarten. It's the custom at her preschool in spring to walk the paseo from Little Sheppard's to Meadows Elementary to join the current kindergarten class for circle time. The children "graduating" get to meet their teachers and scope out the playground. Parents are asked to join. Nonie and I will meet the class at Meadows.

I can hear Nonie calling Kim from the kitchen. It's time for her to go to school. Nonie will drop Kim off and come back for me. We will walk over to Meadows. It's ridiculous to drive; the school is literally behind us. The waddle will be good for me.

I hear Kimmie coming up to kiss me goodbye.

I'm sitting on the edge of the bed looking at my barely visible flip-flopped feet. I know they won't fit into a shoe of any kind. I can't stop the tears spilling down my cheeks and onto my very large belly.

"Mommy, don't cry." She leans against my hip and places her hand on my knee.

"Sorry, I'm going to have to wear my flip-flops to kindergarten."

"That's okay, you are so beautiful it won't matter. If Miss Jeanne would let me, I'd wear flip-flops. I made you a present."

It's a piece of construction paper, red. Pasted in the middle is a large pink heart. Kim has drawn round eyes in purple crayon on it. Under the eyes is a smaller pink heart. The little heart is smiling a red crayon smile. It appears to be sleeping; it's eyes are two horizontal lines. At the bottom in all caps, I LOVE YOU, MOMMY.

"See it's you and our baby. Don't get it wet. Don't be late." She struts out the door.

*****

The best place for a cat when the furniture starts moving is on the top of the linen closet. This way you can't get hit, but you can see what's going on.

Jim and his friend Bruce, not the Bruce they call brother or uncle, are moving the crib from Kim's room to the baby's room. They are moving a new dresser and desk into Kimmie's room. They put them across from her big girl bed.

They are moving another bed like Kim's into the baby's room. Kathy says that's where Nonie will sleep when she babysits us.

This is so confusing; I think I'll clean my toes.

*****

May 13, Mother's Day 1979, 9:00 a.m. Thomas James (TJ) Whang enters our world. He is eight pounds three ounces. He's mad. He hollers. He stares at me, his one open eye assessing my reaction. I laugh. Five minutes old, and he's already holding me accountable. I love him so.

Nonie and Jim's parents come to the hospital. Jim has brought Kim; she is wearing her "I'm finally a sister" T-shirt I had made for her months ago. TJ is introduced; both eyes now open. Jim positions Kim on a big leather chair. Grandma Whang puts a pillow on her lap, and Nonie puts TJ on the pillow. Kimmie is glowing. We all are. Jim Senior seems almost elevated, so pleased with his grandson, so pleased the family name is secure for another generation.

I sift through the snapshots of TJ's welcome home. "A picture is worth a thousand words." The one I hold in my hand is telling a lie. Jim and I are sitting on the living room couch. I still look pregnant. TJ is four days old, propped against Jim's chest. His little fists are midair, and one chubby foot protrudes from the yellow flannel blanket that holds him tight. Jim drapes one arm around my shoulders, and his opposite hand holds TJ in place. I'm leaning into Jim. Our faces reflect rapture. A modern nativity. The snapshot doesn't show the still-unanswered questions behind my smiling eyes. Are you really leaving, and if so when? And if when, what are we going to tell Kim?

T sleeps through the night at one week. I like having him next to me in his little blue porta-bed. I wake when he doesn't just to watch him breathe.

We've had the talk. It's been decided we are going to execute Jim's great escape tonight. The timing is perfect; his apartment lease is month to month. It's June first.

He's home early from work and is upstairs packing. Nonie has left before his arrival. T is finishing his "dinner" bottle. Kim and I are helping him hold it. We three are in the rocking chair.

"Did I eat in this chair when I was a baby?"

"Yes, you did. We'd rock and rock until your eyes shut then I'd tiptoe to the crib and lay you next to Teddy."

"T doesn't have a teddy."

"No, he has a dinosaur. We'll wait until he's bigger and then see if he will want dino in his crib."

Kim and I tuck T in. We shut his door. Jim joins us in the hall.

"I'm hungry." Kimmie is hopping on one foot.

"That's good, let go down and get some dinner." Jim helps her hop down the stairs.

It's over a dinner of tomato soup and grilled cheese that Jim and I explain to Kim he is going to live somewhere else for a while.

"I'll call you and see you on the weekends. I need to be closer to work. I need to live by myself. People sometimes need to live by themselves."

Kim looks from Jim to me and back.

"I'm going to leave tonight as soon as I finish packing. Do you want to come back up and help me?"

"I guess."

"You two go ahead, I'll be up in a minute. I procrastinate stacking the dishwasher. This is ridiculous; we are all acting too civilized, I should scream.

Jim is taking shirts and suits out of the closest on their hangers; he has a travel pole in his car. All foldables are in his suitcase in neat stacks just like Nonie has shown him. I sit on the bed next to Kim watching him. So calm, organized, purposeful. We both turn as Kim starts to sob, quiet gasps, then the tears start.

"Oh, baby, it will be alright." I use a reassuring voice that almost convinces me.

She continues, no words just tears and tears and tears.

"Kim, please tell us what we can do." Jim and I don't know what else to say.

"Don't go, don't go. Will you take the baby too? Who will I live with?"

"With me of course. With T and me right here."

Kim catches her breath. "And Nonie and Georgie?"

"Yes, sweetie." I wipe her nose and pull her hair away from her wet cheeks."

It is obvious our explanation was a failure. Kim thought we both were leaving. She thought she was being abandoned. We couldn't have done a worse job if we had planned to be the cruelest parents ever.

Kim slides from the bed. "Oh, just Daddy's going?"

"Yes, just Daddy."

"Yes, and I will be visiting often," he calms.

"Can I help take clothes to the car? Can I come visit your new house?"

*****

Our baby only cries until someone brings a bottle.

Kimmie cried the other night and last week when she scraped her knee.

Nonie cries when the baby and Kathy nap and Kim is at preschool.

Kathy cries at night in the dark as she strokes my back and tells me not to worry.

I don't cry; sometimes I give a worried howl, but I don't cry.

*****

We settle into the new arrangement.

Kimmie returns to her preschool routine. I have filled Miss Jeanne in, and she promises to let Nonie and I know if Kimmie struggles.

Nonie comes every day just like before. When the timing works, we walk Kimmie to school letting her push the stroller. Our arrival is always a big hit. Her pals want to touch T, hold his bottle; they can't get close enough. Kim is the proud sister; she takes charge telling them to wash their hands and take turns.

"What's his real name?" a sandy haired, freckled nose boy asks.

"What?" Kim is confused.

I squat down and explain, "We call him T because we love him so much, and it's small like he is. His big name is Thomas James Whang. His nickname is TJ, T for Thomas and J for James. I think that's what his friends will call him."

He and Kim look at me. They don't get it. Once again, I have overexplained. Freckled nose looks closely at T and says, "I'll just call him Tige."

Nonie laughs, "Our boy has many names."

When Kim is in school and Nonie is at one of her church functions, it's just me and T and, of course, George. TJ's chubby and squishy and so huggable. At first, he looked just like Kim, but his coloring is now more like mine, his dark hair is falling out and white, blonde fluff is replacing it; his baby gray blue eyes are turning lighter, sky blue maybe.

Jim comes each weekend. He hires a gardener and pays the pool man to come twice a week instead of once. This way he optimizes his time with the kids. We often do family things just like any other family of four. Jim often lets Nonie and I go off and do girl things. I like this part of the arrangement.

I save grocery shopping for weekdays.

"Kathy, Kathy Whang!"

I'm emptying my cart contents onto the conveyer belt; the cashier is asking for my discount card. I look toward the voice.

"Jerry! How are you? What are you doing in the grocery store on a weekday? Are you still at the bank?"

"And you? Aren't you working?"

"I'm on maternity leave, I have a couple of weeks left."

"I'm on vacation, helping get my girls ready for school. We miss you at the bank. Boy or girl? And congratulations!"

Jerry waits for me to push my cart to the front aisle out of the way of other shoppers.

"Are you going back to work? Would you be interested in making a job change? We are really growing, lots of opportunities. With your skills and experience you'd be a shoo-in for project management. I have a great position open in my section."

Jerry was my former section manager at the bank. He lives in Valencia not far from our current house and just blocks away from the old one.

"A boy. We had a boy. Oh, that's an attractive offer. Let me think about it?"

He hands me his card. "Come in and listen to my spiel. I'll give you all the details: money, benefits, you know the good stuff."

I can't wait to tell Nonie and Jim. I would love to return to the bank. I loved the bank. It would be like going home. I can't believe my luck.

Déjà vu. I return to my current job to tender my resignation. My peers are surprised but happy for my good fortune; several ask me to let them know if there are any other openings. I have negotiated a start date with the bank that will give me two more weeks at home, just enough time to prepare Kim, Nonie, and me for kindergarten.

*****

"Georgie. Come see my new shoes. Georgie, what are you doing? Bad boy, come out of the baby's room. Come on."

Caught.

"They buckle. I'm going to kindergarten. Maybe if you sit on my desk you can see our play yard out the window. See it's over there. Oh, the tree is in the way, maybe if you sat on the wall."

I know where it is. I have used the sandbox once or twice on my way home from mousing. How do I tell her not to play in that stick to the swings?

*****

TJ turns one. This coming Sunday we will celebrate. Friday Jim will move back. Like when he left there are not a lot of words or plans. It just seems the right thing to do.

Thomas James sits in his high chair. He is a toe head; his eyes are big and round and have settled on Dutch blue. He has a safari shirt on with matching khaki shorts. White blond curls spill over his collar. We will cut those tonight. He is quick to shout, quick to laugh, quick to hug. Kim stands to his left. We all crowd around. There must be thirty of us. I place a piece of cake on his tray. He looks to Kim. She nods.

There is no hesitation. Wham, his right palm flattens the cake, pushing globs of frosting between his fingers, perfect for licking. Wham and lick, wham and lick. Kim points to the cake. He shakes his head no. Someone places a bowl of vanilla ice cream on his tray. He laughs and reaches his hand in mixing lumps of frosting with the creamy cold goodness. He paints this into his mouth. Kim claps. The crowd cheers.

PART II

After

CHAPTER 9

Kathleen and Nicki Nicholas

Description:

Kathleen: Kathleen is a hamster. A rodent. A clean pink-nosed, pink-footed, no-tail rodent. Our Kathleen is orange and white. She chews a lot, through just about everything: plastic tubes, cage doors, and electrical wires when she can get at them. She's a hamster. I don't know what else to say. She belongs to Kim, and Kim has named her after me. I am so honored.

Nicki Nicholas: Nicki is a chinchilla Persian. You can't help but think precious at first sight. You want to place her on a satin pillow. She deserves a satin pillow. All puff and fluff. Her disposition is sweet; she could be haughty over her looks, but she's just sweet.

A tiny kitten, a tiny cat. She is reminiscent of George in color; she is silvery white. Her coat is thick and bushy. Nonie says she has a pansy face. Her doll-like eyes, lips, and nose like George's are trimmed in black. She has blue eyes. Yes blue. She is mine, given to me because no one else wants her. She has a birth defect in her right eye. She is a flawed purebred. She can't be shown. She has no breeding value. There's nothing left to do but love her.

Houseboating, we've been houseboating on Lake Powell. Three families—six adults and four kids. Ten days, two ski boats, fishing poles, innertubes, cigars, Tequila, beer, marshmallows, board games, ten pounds of hamburger, mounds of hot dogs, rib eye for twenty, two disposable beach barbecues, few shoes and gobs of bathing suits.

Only T is left behind. He and Nonie stay with Grandma Martha and her *new* husband. (Jim Senior passed away from heart disease when T was just weeks old.) T is still in diapers and not pool safe, certainly not houseboat safe. My mom is pleased Martha has included her, happy to share the babysitting responsibilities while we are away.

Our trip was a step out of reality. An indulgence of sun, water, friends, and family. Returning to "real" life was not easy.

Kim is starting the second grade. T goes to preschool three times a week; he is in Miss Jeanne's class per my request. Like ducks to water, Nonie has taken easily to caring for two kids instead of one. I'm doing pretty good in my new role too. Kim is a great helpmate, so comfortable being a big sister.

*****

"Ahhhh, kitty, kitty."

Here he comes. Oh, maybe I can hide behind the couch. No, that's no good, he still fits there if he gets on his hands and knees. I'll make a dash for Kimmie's bed, slide under, and hide in the corner. Yes, that's it, I'm still faster than he is on the stairs.

"Kitty?"

*****

Jim is a senior project manager. He is responsible for his department's financial reporting. Several weeks ago, he discovered discrepancies in the monthly reports.

"I can't believe this, Kathy. I can't."

"Are you sure it's not a glitch or mathematical error of some kind?"

"It looks deliberate, and it has been going on for a while. It's finally too big to hide."

TRW conducts an official investigation. Jim is made interim department manager.

"I feel like a Judas. I can't believe my boss has done this."

Jim is promoted. He receives a "thank-you" bonus. He doesn't celebrate.

My job is not as dramatic. I was right; returning to the bank was like coming home. I'm responsible for several back-office systems, managing two to three programmers per project. A unit manager's position will be opening soon. Jerry encourages me to apply, "A shoo-in, you're a shoo-in."

*****

"Run, Georgie, run," calls Kim.

I dash under the coffee table. A huge clear ball rolls past me. Clickety click it goes over the entrance hall tiles. What's making it go? Oh. There's something in it.

TJ is close behind, his chubby legs pumping, his bare feet slapping against the cool floor.

"TJ, don't touch it, don't kick it. Mom!"

"Hey, what's going on? T, you know you can't chase the hamster when it's in its ball. Just watch. And, Kimmie, you need to make sure Georgie can't get to the ball either. Although, it looks like he is more afraid than curious."

Oh, it's the hamster, Kimmie's hamster. Kimmie's mouse. The mouse they call Kathleen. The mouse that lives in her room on the desk that runs all night on the whirring wire wheel.

"Well, just wait, little mousy, just wait. I'm watching you. Hamster or mouse, whatever, I'm going to get you."

*****

A couple of weeks ago, Kim brought home the class Guinea pig. Gilbert spent the weekend with us. Ever since Kim has insisted that she needs one.

"Nonie, can you talk to Mom? Do you think she will let me have one? I took really good care of Gilbert."

"Yes, I know. But having one of your own is different than just having one over the weekend. You already have Georgie, and Mom doesn't like rodents."

"Rodents?"

"Anything mouselike. To Mom a Guinea pig looks just like a giant mouse. Besides, Georgie Boy might want to chase it."

"I'm going to ask. My friend has one. It's in her room."

"Well, can't hurt to ask."

I said yes, I did. She caught me when I was just home from work. She was so intent so serious. She promised she would take care of it; I wouldn't have to do a thing. I was able to talk her out of the G-pig and into a hamster. To thank me, she has named it Kathleen.

I'm glad about the hamster. It makes me less guilty about my own acquisition, a Persian kitten.

A work friend breeds chinchilla Persians for show and profit. She has a kitten with a flaw in one of her eyes. That makes the kitty "worthless" in the world of show cats. She offers it to me.

"Kathy, wouldn't you like one of my fuzz balls? She's beautiful."

"One of your Persians? I would love it, but aren't they pricey?"

"This little girl needs a home. I can't sell or show her she has a flaw in one of her eyes. I'd keep her, but I already have three permanent cats. My landlady would throw a fit. I would happily give her away if I could find her a good home. I know you would love her… Please?"

I can't resist.

My friend delivers her to the house. Her little flat face tufted in white silver ears perked up listening, nose and chin peeking curiously over the edge of her carryall, a red leather purse. Purrfect.

"Here she is. She'll need a good brushing daily. Don't let her outside. I'm not sure she has any street smarts. It would be easy to pick her up and take her. I mean who could resist, she is adorable.

I promise we will take good care of her.

I lift her up. She is a whisper weight. She mews as softly as she feels. I'm captivated. Her name is instantly on my lips.

WHO ME

"Welcome home, Nicki Nicholas."

Nonie, Kim, and TJ are very excited. Jim, Kathleen, and George not so much.

You can't see the flaw in her eye unless the light hits it just right. It's the slightest of lines across her pupil. Unlike our other more pedestrian cats, her long silver tresses must be brushed; if you skip even a day, she mats up and then there is hell to pay. We wipe her face after she eats; its flatness makes the stinky stuff stick to her whiskers and nose. She lets Kim and I bathe her in the kitchen sink, lukewarm water please. She does groom herself, but her fur is so dense a weekly shampoo is in order. When wet she isn't much larger than Kathleen. Bathing makes her shiver, so we tumble her towel on warm before we pat her dry. She doesn't mind the blow-dryer; she tilts her flat face up and shuts her eyes welcoming the warmth. I swear she smiles. She and George eat side by side; we give her a head start. George is being very gallant about this newcomer; he often defers to Nicki regarding food and sleeping preferences. I think he is smitten.

*****

She makes my toes curl. If I sit still and close my eyes, she will come and clean my ears. She lets me lick the soft spot between her eyes. We nap on the back of the couch, nose to nose. The sun warms our backs.

*****

I'm now a unit manager with the bank. My official title is assistant vice president (AVP). Six programmers report to me. I have an office with a door, windows, desk, credenza, and guest chairs.

Jim brags and sends me suit shopping, friends take me to dinner, work peers take me to lunch, and a headhunter sends me flowers. My mother-in-law wants to know who makes more money—Jim or me. Jim winks at me and replies, "Kathy does." My mother just beams, "You're smart like your dad. He would have been so proud!" Jim's best friend tries to burst my bubble by declaring that everyone

201

at a bank is an AVP, everyone but him (I think he's in marketing at Wells Fargo, a junior something).

The bank trains its managers in time, finance, project, and human resource management. We are expected to meet and maintain specific criteria. The bank takes pride in its revered reputation. TRW is similar. Jim and I are caught up in Reaganomics. We are young, hardworking, and purveyors of optimism. We don't think in terms of what we can't do; we only see possibilities.

We believe respect creates respect. That's our management style. We have high expectations for our staffs and ourselves. Our professions are similar enough that we can and do use each other as sounding boards. We enjoy entertaining our staffs. We have summer barbecues, winter open houses, and last spring we pitied our groups against each other for a softball competition. We are hoping to make it a tradition.

Personally, it's been hit-and-miss. Jim is unsettled and distant. Déjà vu. Every night is a guessing game, who am I going to get—happy family man or pissed-off want-to-be bachelor. We shout at each other after the kids are in bed. Jim has never been angry, he is now. Talking or not talking doesn't help. Civil conversations only occur about the kids or work. I ask him to leave. He moves to his friend's and then in with his mother. It's a relief.

*****

The big people go in and out. Kimmie does, and so does TJ. Georgie is always catting about on the back wall or up in the sycamore. I watch from Kim's room. I've tried to get out the patio door between their feet or by following George nose to butt. But Kathy catches me or Nonie.

Kathy says, "Someone will see you and take you, Nick, you are an inside cat. We need to keep you inside."

I just want to see the backyard and maybe the front where the birds dive for worms. I don't want to be anywhere but here. I just want to see all there is of here. And I want to go and come like George.

I guess for now I'll settle for a romp up and down the stairs, or if Kathleen is rolling around, I'll chase her. I remind myself not to get ahead of the ball; it hurts when it rolls back and hits your nose.

Tomorrow I'll talk to George again; maybe he'll reconsider and help me get out.

*****

"Kathy, here's a message for you." The receptionist waves me down on my way back from lunch.

I knock on my boss's door. "Come on in."

"Donald, I'm going to have to go home. I just got a phone message from my mother, and our house has been broken into."

"Oh, of course, go, go. Just keep me posted if you need a few days."

Nonie meets me in the driveway.

"Mommy, they didn't get my Pooh, I looked. He's still on my bed," Kim reassures.

"Kathy, the front door was ajar when I got home from my women's meeting. I didn't see anyone around the house, so I went in shouting 'I'm here, I'm here.' The big window in the family room is broken, your TV is gone, and Jim's stereo equipment is hanging by its wires. The bedrooms have been ransacked; you better check your jewelry. I called you, waited for Kim to get home from school, and we went to pick up TJ. Then I thought I'd better call the police, well the sheriff, they'll be here at three to take a report. Georgie Boy, Nicki, and Kathleen, are *none the worse for wear.*"

"Mom, I can't thank you enough! Are you okay? Were you scared? Let's go in and get a cool drink or something. I better call Jim."

Jim comes to assess the damage. He makes it in time to talk with the sheriff. He calls our insurance guy. He puts cardboard on the broken window and tells me to call a glass man. He laughs about the stereo equipment. "I'm glad I hardwired that into the cabinet. I guess it was taking too long to get it out, so they just left it." He decides to complete the job and takes the stereo with him. He's pissed about my diamond ring; it wasn't insured. He is not impressed that they left my wedding ring. He apologizes, but he needs to leave, he has a date. He promises to pick us up a TV this weekend.

Kim is worried the "bad men" will come back.

I'm heartbroken; they took a collection of gold wedding rings belonging to both sides of the family—my grandmas, Jim's grandmas. Irreplaceable.

T sits in my lap, he looks worried. "Mom, did they take our food?"

"No, baby."

"I'm hungry."

Nonie laughs. "Let's get dinner, and I think I should spend the night."

"That would be wonderful, Mom."

I go back to work the next day. Kim puts Pooh in her closet each day when she goes to school. Nonie is obsessed with locking the doors and windows when she leaves, even though they broke the window to get in. We have a new TV. Insurance covers everything but the jewelry.

*****

I did it, I slid right out between Nonie's legs. I'm free! I'm not just a pretty face. I'm smart and clever. Now where to?

"Nicki, Nicki, come back! No, no. Don't go over the wall. Don't jump. Stop."

*****

We call the school. We search the playground, the neighbors' yards. We walk around and around the cul-de-sacs. How did she get away so thoroughly so quickly? She doesn't answer our calls. We leave food out. Days pass. We are convinced that someone has her, has our sweet baby.

There is no consoling George. Nonie goes over and over how she could have stopped this from happening. T says, "Call the sheriff." Kim is silent. My heart aches, and I dread telling my friend I have betrayed her trust.

There are a number of us women at work in the same boat. The ex-love boat. I can't help but remember that programmer from my first year at the bank and his warning about divorce. The bank seems to breed divorce or maybe working women do. Several of us losers have gravitated together. So far, we are all just separated, but you never know. We do Friday-night drinks when possible. We gossip about available guys and leaf through the employee phonebook in search of possible bachelors. I find it comforting not to be the only one failing in a role that women are supposed to excel in.

Nonie keeps the home fires burning. I tease her that she's more than my mother; she's my wife.

Jim and I establish a sensible relationship. Being separated has allowed us to become friends again. We talk daily, he takes the kids every other weekend, our expenses are handled from a joint account, he is available for school activities, he makes sure Nonie's condo is well maintained and helps her buy a new car, we take the kids on the boat and to the condo in Mammoth, he has his team and I have mine. We see no practical or emotional advantage to divorcing, so we don't. We are the contemporary family.

"Kathy, look at how Georgie eats." I can tell Mom is worried. "It looks like he is having trouble swallowing, and he looks thinner than usual."

I make an appointment at the vet's. I wonder if cats can get sore throats like people do. I'm preparing myself for a round of forcing antibiotics down Georgie's throat. I know he will not be happy about any cure. I remember when he had a cyst on his leg, and they wrapped it after draining it. Talk about upset, he ran in circles shaking his leg and pulling at the wrap with his teeth. When he finally got it off, he hid under the bed until he cleaned it to his satisfaction. I never told the vet; we didn't have it rewrapped, it healed, and Georgie finally forgave us. I am sure I can handle a few pills, or maybe they can take care of this with a single shot.

If it were Nicki, I'd just put her in my purse. But taking Georgie to the doctor involves a chase around the house before I ungraciously cram him into his carrier. There is howling all the way to the vet; the car radio doesn't help.

Georgie has to spend the night; he needs x-rays and blood work. The vet will call me in the morning.

"Mrs. Whang?"

"Yes."

"We have Georgie's test results back. Can you come in?"

Georgie has throat cancer. There is nothing the vet can do. I only have one choice. We can do it now or later. I decide not to let George suffer a minute more than he has too. I give my approval to put him down. (What an awful term.)

The doctor asks if I would like a few moments with George. I would like another lifetime.

George is calm; he is sedated from all the tests. He's lying on a blanket someone has kindly placed on the cold stainless steel table.

"Georgie, beautiful boy. I love you. We all love you. You are handsome and smart. I wish I could fix you, make it stop hurting." I kiss his head and stroke his signature fur. "Oh, gorgeous George." I remember the portrait my friend took of him and promise him we will hang it in the hall with Kim and T's school pictures. I should hold him as he falls deeper asleep. I can't. Someone comes to take him out of the room.

Nonie blows her nose and wipes her face. I've just let everyone know Georgie Boy is not coming home. Kim disappears to her room. I don't think TJ gets it, but he knows Kim's upset. He follows her upstairs.

Mom puts the teakettle on. I pick up Georgie's bowls and let the tears flow.

CHAPTER 10

Pepper and Ginger

Description: Pound kitties…

Pepper: He is not quite black and too dark to be gray. He looks like pepper. He is from the animal shelter in Castaic. His little face is happy, yes happy. His eyes bright and Irish green, his whiskers choppy. He is fast, running and jumping, up and over the other kitties in the wire compound. He is tiny, wiry, and full of it. I don't think he is quite six weeks, but the officer at the pound says he is good to go.

Ginger: We think she is from the same litter as Pepper; it's hard to tell as the pen they are in is large and has at least ten kittens of all sizes. She and Pepper look the same age and seem the same size. The officer says, "Pretty sure we picked them up together." Her face is delicate; her features remind me of the pale fall flowers on one of my grandmother's hand-painted china teacups. She is orange, no soft apricot, and white. She wears her apricot as a cape over the top of her head, shoulders, and back. Her ears, limbs, and tail are white. I've never had an orangey kitty. She prances around, following Pepper; he must be her big brother. Yes, must be, her eyes are Irish green.

"Okay, ladies, let's do this." I have gathered my ex-love boat comrades.

We have decided that my boss is the perfect match for the youngest member of our group. They are both tall, bright, available, and possess striking good looks. If we held a contest at the office, they would win most desirable man and woman.

It's Friday night and two of us are escorting our candidate to the bank's watering hole. Operation matchup is a go. We are in luck; all players are present.

This is tricky business getting Donald to come sit with us. He's across the room with his secretary, she is pinned to his side. He sees us, waves, detaches the secretary, and strides over to offer us a drink. We accept.

"Kathy, did you recover from your break-in? That must have been awful for you. Are your kids okay? I understand you and your husband are separated. Please let me know if there is anything the bank can help with. My door is always open."

Our plan has taken a wrong turn. My friends have disappeared. I'm not sure what I should or want to do.

"Oh, thank you. We're fine."

"Good to hear. Can I offer you some dinner?"

"No thanks, I really should be getting home."

"Where's your car in the bank's garage?"

"Yes."

"Let me walk you over."

The restaurant and bar sits across the street from the garage. Halfway across the intersection Donald takes my hand. It's a sweet gesture, protective. I say nothing. I don't pull away.

"Here it is. (My trusty gray Honda sedan)."

"I'm up two levels, would you give me a ride?"

"Sure." He folds his six foot four inches into my car.

"Okay, this is me. (Black boat-sized Cadillac.) Drive safe, see you on Monday."

My right hand is resting on my gear shift. He places his hand over mine and leans in to give me a kiss. A kiss on the forehead...an intentional kiss on the forehead. He unfolds himself, drapes his suit coat over his shoulder, and shuts the car door.

"Night."

Back in the office Monday, I'm faced with a barrage of questions.

"So what happened to my date? I thought this was my match not yours." She laughs and winks.

"Kathy, what happened after we left? What did he say, what did you do? Did anything happen we should know about?"

"Where did you guys go? You just abandoned me."

"Well, we could see we weren't needed."

Blushing, I wave them down the hall.

I catch myself smiling for no reason as I review the proposals for this year's federal tax updates to our payroll system. I'm impressed. My group has shown innovation and best of all tight doable deadlines. I reach for the phone to congratulate my senior programmer.

Donald is standing in my doorway.

"Lunch?"

"Okay." I grab my purse. (I must be losing my mind.)

"Mom, I miss Riley and Nicki so much." Kim is moving her broccoli to the edge of her plate.

"Oh, sweetheart, me too." Nonie has made our favorite, tuna casserole with a thick top layer of potato chips.

"Mom, Miss Jeanne says I make good forts. We have new Lincoln Logs at school. Can I have some?"

"T, do you want to put that on your save-for list?"

"Yep."

"Mom, about the cats, couldn't we have a kitten?"

"I want a kitten too. I would make it a fort."

"Oh, let me think about it. I not sure I'm ready."

Kim pleads, "We are, Mom, we are."

Donald stops by my office every morning. We go to lunch every day. He often reaches over the table to caress my hand as I reach for the salt or my water. It's a gentle move, meant to make contact, not to impose or compel. I remain physically distant. He seems oblivious to the possibility that peers or staff may see us. I show no resistance to his attention; I am an equal culprit. He is interested in my kids and Nonie, and our relationships one to another. He wonders where my marriage is headed. Will we divorce? What are my thoughts about the future? I'm fascinated by his interest in me, by his openness about his wives, his girlfriends, his roommate. Does he know he's labeled a *playboy*?

Today after lunch, he lingers in my door. Tall, very thin, bearded, irresistible.

"So would you ever consider having more children?"

Now there's a line. What woman wouldn't fall for that?

I take the kids to the Castaic Animal Center on Saturday. I'm not ready, but I can't imagine being a kid without a kitten. Kathleen just isn't enough.

"You can each pick one."

They get out of the car. This will be their first trip to a shelter. The officer in charge escorts us into the facility. We pass some empty dog kennels.

TJ asks, "Where are the dogs?"

The officer replies, "See the little door on the other side of each cage? They can go out to a play, and they can come in when they are hungry or tired, or like now, they can come in to see if someone has come to take them home."

"Oh, Mom…"

There is barking and leaping, and it's hard to keep walking. I look straight ahead.

"No, T, we cannot have a dog. Daddy won't let us." Jim's not here to defend himself so I take no shame in attributing this decision to him. It's true anyway. He doesn't like dogs; they are too needy.

"Here we go, folks." The officer points down the hall.

There are two large cages. One has older cats and one has kittens. One is like corn popping in a covered pan, the other one is dominated by sleeping felines on platforms covered with rug pieces or in kitty-sized hammocks. We are here for the popcorn.

Kim is quick to pick an orange, mostly white kitten. A girl. TJ takes longer. He can't decide between a tabby or a near black mix. He settles on the one that easily climbs to the top of the cage, the near black one. A boy.

The kittens are named before we turn onto our street. The girl, Ginger. The boy, Pepper.

It's fun getting the kitties settled. Kim and T each want their kitty to sleep with them. After much discussion, they agree the kittens would be better sleeping together so they can keep each other warm. We find a box roomy enough for two and one of T's old baby blankets. Kim and T decide they will slide the box from one room to the other each night.

Nonie asks if we should butter their feet and put them in the garage.

"Mom," I laugh, "I read that there is no need for the butter, a wives' tale. We will keep them in the house, not the garage, for a week or two and then introduce them to the yard in stages."

*****

I have noticed that no one ever asks my opinion.

"Kathleen, would you like a plastic tube system to climb through?"

"Kathleen, what do you think about being put in a ball, would you rather not be?"

"Kathleen, do you want more cats sneaking around and peering at you in the middle of the night?"

I do have a thought or two you know.

*****

"Your boss?" My mom raises her voice just enough to let me know she's advocating extreme caution.

"Yes." I bring her up to date. "I know I've got to put a stop to this. I could be jeopardizing my career and that is not worth a fling with the bank's playboy. I don't know what he sees in me anyway. Playboy does suburban housewife?"

"Kathy! Well, maybe he doesn't want to be a playboy anymore."

"I doubt that."

Lunch again. We sit down, and Donald passes the breadbasket. I put it to the side.

"We need to talk. This has to stop. We are in harm's way, and I'm in no position to put my job at risk."

"You're right."

"This has to be our last lunch. From now on its boss and employee."

"Agreed." He lights one of his long, thin dark cigarettes and looks away.

Several days pass. In support, Nonie now packs three lunches. I eat in my office.

Donald is staying on his side of the floor.

I try to empty my mind of missed possibilities.

*****

"Hey, Pep, come look. What's that up there?"

"A mouse I think."

"I am not a mouse, you stupid cat."

"I am not stupid, and I'm a kitten. Ginge, it's a mouselike thing."

"I'm a hamster. Get out of my room."

Pepper hops from floor to chair to desktop. He pushes his nose into the wire cage.

"What are you doing in there on that wheel?"

"Having a run."

"Where too? Talk about stupid."

*****

Donald calls me to his office to review staffing plans. He asks me to bring my justifications for any increases.

The door is open. I take a seat placing my budget files on the edge of his desk.

"Before we get started, I have a proposal."

"About?"

"The way we ended our brief relationship. I still would like to meet your kids and Nonie and your menagerie. Maybe we could have a barbecue at your house. I'd bring the steaks and cook if you'll do the *sides*. That's pushy right? I know, it's just I didn't like the way things ended. It was the right thing to do, but the wrong way to do it. Cold turkey, no looking back."

"Okay." I'm not sure I should agree.

I invite Donald to come on the Saturday two weeks after our budget meeting. I've asked him to come early to meet the kids and Nonie. I'm anxious about him being with the kids too long. He has zero experience, and I imagine little tolerance with kids, and TJ's and Kim's curiosity can be overwhelming. I need to keep their encounter brief. Thirty minutes tops. Nonie is going to take them to her house for an overnight. They will be thrilled. Donald and I will have a quiet dinner, say proper goodbyes, and return to business only.

"He's here, he's here." T has been peering out the window for the last twenty minutes. I have just finished putting Kim's hair in pigtails. Nonie answers the door, introducing herself and keeping T in check.

"Hi, Donald. This is my daughter, Kim. I see you've met Nonie and T."

Kim rolls her eyes up and down Donald, gives him her best smile, and declares, "You are really tall."

"I guess so. I've been this way for so long I don't think about it very often, only when someone asks me to get something off a top shelf."

As promised, he has brought steaks. He also has a bouquet of flowers from his yard and a bottle of champagne.

He hands the flowers to Kim. I give him a brief tour. He admires the pool and the fort TJ has built for Pepper under the pool table. Pepper sidesteps up to him, I'm sure thinking he's a tree. Ginger decides to watch from under the stairs.

My plan is working perfectly. Dinner was great, our conversation easy. The children left willingly, and there were no cooking mishaps. I'm a little sad this is our first and last dinner.

"I can't do this. I can't not do this," he whispers to my back. I'm at the sink. He enfolds me in his arms. He turns me to face him, leans down, I reach up. My plan evaporates.

As managers, we support the bank's professional standards. We have agreed our relationship is not a flirtation; we are not sure what it is, it may be serious. We are concerned about our staffs, our reputations, and our careers. We follow HR protocol; we individually notify our department head, and we each meet with HR assuring them our feelings are mutual. As soon as an appropriate position becomes available, I will move out of Donald's section. We let our staffs know we are in a relationship and the plan for my transfer. We address any concerns they have. Donald and I laugh about HR's effusive thanks for coming to them; we know that reduces their liability should things turn negative.

I let Jim know what's going on. I need him to commit to a more dependable weekend schedule. Donald and I need time together, alone.

"Kathy, that's great." Jim is genuine in his well-wishes.

"I will talk to my mom. I'm sure the kids are welcome. I will plan every other weekend at her house. How come this guy? You've had other opportunities but never were interested. And your boss, that's interesting."

"I know, it's a surprise to me too. I have no answers. Just going with the flow for now."

"I've been thinking. I'm going to sell the pool table. No matter what happens between us, there is no sense having one in the house. I find part of my enjoyment is going to different pool halls to play, you know just getting out."

"That would be great. I would love to have an actual family room. Then I can make the den a playroom."

"I thought you'd like the idea. You've always loved the opportunity to move the furniture around. Bet you'll want to paint and redecorate too."

I turn in my ex-love boat membership. I receive many good wishes and an equal about of warnings.

"You know he lives with a woman. They used to date. Kathy, you better be careful. Don't count on anything serious, you are hardly his type."

"I know about her. Her name is Kathleen, so unbelievable. She's also blonde but brown eyes and tall. Donald's been up front about her. She's a flight attendant, talk about the classic bachelor chic. They have been involved in the past, but now she is a friend. He refers to her as his renter. I've got my eye on the situation. And as for his type, Donald has been clear that would be me."

"He's been married twice. Obviously, those didn't work out."

"Both wives left him. I know the stories. And face it I'm still married."

"He has dated almost every single woman in the technical division. And those he hasn't hope he will."

"Yep. I know, I know. But he's off the market for now."

"I hope you aren't headed for disaster."

"Hope not. I'm infatuated, caught at the edge of a whirlpool. You know, sort of in, sort of out, anticipating the thrill of the fall…"

"Oh my god. You are in trouble."

*****

"Hey, Ginge, what's that noise? That grinding sawing noise. Our people are all in bed. What is that?"

Ginger and Pepper uncurl themselves from the corner of their box. They are in TJ's room. Pepper leaps up to check on T.

"It's not him, he's sleeping hard. He's got that plastic lawn mower with him again. Wouldn't you think he prefer his stuffed dino. Kids."

The sound stops. And begins. And stops.

Pep and Ginge pad to Kim's room. The culprit is on her hind legs tittering on the edge of the desk. Kathleen has gnawed her way out of her cage from the plastic plug that holds the new orange tubing on.

She sees the cats and dives into the pencil holder dumping pencils and crayons everywhere. What a clatter. The cats pursue her over the desk and onto the dresser. Socks without mates, barrettes, and Kim's piggy bank fly.

"Mom!"

The room light flips on.

"What is going on in here?"

*****

"Sweetheart, we really need to do something about Kathleen."

"I know. She can't help it, Mom."

215

"It's not just the tubing, it's her ball and electrical wires. She's going to electrocute herself or one of us. Yesterday I found a hole in the carpet by your bedroom door. The only thing that she hasn't chewed through is her wire cage. I think we are going to have to go back to just keeping her in there."

Kathleen must really want out. She's taught herself to trip the latch on the cage door. Night chases have become the norm. I make myself resist opening the front door and letting her escape. I decide to relegate her to the garage. I wire the cage door shut. The garage is warm, it's spring. Kim and I make sure the cage is clean, there is food and water. Kim visits her before and after school. So far, so good.

"Chilly this morning." Nonie is making toast. "I think hot chocolate is in order."

We are having an unexpected cold snap. Nonie insists on sweaters for kids and tells me to take a coat.

"Morning, Kathleen." I pat her cage on the way to the car. She is hiding under the wood chips. She must be chilly too. "Are you there? Come out and say goodbye, sweetie."

No response. No movement.

"I feel horrible."

"Not your fault. The weatherman got it wrong too."

"I shouldn't have put her in the garage."

"Should I get Kim another hamster?"

"No, Donald, not unless it's going to live with Jim."

On the weekends that Jim has the kids, Donald and I alternate between his and my house.

Donald's house is up against a hillside in Glendale. It looks like a miniature Spanish castle. The garage is street level, circa the twenties or thirties, not really big enough for today's cars. The only way to the front door is up two flights of brick stairs. The first flight goes from the street to a small terrace where you can catch your breath. There you are level with the garage roof. The second flight takes you to a larger terrace where the house sits. These stairs connect to a path that leads to the front door. The door is arched, made of heavy planks, and touts a peephole guarded by a window grid of twisted wrought iron. To the left of the door is a massive window, to the right a turret. The door opens to a circular entrance area. Inside the floors are dark wood, the furniture heavy, and most drapes green velvet. The light sconces and stair rail are scrolled wrought iron. The living room is massive, as is the fireplace. The dining room table is conference-room size with eight tall backed, carved chairs. The kitchen is a kitchen. The jewel of the downstairs in my mind is the breakfast room; sunshine pours in from its three turret windows and makes the room warm and cozy. Upstairs are two bedrooms and a room that opens to a rustic wood balcony hosting overstuffed club chairs. Donald calls the room the den, the balcony his oasis. The master bedroom is huge, worthy of a king. The backyard is a secluded brick patio, pushed deep into the hillside. This house is Donald's third wife and his most beloved.

Being in Donald's house makes me nervous. I am after all in the other woman's home. He reassures me (time and again) their romantic involvement is over. Now it's a friendship, and he needs the rent. I believe that he believes his story. I wonder what she believes. Kathleen is never there when I'm; she is usually on a bicoastal or European junket. Before me, the rule was no *dates* in the house. Kathleen has confronted Donald on this lapse. He has told her I'm not a *date*, I'm the one he is going to marry. Okay…still uncomfortable. Is this jealousy or common sense?

I focus on…the romance. His midnight visits to Valencia to be with me before stealing back to Glendale before dawn. His reflection in the floor-length mirror watching me brush my hair. Our physicality. The discovery of passion, compassion. The realization of self. The fun of together. The laughter. Anticipation. The joy of feeling beautiful, cherished. The shock of being loved more than loving. I will myself not to overthink this absurd, astonishing predicament.

*****

"Pep, why did you do that?"

"Ginger, I didn't do it on purpose. I slipped on the tile trying to get out of his way. He took a step back. I saw the end of one of my lives in the heel of his shoe. I lost control."

"Disgusting. You are too big to do that."

"I'm ashamed, I am."

"Well, Kathy got his shoe and the floor cleaned, and you're not squashed, so I guess everything is alright."

"I almost did it again when he picked me up. He raised me so high I thought I might hit the ceiling. We were eye to eye."

"What did he say to you?"

"Kitty, I'm sorry. I'll try to be more careful. You too, okay? No more shitting on my shoe."

"No argument there."

*****

"Kathy, what about our trip? It's coming up."

I can't believe it's almost time for our second houseboat vacation. This time TJ can go.

It's Friday, Jim is picking up T and Kim. "You want to go, right? I'm looking forward to being together with you and the kids."

"Me too. Kim was asking about it the other day. I can't wait to see T's reaction to living on the houseboat. We will have to keep a life jacket on him day and night. Maybe tether him to the railing?"

"That's a good idea. But I'm not sure about the tether." Jim laughs, tackles T from behind, and tosses him on his shoulders.

"I will let the others know, it's a go. Let's set up a pre-trip barbecue to talk about who will bring what. Do you still have the menus from last time? I was thinking we could reuse them."

"I do. Great idea."

"Bye, Mom."

"Bye, guys, I'll see you Sunday. Be good for Dad and Grandma. Jim, don't let your mother overload them with coke or candy, Mondays are hard enough without scraping them off the ceiling."

Today I transfer to my new section. Donald is no longer my boss. I'm familiar with my new manager and several of his other unit managers. A reorganization made this possible. Systems have been realigned: all general ledger systems grouped together in one section and all the payroll systems in another. I will be taking some of my staff with me and acquiring others. The bank believes in rotating staff and managers, ensuring we are interchangeable as needed. Donald and I are looking forward to being more open as a couple. We've planned a celebratory lunch. I plan to talk to him about my upcoming vacation. I hope that won't dampen the mood.

"Donald, the kids and I are going to be gone for two weeks. We are going houseboating on Lake Powell. I think I told you we've done that before. We've had the reservations for over a year. Last time T didn't get to go. This will be such an adventure for him."

"When? With Jim, right?"

"Yes. End of next month."

"What does this mean for us?"

"That means I am going on a family vacation with my kids and husband. I don't know what that means any more than you do. I need to distance myself long enough to decide where I am and where I'm going. I need perspective, and Lake Powell is a chance to get it."

"So am I going to lose you? I'm about to be left again, that would be strike three. God, babe."

"I need to get my head clear. I think I know what I want, but this isn't just about me. There's a lot on the line. My family, my life as it should be."

"I hear you. I get it. But it's going to kill me. Days of not knowing, and then the knowing…"

I'm as scared as Donald. I want to do the right thing, reclaim my morality, my sense of duty, be a good mother, a good wife. If Jim comes home, shouldn't I be there? And if he doesn't, shouldn't I fight for his return? Don't Kim and TJ deserve that? Why is it so hard to embrace what I know is right? Why does wrong feel right? Is my wrong right? God.

We are set to go. Van packed, boat hitched, Lake Powell, here we come. Yesterday I met Donald at his house for a bittersweet bon voyage. I promised to find a way to call at least once. Nonie is taking care of the house and the kitties. Everything is under control.

We are quite the caravan—three families in two vans with two ski boats in tow. We spend a night in St. George, Utah; take a side trip to Zion National Park; hike Indian cliff dwellings; and pick up the houseboat in Page, Arizona. We are anxious to get on the water and relax. The drive in has been spectacular, our senses are on overload, our cameras need film. We launch the ski boats; load the kids and gear into the houseboat; raise anchor and move away from the vast marina into landscapes of sun-kissed sandstone castles and cathedrals; skies of magnificent crystalline blue; deep channels of navy, emerald, and turquoise water; and the promise of a starry, starry night. Our escape is complete.

*****

"Pep, there's the front door. I bet it's Nonie. Maybe she's brought people tuna."

"Oh, wouldn't that be wonderful."

"Hey, guys, have you been good? Bet you'd like to get out for a while, chase each other around. You can come out front with me while I get the mail and water. Then I have a surprise for you."

*****

Lake Powell is an indulgence in sensibilities. Engulfed in nature's beauty crap falls away, clarity seeps in, and uncertainty is replaced by the obvious.

For the last two days we have anchored in a small channel of the lake. We are alone, well not with eleven of us, but we are the only houseboat in this inlet. There are climbable rocks to our left and a perfect beach for the kids to explore to the right. Both are just a swim or a paddleboard away. We take the ski boats out to a large bay each morning where we make the first wake of the day in the glassy water. The kids find a grocery bag and make a flag from its brown paper. They insist we all put our names on it. Using a stick from last night's s'mores for a pole, they plant the flag on "their" beach. They end their impromptu celebration by singing "Do-Re-Mi" from *The Sound of Music*. They declare the cove ours. Tomorrow we will break camp and go into Bullhead. Tomorrow I make my phone call.

Jim and I dock our boat. He has to check in with work also. We will meet back here in about twenty minutes and regroup with the others for a real sit-at-a-table lunch. Kim and TJ are with the group getting the houseboat refueled.

I hate pay phones, counting change, less-than-friendly operators. "Yes, I want to charge this to my home phone, no not collect." I've decided to call our reception desk instead of Donald directly, that way if he is not there I can leave a message, and he will know I called.

"Hello? Yes, just give me a minute I'm wrapping up a meeting. No, don't go, stay on the line, I will be right with you."

I take a deep breath.

"What's up?" I hear him take a drag on his cigarette and the clink of his pinkie ring as it hits the side of his ashtray.

"Donald. I love you. I want to be with you."

"Oh God. I've thought of coming after you. Where the hell is Lake Powell? Get home! I love you so."

CHAPTER 11

Amanda of Mill Valley

Description: She is eight weeks old when she arrives at the Newhall Pet Store. We have been waiting for her for over two months. She's from a breeder in Oregon.

She is a Cocker Spaniel, purebred, buff colored. Her baby fur is wavy. She reminds me of one of Kim's teddies. Her tail is a nub. I was not pleased to learn that it's been cropped; I wasn't aware of the accepted dictates of the breed. At the moment her ears fall to the edge of her jaw. When she's grown, they will be the signature Cocker length like Lady in the Disney classic. Her face is gold velvet. She has black button eyes, of course, and a cold, wet nose.

"Miss me?"

"Well, let's see. I couldn't make it to work for the first three days you were fooling around with your husband. I haven't been able to concentrate, no appetite, imagine me without an appetite, been drinking and smoking too much… I've become a lovesick teenage girl. Miss you? No not much."

It's good to be home. Better to be with Donald. Glad the trip was everything I'd hoped for. Brokenhearted about Ginger.

"Mom, why did the lady next door kill Ginger?"

"T, I don't know. I don't. I don't think she meant to. She just wanted to scare Ginger away. Nonie said she's afraid of cats. Ginger was running toward her, and she was on her knees weeding."

"Ginger wasn't going to hurt her, she's just a kitten. Nonie says she was playing down by the sidewalk. She was chasing a grasshopper. She wasn't even in their yard just close. I think we should do something." Kim lays her head on the kitchen table.

"It feels that way, doesn't it?"

"Maybe we should call Dad or Donald or the sheriff." T is feeding bits of cheese to Pepper.

"I can't believe she sprayed weed killer in Gingie's sweet face. I can't believe she had the nerve to think Nonie would feel sorry for her. That she wouldn't be upset, that we wouldn't. We are going to have to make sure that when Pepper is outside, he stays in the backyard, and we don't leave him out too long."

"Maybe we shouldn't let him out at all. T and I could guard the doors. We could get him a litter box, so he doesn't even have to go out."

"Both good ideas. Maybe one of us can go with him when he's out. Kind of keep track of him. I hate not to let him out. He's used to being outside and would miss chasing and climbing. We'll figure it out. I'm more worried about Nonie, she feels so guilty especially since we were away when it happened. I hate that she had to take care of everything by herself. Make sure you give her extra hugs."

"Like she gives me when I break a glass or spill the cereal?"

"Yes, T, exactly."

*****

Chilly. Maybe I'll fit here. I'll just slip under the lawn mower handle and knead a nice flat spot between his back and the blanket. There, circle, again, settle, wrap tail, relax, tail tip to nose. "Ginger, where are you, I'm cold."

*****

Donald is really angry about the cat. He has quite a temper. He wants to report it, make her pay; he wants to march over and give her a piece of his mind. I talk him out of it. He can't bear to see Kim cry.

Donald asks me to file for divorce. It's time. After a false start with a lawyer who wants me to denigrate Jim, rob him blind and sell the house to guarantee his fee, I come to my senses and fire him. I told him from the start, this was going to be fair, equal down the middle; that Jim and I had grown up together, are parents together, are best friends. I thought he understood, I was wrong. He was all about the money, his not mine. Jim and I use a paralegal. Standard forms, a flat fee, and six months later on November 3, 1983, after fourteen years of marriage, our divorce decree is granted.

Jim buys a condo in Redondo Beach close to his mom's house and a short drive to *his* boat's storage. The condo is two blocks from the beach; the kids are ecstatic. We refinance the house; he takes the current capital, and I take the mortgage and potential capital. He sells my mom's condo, and we relocate her to senior apartment just blocks from *my* house. He sells the ski condo and upgrades to one that can accommodate several families. He invites Donald and I to use it whenever we want.

Donald refinances my loan at 14 percent interest to 9 percent. Good for me good for him.

Months ago, I wrote a white paper on the potential economies of reorganizing our department. The plan has been adopted. I'm promoted to vice president/section manager.

"Babe, so proud of you. Let's take everyone out to dinner, just not to Bob's." He laughs and pulls me into the elevator and hits the close button. We are alone. The doors click shut. He leans over and kisses me. "Love you, Madame Vice President, love you."

We regroup. Donald moves his suits and shirts to my closet and underwear to my dresser. He teaches T how to use a flat head and Philips screwdriver—*righty tightie, lefty loosey*. Kim hammers away on his smoking, slinging the "just say no" slogans at him relentlessly. She tells him over dinner that if he doesn't stop, he's going to die. T agrees. Donald tries, but I find small piles of butts under the bushes at the far side of the garage. He spends most weeknights with us. Dinner is a challenge; we make him turn off the TV and sit with us; he hates our incessant chatter and the way T examines his food, always wanting to know where each piece of meat comes from.

When we are all together on the weekends, we introduce him to Friday dinner at McDonald's, Saturday morning donuts, and runs to the mini mall for new shoes and school supplies. Sundays he flees to Glendale taking refuge in his castle. The weekends the kids are with Jim, Donald and I immerse ourselves in each other, mostly ignoring anyone else. Nonie navigates through this brave new world with grace and tolerance. She's our constant.

The ex-ex-love boat comrades are now a monthly gossip gaggle. Most are dating, some remarried, and we are celebrating a couple of babies. In my new VP role, I have been asked to counsel several twosomes on how to successfully date in the work environment. It's been brought to my attention by several of Donald's old flames that I'm the lucky one, I've won the prize. What? Seriously, what a funny thing to say to me. I love him excruciatingly, but he's no prize, he's… Donald.

*****

I miss Ginger; ever since she left, Nonie won't let me out. Donald will, but he goes with me, usually after everyone's had dinner. We walk around the backyard. I show him my favorite branch in the sycamore. He can reach me up there and sometimes I get a ride down to the grass.

He says, "Pep, don't tell, but I got to have a smoke. Shhhhh, let's hide out here by the garage."

I wouldn't tell, we guys have to stick together.

*****

Christmas 1985. Kim will be twelve. T's halfway to seven. October made me thirty-seven, September turned Donald forty-three.

Donald leaves work early. He stops by my office. He looks like *the cat that swallowed the canary.*

"See you at home."

"Okay, I won't be there for a while."

"No hurry."

I stop before pulling into the driveway. What in the world? The garage door is open, boxes and ladders prevent me from pulling in. Donald is sitting on the roof of the garage; he is still in his suit pants, shirt untucked with tie hanging loose around his neck, and…it looks like there are strings of Christmas lights draped around his shoulders? There are. T is sitting next to him. Donald has a firm grip on his arm, thank God. Kim and her best friend are sitting cross-legged just feet from Donald and T; they are concentrating on unwinding more wires and lights from their packaging. I want to honk in encouragement, but don't dare. I park in the drive.

"Mommy, Mommy. Look what we're doing. We had to climb out of your window. I'm going to climb back in when it's time to plug in the lights. Donald says we have to test them. Don't worry he won't let me fall."

"Mom, can Sarah stay for dinner? Her mom said it's okay. Please?"

"Sure, we will have a light-turning-on party."

I couldn't be happier for the kids. Jim would never put Christmas lights up, no matter how much Kim begged. Way to go, Donald!

As if the lights aren't enough, Donald wants to give the kids a dog too. I've never had a dog; the kids have been asking for one. Donald believes a dog is an important part of childhood. I suggest a Cocker Spaniel. My family had one when my brother was ten, Scampy. Nonie still talks about him.

I've just made it, the pet store closes at 8:00 p.m., it's seven thirty.

"Hi, I'm here to pick up a Cocker Spaniel. You called and said she had arrived."

"She's here, buff color, female. She's a sweetie. Christmas gift?"

"Yes, for *our* kids. She's going to spend the next two days with friends. She's going to be a Christmas Eve surprise."

I bend down to take her out of her kennel. She's reluctant. The store clerk hands me a treat. "Here, pup." She ventures a few inches from the cage door and sits askew. She checks me out. Oh, those eyes. I pick her up; she's the weight of a newborn, that wonderful weight of baby. She yawns and licks my nose.

"Okay, sweetie, back in." I put her in the front seat of my car, my right hand steadies the kennel. "Almost there."

I park. Poor puppy has worried herself all the way with that *I hate riding in the car* whine. I've tried to console her with words then songs and, finally, whistling; nothing helped.

Someone is knocking on my window. "Hey, KW, I can't wait, let's take her home now."

Our friends don't mind. They were afraid of becoming too attached; they are glad to be off the hook. Donald heads home first; he's going to gather Nonie and the kids into the family room. I'll park outside and make a grand entrance through the front door.

*****

What is this? Why is everyone shouting, clapping, jumping up and down?

Let me have a look. Whoa, get that tongue away from me. I escape to the landing.

"Pepper, come back. This is Amanda. Oh, Pep, isn't she cute? She's a puppy. A Merry Christmas puppy." Kim has the startled fur ball in her arms.

A puppy?

Oh my god it's a *dog*.

*****

What a Christmas. Lights, dog, presents at my house, presents at Jim's. The kids are reaping the benefits of a broken family or as *Family Circle* might say, the blended family.

"Mom, why did you name the dog?" TJ's tone is accusing. I should have known I'd be held accountable by him for my dictatorial decision.

"Oh, just because. I wanted to name her after my grandmother. I've always loved her first name, and its Nonie's middle name. I was thinking it would be fun to name a dog after people. When we register Amanda with the American Kennel Club, it will be Amanda of Mill Valley.

"Like our street Mill Valley?"

"Yes, they're pretty fancy group. I thought adding our street to her name would make her sound very important. What do you think?"

"Well, okay. But Kim and I want to call her Mandy. That's the name Donald is going to put on her house. I'm helping build it."

"More than fair. I should have let you guys name her. She is your dog." (I'm just the pooper scooper and the food and water gal.)

*****

"Well, la de da! Miss Amanda of Mill Valley. You better stop peeing on the floor, or they will be calling you Peester."

*****

Christmas is the trickiest of the holidays. Everyone is ensconced in their expectations. Everyone. Donald and I have worked hard to establish new traditions and to respect those that *cannot be changed*. Sometimes you have to give in; there's only so much guilt you can take. Kim and T spend Christmas Eve with Jim's family. Christmas Day is mine; this is where I'm stubborn. Donald sees his parents Christmas Eve through New Year's Eve Day; he's convinced them, a hard sell, that we should be together on New Year's Eve, after all it is a night for lovers. Nonie wins most flexible, always bobbing and weaving to accommodate others. Her only demand: the cookies you leave for Santa must be hers, not store-bought but homemade cutout.

Donald is tired of being a visitor. Me too. He's been dragging his feet. Me too.

His procrastination, I think, stems from his relationship with his house. It's his soul. For years his time, money, and energy have been poured into it. It's been all about making the house on the hill his home, his castle.

228

My relaxed attitude is recent. A personal discovery of sorts. I like making my own decisions, not asking permission, being in control. Donald can give me his opinion and does. But he has no veto as lover; being a husband might change that. His expectations are old-school.

The truth is we both share a need for tradition. We are lured by the Norman Rockwell image of the perfect family. We'd like to blame it on the kids, but it's us wanting well…acceptance.

I suggest he move in here permanently, keep his house. Lease it, make some money, at least cover the mortgage. Everyone wins.

"That's what I've been doing, sort of. It makes it too easy to go back when things get tough. If I don't sell it, it will always be between us. I'll always be looking back. Maybe you guys should move in with me? Make it, our house?"

"No. I've thought about that. But adding me and the kids, dog and cat to the castle will land somebody in the mote a.k.a. on the street."

"I'm sure we could work something out. I'm not that bad."

"Oh my god, you are nothing less than a fussy old lady."

"I see your point." He turns slightly red underneath his chuckle. He is pure Virgo.

"I really don't want to transplant the kids. Not now, maybe later when we've melded together. Then it should be a whole new adventure. Not one pieced together from our pasts. Although the kids do think the castle is cool, but leaving their school and friends would be asking too much."

*****

The dog is spoiled. She's everyone's favorite.

She drinks my water; they've moved my food to the top of the washer. She's disgusting; she roots through my litter box, that's gone upstairs. I've gone upstairs.

She chased me the other day. I slipped through the patio door just as Nonie was taking out the trash. Mandy didn't make it. She slammed right into the glass.

Was there a poor, poor Pepper? No, just a poor, poor Mandy.

Donald has built her, her own house. And now she's the one that goes with him on his cigarette sneaks.

Yes, my feelings are hurt. Won't they be surprised when I run away.

*****

It's done. He's here. Just one load of his life tucked in the back of his truck. Several paintings by a friend; his grandfather clock, a Christmas gift from Kathleen; his desk and chair; two TVs and tools that can't be found in Jim's red box.

The kids have moved their downstair toys upstairs surrendering the den to Donald. He moves in his desk, chair, and a TV. We paint, put in a sofa bed, and create a mini oasis. The double doors remain shut. No visitors without an invitation.

The family room is just that.

His house is on the market. His car is in my, our garage. The second TV goes in our bedroom.

On Meadows family picture night we pose for the camera. The photographer asks Kim to move closer to her dad. TJ says, "He's not our father." Smile. *Click.*

Donald has taken the capital from the Glendale house and bought his parents' rental house in Studio City. This was a sentimental move as well as practical. Donald was raised in this house, boy to man until his dad pissed him off and he stomped off into adulthood. Selling/buying property within a family has tax and real estate benefits for all involved. Kathleen is renting it. Donald claims he talked her into it. I'm not sure that's how it went down. He's relieved; she'll maintain the house to his specifications, and she can be trusted for the rent. I'm irritated. She's like bubblegum on my shoe.

I've taken a position with the bank's legal department. They are an internal client of Donald's; he gave me the heads-up on the opening. We are still sensitive to our work image. A move to legal will provide the ultimate professional division. I'm excited to see if my management skills are transferable. My office is on the twenty-third floor of the bank's headquarters building in Los Angeles. My boss, the bank's general counsel. My title, director of legal administration/key VP, now eligible for merit bonuses. My staff varies from file clerk to paralegal, secretary to Word processor. We meet the technical, financial, and administrative needs of the department and its inhouse attorneys. I'm the conduit between legal and nonlegal bank entities. There seems to be a communication problem. I'm enjoying the challenge.

Our relationship is push-pull. Donald and I teeter between love and hate. We are *so close but yet so far*. He wants to elope. I want a wedding with friends and family; he throws his clothes into the trunk of his Mercedes, slams the door, drives to the corner, and an hour later he's back. I say, "Wouldn't marry you if you were the last man on the planet." We hold fast to our egos, we sleep back to back, we wake and spoon. We are a mess. We are perfect.

"KW, this is just too hard. It just shouldn't be so hard." Donald puts his T-shirts back in the drawer.

"It wouldn't be worth it if it was easy." Stupid argument? The only one I've got. Maybe this is just us. Maybe we should just go with the flow?

Kim is almost fifteen. Donald and I are so amazed, so proud. She'll be in high school next year. She's perfect. Smart, pretty, sweet, funny. Best of all, her innocence has protected her from the egocentric nature of being a teen. We like her. She's a friend. She calls Donald her stepfather, tried of trying to explain his role to her friends. Sometimes she slips and calls him Dad.

TJ is in the third grade. In the second, he was dubbed a poor reader. His teacher suggested we hold him back. We found a tutor to the chagrin of the school; she taught T how to take a standardized test. Magic, now he's an A student and devours books that are of his interest. He has cold-/flu-induced asthma. It makes him stamping feet mad, why wouldn't it? He says it feels like breathing water. He loves to make and fix stuff. Donald and he share that. A teacher sent us a postcard: "TJ has a beautiful soul." We know.

A year ago, Pepper disappeared. I think Mandy was just too much for him. I wish I had been better to him, paid more attention, rubbed behind his ears more. He was such a funny little guy. Always peeping around the corner, pawing at your book or paper, darting from room to room. Miss him.

Amanda of Mill Valley is moving from puppy to dog at last. She has claimed a spot under a hedge across from the patio door where she can watch our ins and outs without us seeing anything but her nose. Her house is her castle, old blankets and stinky stuffed babies clutter it. That's where she insists on spending most nights. Donald installed a doggie door into the garage, and Nonie found her a big round basket and tucked it next to the workbench. She filled it with clean blankets and new babies. If it's really cold, Mandy will relent and sleep there. She does swim but not for fun; put your head under the water, and she dives in to pull you out by your hair. She likes a walk but prefers to get her exercise by retrieving tennis balls; Donald obliges, they play for hours.

Lunches, laundry, dusting, taxi service, comfort food, postage stamps, Sunday school, mending, crafts, cutout cookies, scraped knees, hand-holding, patience, paying attention, hugs, and kisses—Nonie never disappoints. When not with us, she's busy with her church groups, playing canasta and visiting friends. Everyone loves her, they should. Donald helps her replace her car, keeps her appliances working, and takes time to explain how unfamiliar electronic or mechanical gadgets work. Only he is able to explain a fax machine to her.

Donald's house in Studio City is on a main street. It has been tagged for widening, going from two to four lanes. The loss of his deep front yard and the neighborhood turning to multifamily dwellings signals it's time to sell. He takes the profit and buys in Valencia minutes from Mill Valley.

I'm silent. Violated. Kathleen will maintain her status as renter. This is my neighborhood. I don't want her just blocks away. Donald doesn't get it or worse he does and doesn't care. Will I ever get this Albatross from around my neck?

I know that Donald doesn't see Kathleen as a threat. She's a tie to his past—the woman that didn't leave, the woman that acquiesces. I get it, but I don't like it. My feelings should take precedence to his. Unreasonable? Don't care.

"KW, won't you please come take a look at the house? I think it's a good investment. And easily taken care of being so close. And someday we can sell both our houses and buy one in Oxnard or even Carmel."

"I trust your choice of property. I don't really want to check out Kathleen's new house."

"Sweetheart…"

"Does she really need to live here? Doesn't her family live in LA? Aren't she and her sister close? Why commute to LAX from here? What's in it for her?"

"We've been all over this. It's me, I want a renter I can trust. She's doing me a favor. And she's transferring to Burbank."

"Is she? Well, since it's a fait accompli, here's what I need."

"Must be serious you're rolling out the French."

"Please do not run errands with her locally. I know you have to take care of the house's upkeep, and you will want to make it perfect inside and out even though it is just a rental. Please if you need to do something together do it in the Valley. I don't want neighbors asking me or my kids who you were with. Are you listening?"

"Yes, Kathy, I am. Want to get married, wouldn't that help, prove that I'm yours?"

"Don't change the subject."

*****

Where'd it go? Where? I saw him throw it. I did. It's got to be in that bush. It does, it does. Looking, looking. Smelling, smelling. "Ouch, darn, branch."

"Mandy, he's messing with you. Go look behind him. Behind him, Mandy. It's in his towel. Donald, give the dog her ball." I sit down beside him. He's dangling his feet in the pool. Mandy comes running and grabs it. "There you go, sweetie."

The kids are gone at Dad's; that's what Kim said. "We're going to Dad's. Be a good dog. Love you." I want to go to Dad's. He has a beach, a boat… What's a beach? A boat? I want to see.

*****

The bank is reducing its computer support operations. The software trend is turnkey packages, plug and play systems. Support is now by external tech shops. There is no longer a need for floors and floors of programmers. Computer mainframes are swapped out for compact computers with smaller footprints. Personal computers are on every desk; printers and copiers are decentralized. The organizational term is *downsizing*, the staff management process is *layoff*. It doesn't happen overnight; it cranks through the organization one unit, one section, one division at a time.

The legal department is not a target. One of my tasks when I took the job was to automate them with state-of-the-art hardware and software. Donald's group supported me in this endeavor; now we are a stand-alone department requiring minimum internal support. My position and my staff are safe for now.

Donald is on shaky ground. In addition to losing the legal department as a client, many of his other applications are slated for outsourcing. For months he has been lamenting the state of his division, its increasing bureaucracy and decreasing workload. He has placed the majority of his staff in viable positions in other areas of the bank. I suggest he look out for himself too. I know other bank groups have reached out to him. Jerry has called him several times; he's growing an organization in finance. Donald would be great there. Donald doesn't call him back. I think he is in denial. I needle and needle him to do something, make a plan. He talks about an early retirement. I try to keep my mouth shut—that wouldn't or couldn't be my choice.

Kim's learning to drive. I'm teaching her on my Honda five speed. She's almost got it. Foot down, engage, hand shifts to first, down, engage, to second…we barely jerk, third here we come. We spend hours in the College of the Canyons parking lot. Once she passes her test and has her license, she will be the shuttle between here and Redondo, the taxi for her dance team, and the ride to and from school for her many friends. Donald refuses to get in the car with her. "I'll wait till the DMV says she's good."

The inevitable happens. Donald is laid off. He seems surprised. I help him clear out his office; we tuck everything into the den. He spends a lot of time on the family room couch going over and over and over his situation. HR calls almost daily with possible positions within the bank. My boss wants to help; he's been a fan of Donald's for years. He calls his connections. Donald is not interested.

An old friend surfaces. He has a consulting firm. They do project management and software installations. Donald accepts a job with him. There is little bureaucracy, and Donald can pick and choose his projects. Work the hours he needs. No more suits, no more eight to five, few rules and regulations. He can work from home unless there's a need not to.

"KW, sorry I've been such a bum. I just couldn't believe this happened. I couldn't get my feet under me. Come here." He pulls me close, and we silent dance around the kitchen. "Still love me?"

"Always, but I could just smack you sometimes. Sorry I wasn't more sympathetic, more understanding."

The house is quiet. We're in bed early. Mandy is outside drinking from her water faucet. We can hear her every time she licks the faucet tap. Her lapping makes the water pipes thud. It used to irritate us, but now we know she's making her rounds before settling in her house. Kim and T are at Jim's. Donald turns the eleven o'clock news off. He pulls me close.

CHAPTER 12

Thomas, Tanya, and Baxter Baby

Description:

Thomas and Tanya: Thomas is a box turtle. Tanya isn't. I didn't know that when I chose them. They were the only turtles at the pet store. I needed two.

Thomas is brown-green, Tanya is green-brown. We are not sure what sex they are. Kim named them relying on her sixth sense. Thomas is larger than Tanya but not by much. They both have really shiny black eyes and a love of lettuce, carrots, squash, and cabbage.

Baxter Baby: Baxter is an Abyssinian; he may be a mix, but mostly an Aby. He is handsome, charming, and a trickster. He has what they call a distinctive "ticked" tabby coat, in which individual hairs are banded with different colors. I wish I had read this description before trying to describe George; I would have called him a black-and-white Abyssinian. Baxter's color has hints of rust, black, brown, and white like a tabby but in subtle stripes, not splotches. Also, like George his eyes and mouth are edged in black, his nose is solid black, whiskers white and not long. He's more doglike than cat. He and Mandy are pals. Baxter often takes a walk with Mandy, and he is not afraid to join her chasing tennis balls.

WHO ME

It's near Easter. I want to do something different. Enough with
the stuffed bunnies and fussy baskets. I will, of course, hide plastic
eggs that's TJ's favorite Easter tradition. I'll get Nonie to help with
that; we always fill them with M&M'S, sometimes dollars. But what
would make it special?

"You want to go get what?"

"Turtles."

"Are you sure the kids will like them? Where will we keep them?"

"I'm sure they will. I'll pen them up in the planter on the side by
the garage. When it starts to get cold we will wrap them in newspaper
and put them in a plastic tub so they can hibernate in the garage until
spring. That's what they told me to do at the pet store. They eat raw
vegetables, that's easy enough. They are basically self-sufficient. I just
think it would be fun, something new."

"How about some real bunnies? We had bunnies when I was a
kid. We ate them, you can fry them like chicken."

"No, they multiply and need a lot of upkeep. Where would we
put their hutch? And I'm not going to eat them."

"Okay, turtles it is."

The kids' reaction to their Easter surprise is almost as ecstatic
as Donald's was. Thank God Nonie shows up with baskets of candy
and stuffed bunnies. Kim hides the eggs for T and names the turtles.

Donald's pickup truck has a cab-over camper. We take it camping to Big Sur. We park between ocean and coastal forest. Swimming
and hiking, sandcastles, and campfires, Donald and the kids are in
their element. Not me. The bed over the cab is like what I imagine
waking up in a coffin would be like. Even when I sit with my head
out of the hatch, I can't breathe. I try pulling the blanket over my
head. I turn on the flashlight, that wakes Donald. He rearranges the
kids so I can sleep with them, away from the ceiling. Day 2, hiking.
Our destination is a waterfall. The trail leads to a ravine. The only
way to the falls is over a *Grand Canyon* like gorge. Donald points, we
will traverse by fallen log. I argue. The kids are up for the challenge.
Donald goes first to demonstrate how sturdy it is. He coaches Kim;
she prances across without a pause. TJ hesitates briefly and moves to
Donald's waiting hands. Then me. I inch out, freeze.

"Come on, Mom, you can make it."

"Sweetheart, don't look down, one foot in front of the other." I freeze. Brain-to-feet communication completely shut down. Stuck. Minutes pass, maybe hours. I feel my arms pressed close to my body, my feet leave the log, I'm lifted. I'm not falling. I'm placed on the ground. The log is behind me.

"Donald, when can we go camping in the truck again?" TJ is looking at the snapshots we took.

"Soon I hope, but first I need to work with Mom on some basics."

"That's for sure." I can hardly wait.

*****

What are these? Rocks? No, one is moving. I poke the other sort of rock with my nose, nothing.

"Mandy, what are you doing? Checking out the turtles? Tanya, Thomas, meet Mandy. Mandy, it's Tanya and Thomas. I'm going to put this little fence around the planter so you can't bother them, and they can't roam too far."

What's to bother? Turtles? I'd rather have another cat.

*****

"Mom, my biology teacher's cat had kittens. There's one left without a home."

"And?"

"I told her I would ask if I could have it."

"Do I have a choice?"

"So it's okay?"

Days later Kim's brings him home. "Surprise, this is Baxter."

"Baxter? Great name. How'd you come up with that?"

"I just looked at him and knew that was his name."

My only surprise is that someone hadn't taken him sooner. He's gorgeous and so friendly, part of the family immediately.

"Oh come here." He feels wiry, all ears and eyes. He is not afraid and not shy. I've never seen a cat the color(s) he is. He reminds me of George, but he is multicolored. Like a tabby but in stripes. "You're just adorable."

Everyone wants to hold him. Even Mandy is interested beyond something to chase. She sniffs him and Baxter let's her. There is no hissing or barking. Donald urges, "Put Baxter on the floor." Mandy steps forward and takes a lick, pushing Baxter against Kimmie's leg. Kim gets nervous and sweeps Baxter up.

"Oh, Baxter baby, come here, let's go upstairs."

*****

Now this one is a keeper. Wonder what he'll think of the moving rocks? Bet he's not impressed. Hey, guys, let me out. I gotta find my ball. Wait 'til he sees my tennis ball.

*****

A Sunday-morning favorite is the swap meet at the Newhall Speedway. Antiques, plants, sunglasses, packs of T-shirts and socks, old tools, knockoffs, new and used everything. We take our red wagon and go up and down the aisles in search of treasures. The kids and I go maybe once a month. Sometimes I wander through alone and sometimes Donald joins us.

The three of us are going, but Donald is headed to his house for yard work.

TJ is into camouflage and army gear. He is looking for a hollowed-out grenade to set on his desk. Or nunchakus—he takes karate and reads martial art books. He would like to collect the weapons. It's hard to find them; they are illegal in California unless made of plastic. T hopes to find authentic ones at the swap meet.

Kim is looking for handmade jewelry, hair scrunchies, and jeans or anything with leather fringe or patchwork. She is my throwback hippie.

I like to pour over old china and glassware. I hope the plant guy is there. I could use a few hanging plants on the patio. And I never miss scouring the jewelry cases at the entrance; there are deals on gold chains, charms, and birthstone pendants.

The kids bring their own money saved from babysitting, allowances, and birthdays. If T finds something he can't live without and his money is gone, we will negotiate a loan with interest.

It's a perfect day for the swap meet. Hazy, nice breeze, and under ninety degrees.

"Hey, KW. KW. Kathy!"

"Mom, someone is calling you."

"Oh, its Donald." Kim waves. "He came after all."

He is a few strides in front of us. TJ runs to meet him.

"Hey, you changed your mind?" Kim and I catch up.

"I'm here with Kathleen." He turns. "Well, she was right here. I wanted you and the kids to meet her. She asked me to help her get some plants for the yard. Now I've lost her."

Sucker punched.

The kids show him their treasures. He worries over the grenade, checks to make sure it has been drilled out. Convinced, he hands it back to TJ.

Inhale, Kathy, inhale. "Well, we are almost done. (Done. Done. Done.) I have two hanging plants I need to pick up."

"Okay. I'll be home in an hour or two. Everything alright?"

Smile. Kathy, smile. "Yes, fine. See you at home." Donald hugs the kids and moves back into the crowd.

"Mom, can we get a sno-cone?"

"Not now, T, I want to get home."

Kim stops. "Mom, what is it? What's wrong? Can I still pick up my bracelets?"

"Yes, run ahead and get them."

I have heard the term *see red*. I see white, atom bomb light white. My only feeling is in the pit of my stomach. A clench, a forever knot. I push toward the exit. The crowd is heavy, it's like pushing through Jell-O.

"Mom, don't you want to stop at the gold place?"

"No, let's find the car." My plants are at the exit stand. T hands the guy our ticket and grabs them.

Home. Kim disappears to her room. T heads down the street to share his purchase with a friend.

Get it together. Kathy, put this in perspective. Think about the kids. I can't believe he did this. Was I not crystal clear? Did I not say, "Please if you need to do something together do it in the Valley?" I thought he heard me. He said he did.

The phone rings.

"Hey, babe, everything alright? You didn't seem..."

"I can't believe you did that. I can't."

"What? Did what?"

"Took Kathleen to the swap meet. How could you go with her, but you couldn't come with us? You went with her after I asked you not to. Knowing how uncomfortable that makes me. I didn't want another confrontation like the aftermath of your neighborhood stroll with her in Glendale. My friend said I was rude because she waved at us, and I didn't wave back. How embarrassing to admit 'that was the other Kathleen not me.' That happened on your turf, that's your business, but this is mine. It's bad enough that Kathleen and I share a first name and look similar from a distance, but we are not a threesome, and I don't want to advertise this less-than-traditional relationship."

"She needed some plants for the house. She suggested the swap meet. I was glad we ran into you I wanted to finally introduce her to my family."

"But, Donald, I asked you not to go around with her in Valencia. I wasn't joking or making a suggestion. I was dead serious."

"What are you talking about?"

"About not going around with Kathleen here where I live."

"Kathy, calm down. Let's talk about this. Please. This is ridiculous. I don't know what I did that's so awful, she's a friend, a renter."

"That's the point, you don't know. Don't come back to the house."

"Let me come and we'll talk. I'll make this right. I never meant to hurt you."

"No. I want you out. Come get your stuff tomorrow while I'm at work and the kids are at school. I'll tell Nonie to go shopping or something until the kids are due home."

"Kathy."

I hang up the phone.

The phone rings.

"Sweetheart. Please, please don't do this."

"I can't trust you. I don't have a choice."

"Where will I go, what will I do?"

"Oh, for heaven's sake, you will go to Kathleen's, it's your house. It will be perfect."

"Kathy, that's not my home. How can you take my home from me?"

"How can you take mine?"

Donald moves his clothes out. Calls me at work. Calls me at home. He proposes convinced that demonstrates his devotion. "Let's get the kids and get married at the beach." We make arrangements to move his few pieces of furniture to his house. He's worried about the kids, embarrassed. I assure him they are mad at me not him, and they are free to be his friend. For days he begs. I'm relentless.

My perseverance lasts about two weeks. The knot in my stomach relaxes, replaced by unyielding nausea. I take refuge in work, able there to restrict my focus to making a living. The kids occupy my evenings and their activities get me through Saturdays. Sundays and Jim's weekends render me worthless. My mother holds my head in her lap as I wail into a dishcloth. She soothes my forehead, rubs my back, I have no words to explain. And I haven't. I've offered no explanation as to why I've insisted on my feelings and no one else's.

"Mom, can T and I take Mandy for a walk?"

"Of course, she'll love that."

"What will we do about Baxter? He'll want to come. Should we let him without you?"

"Yes, go ahead. I'm pretty sure he will turn back when he gets to the schoolyard or maybe at the corner. He knows his way home. I'll watch for him. I'll start dinner, take your time. Mandy could use a good walk."

Nonie and I move to the kitchen. There are more tears as I peel potatoes; Nonie pretends they are onions and hands me a fresh towel.

"Kathy, would it help to rethink this? Now that you've had some time."

*****

"Hey, Baxter, race you to the corner."

"You are a silly dog. You can't race, the kids have you on a leash. I'd win. That's too easy. I'll just trot along by your side. Mandy, pay attention there's a trash can."

TJ hands Kim the leash and claims a large twig from the neighbor's lawn to throw for Mandy later. Kim, is Mom sick?"

"No she's mad. Mad at Donald."

"Not at us though?"

"No, not at us."

"Where's Baxter. Mandy, where's Baxter?"

Kim points. "He stopped at the corner."

"Will he go home?"

"Pretty sure."

*****

I'm worried. The calls stop from Donald. None to the house. None to my office. My resolve is being eaten away by remorse. As much as I hate him, I love him. I miss him. I need to do something. I call and call. I leave messages. His voice box is full, he's not picking up. I'm worried.

Jim calls, "Hey, the kids told me about Donald. Anything I can do? Can I take you to dinner?"

Jim meets me in LA. I've told Nonie that we are getting together. Jim and I decide that the kids don't need to know; it might be confusing, it is a little to us. Besides it's just dinner. His love life is almost as dismal as mine. It's easy to fall back to being the best of friends. Comfortable, reassuring.

"Wouldn't it be great if we could put our family back together? Go forward from the good times?" Jim orders wine.

"Wouldn't that be lovely. Could we ever pretend none of the bad happened and remember only the good?"

"We could try."

"Yes, if not for us, for the kids. Let's see where this goes. Let's be careful. We've messed up their lives enough already. We can't do it again."

"I agree. We'll take it slow."

"Deal." I give him a hug good night.

"What is Baxter doing? Kim, look at your cat."

Baxter is hanging upside down from the staircase. He is climbing on the back of the open carpeted stairs. He knows he is cute. Up and down, back and forth. He is driving Mandy crazy; she's pawing the air and twirling on her tippy toes. Nonie and TJ are doubled over, almost in tears. I'm just dumbfounded.

"I know, isn't that great? He started that a couple of days ago."

"I hope he doesn't fall on his back."

Nonie laughs, "He can't, cats always land on their feet."

"Hey, kids, this Sunday I'll be picking you up at the marina. Your dad has offered to give me a ride on the boat. I've never been on the *big* boat. I'm excited, I'll take you home from there."

"Cool, I'll show you how I can drive." T is finishing his homework. "Maybe Dad will let me pull it out of the slip. I'm finally tall enough to see out the window."

I'm still worried. I continue to call. Could something medical be wrong? Donald has always emulated his father's ailments: heart problems, kidneys, blood pressure, even worries about cancer. His dad is a doctor, and he always has some ailment impinging on his life. He uses it like a velvet club over his family. Like father like son? What if something really is wrong? God, pick up!

At last. I leave a message. "Donald, I'm worried about you. I hope you aren't ill. I hope you are just not speaking. I deserve that, but I'm worried. Could you just give me a call or even leave me a message to let me know you are all right. Thanks, Kathy."

Not five minutes later, the phone rings.

"Hey, what's up?"

"Donald. Thanks for calling. I've been trying to get a hold of you. I thought you might have had a heart attack or something."

"I'm fine. I was in Hawaii."

"That's a relief. How was it?"

"It was beautiful, Kathleen took me. Trying to cheer me up."

I'm not surprised or mad or anything, just relieved. Before I came along, Donald was always going somewhere on her United Airlines freebies. "That's good, I hope it helped."

"Not much. Kept thinking, wish KW could see these sunsets. How are the kids? Did Kim get her license? How are you?"

"She takes her test in a couple of weeks. She's going to use Nonie's car, so she doesn't have to *shift*. T's doing good, his grades are up. We are trying a new karate studio. I'm okay…"

"I stayed with my parents for a while, not a great decision. My dad said I was a fool. Work's been busy so that helped."

What's left to say. How do you explain the unexplainable? How do you correct the uncorrectable? You can't undo the done. Sorry only covers spilt milk or broken glass; it's no help for breaking hearts.

"Any chance I can see you, actually see you? Make sure you're okay."

He sighs, I imagine he's tugging on his index finger, staring out his window. He has me on speakerphone I can hear his TV mumbling. "Yes, I think I can do that."

We decide on Saturday. The kids will be at Jim's. He'll pick me up. We have agreed on an early dinner, a causal friendly meal, just to catch up.

*****

Baxter is taunting Mandy from the tree out front. He's watching for anyone who might pass by and give him a scratch under the chin or let him rub against their legs. "I just love people. They are so friendly, and they like me. Can't you jump over the gate and come play?"

245

"I'm too short. Besides I'm perfectly happy where I am."

"Well, I wish you could come out here. You could dig under the plum tree. The dirt is really soft."

"I don't think so. I'm sure you've been using it for a litter box. And stop going over to the neighbor's house. That lady might kill you."

"That's what Kim said. Just let her try. I'll give her something to be scared of."

"Come back in here. The rocks are eating."

"Those are turtles. Yuk lettuce. Call me if Kathy takes them out, then we can chase them around the lawn or push them."

*****

The sun is almost setting. There is still a yellow glow outside. I watch the driveway from the front windows. I'm all nerves. Breathless. Unsure.

His car pulls in. I back away so he won't see me watching, waiting.

The doorbell rings. I count to ten before answering.

He steps in, still six feet four inches tall, tan, but his beard and mustache are snow white, his dark golden hair streaked to match.

"Did I do that? I can't help but reach for his face."

"Indeed."

"Oh god…"

He moves forward and takes my hand. "Kiss?"

"I thought we weren't…"

Wet cheeks, the taste of salt, his tears mix with mine.

CHAPTER 13

Ebony

Description: Ebony is black, longhaired, petite, and hardly six weeks old when Kim rescues her from the pound. Her look is surprised, always begging to be comforted, reassured. Her eyes are round, and the black of her pupil fills the green of her iris, making it appear like her eyes are all black. Her most distinguished feature is hidden in the fluff of her tail. Run your hand from the base to the tip and about three-fourths up there is a kink, actually two, like a Z. I worry it hurts, but she doesn't seem to mind, happy to get pets wherever they land.

She is precious, maybe fragile, maybe not.

Donald and I have chosen to be together. We can't not be, that's clear. But it is not clear, yet, what together means. We submit to that rusty old cliché "one day at a time."

"Jim." I call his office. I want to give him a heads-up.

"I heard. Kathy, I wish you and Donald well, everything. I do. One of us has to have a happily ever after."

"Friends forever, right?"

"The best of, and Kim and T's parents."

I have a clear view of the pool from the kitchen. The pool man just left. He does a great job. It's so...

"What's that in the pool?" Oh god, it's one of the turtles. Must have fallen in. It's swimming in circles, it's legs too short to reach a step and not long enough to reach an edge to crawl out. Where's the pool net?

"There you go, little fellow." I'm sure its Thomas. I place him on the lawn to dry a bit before I put him back in the pen. "Mandy, go find your ball, leave Thomas alone."

"Nonie, can you call Mandy in?"

"How'd you get out? Did Mandy toss you out of the planter? Did she? Poor you, guess I need to find a better way to fence it off. Donald or T will have an idea."

Kim's a sophomore. She's on the dance team at Hart High. She has her first on-field performance tonight. Hart's JV and varsity football teams play at the College of the Canyons' stadium. I'm taking T and his friend, Donald's working.

I'm home early. I want to help Kim get ready for her big night. I pull in the garage; she comes through the laundry door, pulls open the passenger's door, and begins to weep.

"Mom, look at me." She is covered head to toe in silver dollar-sized hives. "What I'm I going to do? I can't wear my uniform looking like this. My legs are awful. I'll have to stay home. If I don't go they will kick me off the team. Mom?"

"Oh, baby." Hang on. I find the Benadryl and give her a double dose, hoping the next tragedy won't be her falling asleep in the stands. "How long before you have to meet at the school?"

"I have a couple of hours. Will they be gone?"

"Pretty sure."

I throw the camera and a seat cushion into the car. The boys' plan is to hit the snack stand and hook up with their friends. They probably won't watch the game. I'm sure I won't see them again until we meet at the car. The parking lot was a mess. I hurry to find a seat. I see Kim. She is lining up. I don't see a hive anywhere. Her eyes are straight ahead, she's in formation. I wave. "Kim, Kim." Her eyes are forward waiting for the signal to march in. I know she's heard me; she can't help but smile.

Kim is now the taxi to and from Jim's. Depending on her commitments, she often waits until Saturday morning to go to Jim's. If she can't go at all, Jim and I revert back to the old routine. T needs to spend time with his dad.

Donald has stuff here and at his house. He spends weekends and several nights a week. We talk throughout the day. I think he must miss *life in the white-collar office.* Each night we review the day's events, either in person or apart, usually while ignoring the eleven o'clock news.

*****

"What's she doing now?"

Baxter and Mandy are watching me wrap the turtles in newspaper. Baxter keeps pawing the paper.

"She does that every so often. Watch she'll put the rocks in those tubs, and then she'll put those in the garage until it's warm again."

"Mandy, will she do that to us?"

"Of course not, Baxter, we are warm-blooded."

"What's that?"

"I have no idea."

*****

"Mom I've looked and looked, called and called. TJ and I have been around the block at least five times. Baxter is gone."

"Not again. Why do we have so much trouble keeping our cats? I bet he wandered off with someone he ran into on one of his walks. I can just see him darting up to them and begging for a chin rub or scratch on the head. He probably tagged after them. He has no collar. They could have thought he was homeless, maybe they offered him one."

"Why would he leave us? I thought he loved us. Weren't we good enough?"

"Baxter loves everyone. He's a connoisseur of life. He can't get enough of it. Let's leave some food out front and keep looking and calling. Give him a few days, he'll find his way home."

Kim's at Meadows saving seats for the family (Nonie, Donald, Jim, Kim, and me). TJ is graduating from the sixth grade today. The ceremony is always held on the school's main playground; it's right behind our house. Even when my kids aren't involved, I watch the ceremony from Kim's room. It makes me cry. I like a good cry. I can't believe TJ is the speaker for his sixth-grade class. Just five years ago Kim did the same for her class. I've already cleared a space next to Kim's picture for the one I will take of T at the podium. We were surprised when T announced he had been chosen for this honor. Even that he had tried out. He's not an academic; school is a place we make him go. He's done well because he made the choice to; he could just as easily have chosen to be mediocre. He is loving the idea of giving a speech. I can't wait to hear what he has to say. With Kim it was different. We weren't surprised; pleased, proud, but not surprised. Kim is an academic. She gets school; she likes it's order, it's clear expectations. Grades, even life seem to come easy to Kim because she works hard to make it so. They are so different. So amazing.

"I don't think Baxter's coming back, Kathy. Maybe we should get Kim another cat or kitten."

"I hear you, Donald, but I don't know if I can take another one."

Back to the Castaic shelter, they call it a shelter now, not the pound. (Perception counts.) Back to the big cage with all the crazy kittens. God they are so cute; maybe we should take a half dozen, bad joke.

"Kimmie, see the perfect one yet?"

"Not yet, Mom."

We watch as they roll and tumble. A couple are practicing their hissing, oh, and back arching. There's one that's trying to nap in a blanket-lined box; no luck, a little tabby just smacked its flicking tail. Oh no, now it's biting its ear. It's tough in there.

I walk over to the adult cage. Hoping maybe, just maybe, our Baxter Baby is there. I know it's a long shot, but I have to look.

"Mom, I think I found her. I hope it's a she. See up there, the tiny black one. See? I think she is trying to get out. That's the one."

In the top corner of the kitten cage is the tiniest of babies. It's climbed up on the cage fencing and is hanging by its front claws; one back leg is planted, giving it some stability, the other is trying to find a foothold.

"Ladies, have you found one you like?" the officer asks.

"Yes, see in the corner. The one hanging close to the top."

He retrieves the kitten. "It's a little girl. Okay?"

"Yes!"

Kim gets into the car; she holds the kitten in her lap. She has wrapped it in a towel. Just kitty's face peeks out, her big round eyes wide, taking it all in.

"She looks petrified, Kimmie."

"She's trembling." Kim unwraps her and cuddles her under her chin. Softly patting her back like you would a fussing infant.

"Just ten more minutes and we'll be home, sweet kitty."

"Oh, Mom, look she falling to sleep."

"Okay, guys, here we go again."

"Kim, what are you going to call her? Know yet?" Donald asks.

"She's so black like the liquid ink I use in my calligraphy pens. The color I use is called ebony. I think that would make a great name."

Nonie agrees. Ebony it is.

*****

Again? Not another one.

It's not Baxter. I want Baxter. I bet she won't walk with me or even play ball.

I thought they were going to bring Baxter back.

Put her in a tub with one of the rocks.

*****

The general counsel asks me to make sure our conference room is set up for a Saturday morning meeting.

"You know coffee and water, that's all. I'll worry about anything else," Maurice dismisses me with a wave.

We never have Saturday meetings, but we do have a cafeteria that operates around the clock to service our branch operations folks. I call, it's set. I check to see if he will need Word processing or want to bring in his secretary. I get a resounding "No!" That's weird, but so Maurice.

The phone is ringing, too early. I hate Monday mornings. Thank God I usually face them alone. I knock the receiver off the cradle and onto the floor causing Ebony to levitate from the foot of the bed. "Geez where did it go?" I grab it from the carpet. Got it.

"Hello? Donald? It's so early, anything wrong?"

"Turn on the TV, Kathy, there has been a merger between Security Pacific and Bank of America. Finalized at 333 S. Hope, in Security's legal offices. Did you know?"

"No, but I think I ordered the coffee."

What does a merger mean? Is there a winner or loser? It's a consolidation, a reorganization. Winners and losers are on both sides or better said stayers and goers. The name will be Bank of America; that name won and their chairman. But people from both sides stay, and people from both sides go at all levels.

The first few weeks I don't have time to think about my fate; there are too many attorneys and staff that need reassurance, hand-holding, and Kleenex. From an organizational standpoint, the bank(s) orchestration of this *merger* is a thing of beauty. From the immediate key manager meetings to present the consolidation plan, to manager meetings with their staffs, to presenting each employee with their personalized timetable for layoff, payout, or possible placement; it's been a wonderous concerto of administrative logistics. I'm impressed. There is a plan, and everyone is privy. All managers on both sides are held responsible to execute it with grace and respect. It's a horrific event, but there will be no goring of the fallen. If you have to be laid off, severed, this is where you want to be.

Donald is panicked. "What will you do? Where will you go? You know you are over forty, that's too old to change careers especially at your salary."

"Well, thanks for the pep talk. I don't seem to have a choice."

I am not panicked. Maybe I should be. I don't consider myself too old. And finding a new job after seventeen years with the bank may be just what my career needs. I will receive a golden parachute. It will kick in when I find employment outside of the bank. I have a year to find a job; until then I will receive my full salary. I'm confident a job will be found. I'm going to try the private law firm arena. I think there will be more opportunities there. I'm optimistic and grateful that I have choices and time to make them.

While I job hunt, I am asked to integrate Security's attorneys with B of As. It's a physical relocation, a swap of about forty attorneys and staff between two buildings just two blocks apart. It's a mess. I'm glad the office assignments weren't my responsibility. Oh, the whining and gnashing of teeth over window count and square feet. Egos, egos, egos.

My workday keeps shrinking—in at ten out by two. I can't stand just sitting there redoing my Rolodex. I call my B of A counterpart in SF and offer to create a five-year plan for the integration of the two legal departments. I get the go-ahead. I'm still at loose ends. I have no apparent boss, just an HR contact. I call. She says not to worry, just call in once a month to keep them current. The paychecks keep coming so what's to worry…

Donald encourages, "Kathy, look at the time off as part of your severance. We'll have more time to play."

It's Kim's senior year. Donald, Jim, and I host a dance team event, applaud Kim's achievements in art and academics, host a graduation party, and prepare to move her to UC Davis where she will major in environmental science. It couldn't be a better time to be a part-time stay-at-home mom.

TJ is at Placerita Junior High. He's finding his way as a teenager and becoming interested in school sports. He played flag football as a sixth grader (Donald and I were such fans) and now he's trying track.

When we are home, Donald and I often pick TJ up after school. We pull the car up to the field entrance behind the portables. T loves the ride but is doubtful having us pick him up is cool.

"Donald, look how he saunters across the field, all cocky, such the guy. I'm relieved."

"Why?"

"Because the poor kid has been smothered by so many of us girls. Me, Nonie, Kim, all of Jim's sisters, and Grandma Martha. I often wondered if you and Jim would be enough testosterone for him. Looks like you were."

"You had nothing to worry about. He's a good kid, a good guy."

Donald is a worthy companion. He keeps me sane. He frees up his afternoons so he can support all my *let's-keep-Kathy-busy* projects. We finish the dollhouse Kim and I started when she was ten. We collect pine cones from parks and the neighborhood so I can emulate a magazine cover's ode to fall. We scour shops and the swap meet for antiques, restoring a drop leaf desk for the family room and a church pew with oak leaf cravings for the entrance hall. We purchase rockers for the back patio. Yes, rockers. Saturday mornings we rock, he with his paper and a diet Pepsi and me with coffee and my latest vampire novel.

I am months into my severance year and still interviewing. I enjoy the process; the challenge of adapting to different personalities and anticipating what the right answer is for the person sitting across the table from you. Interviewing with legal firms is unique. Each partner has to have a go at you; you are the adversary never an ally. It's always a *gang* inquest. You are on trial from the minute you arrive to the closing handshake. Whether it's regarding how many staplers you would order annually or how you would manage their credit line, you are culpable until proven innocent, in this case capable. Always daunting, never dull.

I accept a director of administration position at a small LA firm. I take a cut in pay but will be eligible for year-end profit sharing. They are interested in my legal and financial experience and my exposure to all areas of management. I'm interested in learning legal operations from the inside out.

I receive my payout from the bank and decide to remodel the house. This will be a good use of the money, an investment.

"Kathy, why do you want to do this? Eventually we will do something together, have a house of our own. You should put this money in savings."

"We've been working on *eventually* for years now, and *savings* won't give me the return real estate will. When *eventually* turns into reality, we'll be set. In the meantime we can enjoy the new space and the increased property value it will create."

"Okay, but construction will be miserable. Never-ending problems, idiot excuses. You'll have to choose a GC, good luck. You are on your own, I can't take the pressure."

"It will be a learning experience. The end product will be worth it."

Donald's reaction doesn't surprise me. He has renovated a number of rentals in addition to the Glendale house. He has the horror stories to back his knee-jerk response. I know he will be there for me if I fail.

*****

"Hey, Ebony, what's up? Come down here, I won't chase you. If you stand here by the kitchen window you can watch them dig."

"Promise?"

Ebony misses Kim; she spends most her time on her bed. She's not very fond of the rest of us, always watching from afar.

"Promise. I'm so bored having to stay in here. I don't know what they are up to. Nonie says in a few days I can move to the pool side of the gate. Donald is going to move my house. Then I can stay outside. I wonder what the rocks are doing."

Ebony scampers down from the stair landing. Mandy sits very still while Ebony finds a spot at the window.

"See I'm not so bad."

Ebony relaxes and folds herself onto the seat of a kitchen chair. Mandy moves a little closer, but not to intimidate. Their heads move back and forth in time with the wheelbarrow and workers, both wishing they were digging in the dirt too.

******

"I can't believe your luck. I have to say Phil is a keeper. Sorry I was so negative about the addition. I just worried you'd be taken advantage of."

Donald conducts a daily site inspection, which he discusses with me on his way to work. Any issues I discuss the following morning with Phil. Donald doesn't want to usurp my rapport with Phil; he refuses to be the middleman. So far so good; we are on time, on budget, and as Donald would say, "Nice work, really nice work."

We broke ground in September 1993, just as Kim started her sophomore year at Davis and TJ his freshman year at Hart. When we are done, we hope in February we will have added a study, a one-hundred-square-foot alcove to the family room, and my favorite, a double-sided fireplace. That's what sparked this project, wanting a fireplace in the family room. Thanks to Phil's idea now I'll have two new fireplaces.

TJ is playing freshman football. He's been starting, and the local paper, the *Signal*, has dubbed him as one of the new players to watch. Donald, Jim, and I are his best fans; yes, I'm am a crazy football mom. At this point we aren't sure he will play next year; he's pretty silent about that decision. But he's all in this year and so are we.

Kim has a part-time job in the art department of the student store; she pays for her books and social activities. (I think Donald is subsidizing.) She rooms with last year's dorm mate. They have their own apartment. T and I moved her in. Holy cow, she's a real accumulator. She seems to like the independence of the apartment. There is a special boy, well, man. Donald's worried it's too soon to be serious. I'm in agreement.

What the hell is that? What is that sound? A train? It's dark, no streetlights. The clock flashes four something and then goes blank. The bedroom doors slam shut. It's impossible to get out of bed. It's like bumper cars. I pull myself up and out only to be trapped behind the double doors. The TV is on the floor at the foot of the bedroom window. Why do I know that? I must have stubbed my toe. "Let me out. Let me out." Finally the shaking stops, the doors release, and I fall into the hall. I remember T is at a friend's, and Kim is safe at school. Donald where's Donald? At his house, worked last night, that's right. I have to find T. Gotta get out of here. "Ebony?" I'm at the top of the stairs, barefoot. Mandy, got to get to Mandy. I look down at the entrance hall; its floor is covered with broken

256

glass, pottery chunks. "Ebony, Mandy!" Make a plan, Kathy, make a plan. Down the steps, out the front door, that's easy enough. Bump. Bump. Bigger bump. The staircase is undulating. What will I do if the stairs fall down? I close my eyes. Step down. I am out, out on the front lawn. I have my car keys and cell phone and a clear image of the phone number where TJ is. My car is at the curb. I've been parking outside during the construction. Wait, seasick, another sway. I make it to the car, get in, and start to dial. Oh God, my mother. Crack, Crack. Is that the earth ripping under the car?

"Mom, Mom, are you okay?" T is knocking at my window.

"Oh, T, oh god!"

"That must have been the *big* one, Mom."

He describes his run home: falling slump stone and cracking cement, uprooted trees, muffled screams, grumbling ground, smells of gas, ruptured sewer pipes.

My intent was to rescue him; that's my job, I'm the mom. But here he is rescuing me.

We go to Nonie's apartment. My brother's been staying with her. A resident says they are safe, out scouting the halls, checking on others. We locate them, and I usher them back to the apartment. I'm horrified. Nonie has every candle she owns lit. I try to suppress my alarm and explain the possibility of gas leaks, let alone the risk of leaving candles burning while you roam the halls and the earth rocks. Dawn is beginning to show through their blinds. Bruce blows the candles out, promises not to relight them. Nonie hugs us and says, "Glad you're okay" and sends us on our way. My bother just smiles. "Don't worry I'll make sure she's alright, we'll call you later."

T is worried about the friends he left to get home. Something about being trapped under a bookcase. We drive slowly, very slowly back to his friend's house. The pavement is uneven. The signal lights are out, not even blinking. The guys are okay; one needs a ride home. We pull into his drive. He thanks us and sprints to his front door. His screaming mother flings the door open and pulls him inside; he disappears into the dark house.

Back home we assess the damage. There is no phone service locally. We can't reach Donald. I'm able to call Kim on my cell. She wants to come home. I tell her that won't help and to stay where she's safe. I can't reach Jim or my office.

A neighbor joins T and I in the driveway. Somehow he has a working radio. They are saying it was a magnitude 6.9 earthquake; they assume it will be downgraded once more information is gathered. It occurred at 4:30 a.m. The epicenter is somewhere in the San Fernando Valley. Way too close.

I'm afraid to go into the house. T becomes the adult. We enter; it looks like one of those scenes the kids make in a shoebox for a book report, except someone put the lid on and shook the contents like a rattle. We find Mandy, but not Ebony. The plywood wall protecting us from the open room addition is wet two feet up from the bottom, the carpet is soggy. T is sure it's from a wave from the pool, either from the initial quake or one of its aftershocks. He must be right because the pool water is down, looks like at least a foot. We are lucky all the house walls are intact, no cracks, furniture and other stuff looks stirred with a spoon, but we appear structurally sound.

T sets up camp on front lawn. He pitches a tent, finds blankets and pillows.

"This is where we sleep tonight. You can take a nap if you want, Mom."

He moves a garden bench to the driveway. Tells Mandy to sit on it. She does. She's trembling; she hasn't made a sound since the first shaking. He returns to the house to search for Ebony, no luck.

Donald shows up to check and turn off electricity, water, and gas. He had to dislodge his car from his garage before he could get over here. He has to go into work and get their equipment back online."

"I'll be back, looks like T has everything under control."

My cell rings. It's Phil.

"How are you guys doing?"

I give him an update.

"So that beam I put in yesterday, it's still up?"

"Yes, and we checked outside, all the framing looks good too."

"Well guess my calculations on the beam were correct. I be over there shortly to get you some hot water and double-check everything."

I'm not sure how I feel about the beam comment. If it had fallen so would have the back of the house. Yes, Phil, glad your calcs were right. Good God.

T, Mandy, and I sit on the bench. T and I take a breath, Mandy just shakes. I hug her tight.

The ground rises and falls under our feet. We stand, T points to the mountain range that frames our valley to the west. We watch the mountains raise and crash down. The sight and sound unbelievable. Even more surreal, the rust-colored dust cloud that shrouds the range for hours.

The Northridge earthquake is downgraded to a 6.7. That is just wrong. I know it was a 9. We dig out with lots of help. Donald and Jim right the furniture, clean up the breakage, and bring in supplies. T convinces me to move back inside. Phil gets all utilities operating and makes sure everything is safe. The neighbors are not pleased; they have to wait for the city inspector. Phil speeds us through the process. I invite the neighbors to take hot showers. "Just bring a towel and soap." This soothes the unbecoming neighborly envy.

Mandy remains silent and becomes my shadow. I sleep with my clothes on, and Mandy takes over Donald's spot. I make her sleep with her leash on and wrap it around my wrist, too many stories about dogs running until they drop if not restrained during quakes. Still no Ebony. The turtles are safe in their tubs. T is back in his room. Phone service is on. Donald checks on us in fifteen-minute intervals. He's staying at his house, anticipating more damage.

The earth shook just two days ago.

I return to work Wednesday. Donald never misses a day. TJ will go back to school next Monday. My mom checks on him every afternoon; since he started high school, she has been semiretired. I think she is enjoying coming to the house more often. Bruce comes with her; he's been working on my garage. That disaster needs serious attention. We are still looking for Ebony.

(Bruce lost his painting business and his second wife several years ago. Diagnosed as a paranoid schizophrenic in his thirties, he struggles with everyday life. His wife and work grounded him. Now he depends on alcohol. Alcohol may quiet the voices in his head, but it makes him angry, mean, caustic. He frightens me. I work hard to keep anti-Bruce from my family, from me. I try to protect Nonie, but she's his mom and believes she can fix him. I get it, but I refuse to participate. The quake has given Bruce purpose. He calls it getting clear. We are enjoying having him home. I remain watchful.)

"Oh God what is that?" I hold my breath. Mandy sits up in bed. "Go back to sleep, sweetie, it's not an aftershock. Maybe it's an owl."

Again the sound. It's a cry now going from soft to loud. Insistent.

"Mandy, T, it's Ebony, it's our Eby." I'm shouting.

Ebony is at my bedroom window. She has climbed the eucalyptus to the garage roof which butts up to it. She is hanging by her claws on the window screen. Howling. We open the window and pry her loose. The screen slides off the roof and onto the driveway. What a clatter. I grab Eb under her front legs; she's all bones. Unbelievable. It's 3:00 a.m. I call Kim. She's sobbing, "I'll be home this weekend, don't tell me no."

Ebony was gone seven days. We bring water and food and make her a nest in my bedroom chair. I wake at five thinking it's all a dream. Mandy is snoring; her leash tight around my wrist, Ebony is tucked between us.

*****

"Oh, Eb. I thought you had left me, like the others. Where were you? We looked and called and worried and worried. I lost my bark I was so scared. You should have seen the pool; a giant wave came right out and ran all over the yard. TJ made spaghetti on the firepit and then we all slept in a tent."

"Oh dog, I ran and ran and ran. So far, so far. All the smells were wrong. I didn't know what way to go. There were cats and dogs everywhere. Trucks came to pick us up, mostly dogs went. I hid. An old black-and-white cat pointed me to a cement river and told me to follow it downhill. I did and the smells got more and more like home. I ate a mouse and a bird that had fallen from a tree. I slept behind bushes and under piles of leaves. I looked for you. I looked for Kim. I know she's at school, but I thought maybe I had run that far."

"Did you see Baxter?"

"No Baxters, a Buddy and a Blue and an old dog called Rusty."

"How'd you finally get here?"

"I followed my nose."

*****

Ebony is home and Mandy has found her bark. Construction is close to wrapping up. Aftershocks are felt, but no one is running to a doorjamb. Donald and I are planning a getaway to Carmel. Nonie is having a respite from us and Bruce, indulging in potlucks and bingo. Bruce has a job and a place to live. Kim's safe at school, and T is starting spring practice. The year 1994 has turned a corner; we are on its shiny side. Trite is such a relief.

CHAPTER 14

Amos, Andy, and Teaser the Bird

Description:

Teaser the Bird: Teaser is a male Lutino pied cockatiel. He is light lemon to white chartreuse with the signature orange on his cheeks. His eyes are bright, his crest charming. He's smart, very. He is loving, and he knows how to play peek-a-boo.

Amos and Andy: They are a set. Brothers. From the same pet store, we purchased Amanda of Mill Valley. They are black-and-white tuxedo cats. Amos is more black than white, and Andy is more white than black. Short haired. Both weigh over twelve pounds. Amos is a little shorter, a little stockier. Andy's tall for a cat, sleek. They both are quite a lapful.

Amos is always engaged, social. Andy is aloof, almost a recluse.

It's time to wake the turtles. I unwrap Thomas; he pulls tighter into his shell. I place him in the planter; the dirt is warm from the spring sun. I unwrap Tanya. She's too light, too still. Her tub tumbled from its shelf during the quake; when my brother found her, she was on her back on the garage floor. We rewrapped her hoping she would be okay, she's not.

Donald and I bury Tanya in the front yard, near the five baby turtles that appeared last spring. The five babies that the vet said were impossible for a box turtle and a Greek tortoise to have. The five babies that Nonie had to argue were real. Nonie found the babies in the planter; she called Donald to make sure she was right and the vet wrong. I saw the miracle when I got home. They looked like those miniature turtles you win at a fair or find in Chinatown. They moved around for a few days. We offered them fruit and leaf vegetables, but they died one by one. We were heartbroken. We couldn't just throw them away or flush them like you do goldfish. We buried them under a lavender bush; that's where we put Tanya.

So our zoo is down another turtle and up one cockatiel. This summer when Kim moved back home, her bird did too. Teaser is or was a shared bird. This summer it's clear that Kim's roommate is no longer interested in Teaser; it was her turn to have the bird, but here he is, our newest family member. I hate to admit it, but I'm glad he's here. He is not at all like Jim's and my parakeet. Teaser is always sing-ing or stomping around his cage. He beats Mandy at notifying that a stranger has reached the front door. There is no warning scream like Teaser's; the neighbors will testify to that. His cage is in the family room, so he won't get lonely. The more commotion the better; he was raised in a dorm room, he's a people person.

"Hey, Kim, what's up?" She doesn't usually call me at work, hope there's not a problem.

"Hi, Mom, do you have time to talk? I'm registering for next year's glasses, I've been thinking…"

"About?"

"I want to change my major, from environmental science to design."

"That is a leap. What brought this on?"

"Well, I was in a lecture hall. The professor was talking about this little fish that was at risk of extinction. And. And I caught myself thinking why the hell do I care. Oh, Mom, I'm sorry. How mean was that? But I really want to do something with my art. They have a great program here in design. I think that would make perfect sense to change to environmental design. Would that be okay?"

I try not to laugh out loud, I'm thrilled. First, because Kim is strong enough to say "Stop, I don't want to do this." And second, I can't picture her spending the rest of her days considering the life cycle of the Delta smelt. I can, however, see her designing environmentally sound buildings, places where her paintings can be hung and admired.

"I think that's great. Any chance you can still graduate on time?"

"If I get started next quarter I can."

"Then do it."

I'm glad we can stick to the out-the-door-in-four plan. Nonie paid for my college. I promised myself I would do the same for my kids. I didn't save ahead; I should have, but one minute Kim was five and then she was taking the SATs. If I keep to my current four-year plan, Kim won't have any financial obligations on graduation day. She'll just have to find a job and an apartment. Just. I anticipate using the same plan for T.

*****

"Mandy, where's Thomas? He's not in the planter. I looked. Did you take him out?" Ebony is sitting on the top of the picnic table surveying her domain.

"Not me, I know better."

"Maybe Kathy took him."

"No, it's not that time yet."

*****

I'm lost in the freezer, in the icy fog of cold hitting warm. How long have I been staring at frozen dinners, potpies, and chicken thighs? I hope if I stare long enough into this frozen abyss the answer to what's for dinner will appear. It's just me and T tonight, so I really don't have to overthink this, but I am. Weeknights render me useless with everyday demands, all those tasks that keep home, home. I've spent the day doing staff reviews; dinner should be easy. The condenser clicks on and hums a little louder. Why is this so hard? "Just pick something, anything." I knew the answer was in there. I call China Palace.

"So what about football? Are you going to play?"

I mentally cross my fingers hoping the answer will be yes. Football to me is optimism, a place where cheering can make it so, where loss only lasts a week, where all are part of the team, where purpose is singular. To me it was all about Friday nights and marching in the drill team and burgers at Bob's. It's belonging. I want that for T.

"I want to be popular, so the answer is yes, I'm going to play. I've thought about it. I can either be academic or be popular, not both. Playing guarantees popular."

Love the answer, surprised by the motivation.

"Any chance you can do both? Like a balance. You have to maintain a C average to stay on the team. Maybe you could shoot for a B average."

"Mom…"

Donald and I become typical football parents. Each game is an event. We prepare for it. We eavesdrop on T's teammates as they wander in and out of my refrigerator. We're hoping for insider information; we comb the newspaper for game and player reviews and predictions. We gage our support between nonchalant and enthusiastic based on previous game and practice outcomes. We allow TJ to reward or punish us with his charm and inclusion or with his "you just don't get me" eye roll. We need his approval; we need to be part of his football. This is our mistake. This is his game not ours.

"Donald, I think Thomas has wandered off."

"The turtle?"

"Yes, the turtle. Not TJ. I looked all over the yard. Thomas is nowhere."

"Did you ask Mandy?"

"Very funny."

"They burrow you know. Maybe he made his great escape."

Now we are looking for Ebony. She's been gone for three days. She hasn't been feeling well. Eats little, sleeps more than usual. I let her out each evening, but she's back within the hour. But not last night. After the quake I never thought she'd leave the house again. I can't believe she hasn't come in. I've heard that cats wander away when they are sick or feel it's their time, but Eb isn't old enough to do that, not yet.

I ask Donald and TJ if they think I should let Kim know what's going on with Eb.

"No, Mom, give it a few more days." Donald agrees.

It's trash night, Donald and I are working on clearing out the garage to make space for a workbench. We are loading up the barrels which are lined up at the curb. Donald is halfway down the drive with scrap wood.

"Kathy, what's that laying on the curb? It looks like…"

"Oh, Ebony, there you are. What's wrong, sweetie? Where have you been?"

I kneel down to see if anything is broken or bleeding. She lets me examine her. Nothing on the outside, but she just lays there. We can't coax her into the house.

Donald suggests I get a box with a towel, take her inside, and call the vet first thing tomorrow.

I get the box. We make her comfortable. She just looks at us. I know she wants me to do something.

"There's an emergency clinic in the Valley. I can't wait, Donald. I'll take her tonight."

"Kathy, it's nine. That's crazy. T still has homework and I—"

"I know this isn't something you can do. I know where I'm going. It shouldn't take more than a couple of hours. You stay here with T."

Donald can't stand anything medical with himself or with us and most certainly not with animals. He runs the other way. I wonder if that is something to do with his hypochondriac tendencies or his dad being a doctor or the threat of unwanted responsibility or just a Donald thing. I'm the opposite. If you're sick, go to the doctor, let them make the call. You either dodge a bullet or you're a little embarrassed. Either way you end up with a bottle of antibiotics.

I get to the twenty-four-hour vet close to ten thirty. By eleven we have a diagnosis. Ebony has kidney disease; most likely she did leave home to let nature take its course but decided home is where she wanted to be. The vet wants to put her on dialysis. This will need to be done daily; they will train me to be her nurse. There is no cure, just a daily process. I thank them and take my bottle of antibiotics. We head home.

I explain to Ebony on the way that I'm pretty sure that being on dialysis is not how she would want to end her days. She's on the passenger seat curled in the corner of the box. Eyes shining, I know she is listening. "I'm pretty sure you didn't come home to be hooked up to tubes." She puts her paw on the box edge. I scratch her head. We come to an agreement.

"Kimmie, it's Mom. I have some sad news. I had to put Ebony to sleep. She was so sick. We couldn't fix her, sweetheart. I'm so sorry."

*****

I miss Ebony, she was a funny little thing. Always flitting up and down the stairs, peering at me around corners, worrying about the rocks, and waiting for Kim. I hope she's with Baxter Baby and Pep. I hope there are no quakes where she is, only soft pillows and sugar milk; she really liked sugar milk. I tried it once, just gave me gas.

*****

Jim has a new girlfriend and is recovering from a TRW lay-off by joining the ranks of the real estate moguls flipping Southern California's beach properties. He's encouraged both personally and professionally and is rewarding himself with an extended vacation. He has asked if we can babysit his two cats, Amos and Andy. No one in the Redondo Beach area is available. Family? Friends? Neighbors? They have all gone missing. I can't say no; after all, his cats are really the kids. They were a Christmas present about four years ago; a gift from T and Kim meant to keep Jim company.

"Of course we'll take the cats. The kids can pick them up this weekend. Kim's home and T has a break before Saturday practices start. He can drive his truck down. I don't think you've seen it."

"That would be great. I haven't seen the kids in a while, crazy schedules."

"How long do you think the cats will be here?"

"Maybe three or four weeks. I'll call you when I get back."

That really wasn't the answer I was looking for. I suspect Amos and Andy will become a permanent part of our extended family.

Kim and T bring the cats home Sunday night. I guess it was quite the trip. Andy reacted to his car ride by throwing up. Although the truck cab has back seating, it's close quarters. T had to stick his head out of the window so he wouldn't throw up. Kim thought it was pretty funny. He's just like my dad that way, just the thought gags him. They made it. T and Andy a little green, Kim and Amos none the worse for wear.

Amos and Andy are huge. Amos is anxious to meet the dog. Andy immediately finds a bed to hide under.

Donald argues, "I hope you realize that these cats are never going home. It's going to be just like Teaser the Bird. Come for a visit stay for a lifetime."

"Sweetheart, I couldn't say no."

"You could have, but when it comes to the kids and the animals, you can't."

"And to you."

*****

I like the boys; they are okay for cats. Amos and I are good together chasing birds. I bark at them when they are pecking worms on the lawn, and just as they take flight Amos pounces from behind one of the flowerpots. He doesn't catch them all but enough to make Kathy yell.

Andy is more mouser than birder; he slinks around at night. I watch him from the door of my house. He's sneaky, silent. He learns fast. He never leaves mice by the door for Kathy to find; he drops them over the wall. I've heard the school's yard duty yell more than a few times. Kathy says, "Andy what have you done?" He just stretches out in the sun and stares across the pool. He's so cool.

*****

Donald is taking TJ to have otoplasty today. They used to say, "Having your ears pinned." This is a big deal, a really big deal. I can't believe Donald is doing this. I missed how important having this done is for TJ. To me it wasn't necessary; it didn't warrant the cost— the cost in dollars not in self-confidence. Donald had his ears pinned when he was in the second grade. He tells me the kids called him Dumbo, making him miserable. His dad called a colleague. Problem fixed. The timing is perfect; football season just ended. T's ears will be healed in time for next season's heavy practices. You can't have tender, swollen ears when you pull that helmet on. Ouch.

Donald *gets* TJ, not just the ear thing but him—his *bad boy* persona. It takes one to know one.

> (Definition: bad boy (noun): A man who does not conform to approved standards of behavior. A person who goes against convention. A bad boy is a word that is traditionally used to describe a guy who lives by his own rules, rather than just blindly following the crowd.)

Donald spends a great deal of time talking me down from the panic TJ's behavior elicits in me—behavior that is typical for many teenage boys. Behavior that suburban mothers like me perceive as over-the-top dangerous (too much beer, too many parties, cigarettes, all that rowdy stuff). I just can't relate, but Donald can. He's been there, done that. He laughs at the bad boy tag and my hand-wringing. "Take a breath," he counsels. "It's just a matter of time and settling hormones." I have to confess that raising a boy is hard. I'm not good at it. Thank God for Donald.

And what about Kim? It's so easy to ignore the child that makes no waves, the one who asks for little and expects less. I've been consumed with ensuring T graduates, accepting Nonie's senility, managing my brother's medical issues, making excuses why Jim seems to have disappeared, and ferreting through work politics. I've neglected my good girl.

Kim's only brush with risky business was stealing flatware from Denny's after football games and a weekend road trip with no purpose other than to join one of the girl's boyfriends at a "battle of the bands" in Santa Cruz. The risk—the girls had no place to stay, little money, a car that never should have been on the road, and naive parents that let them go.

In June 1996, Kim graduates from college on plan, accepts her first interior design job, and moves to her first apartment. T and I, her soon-to-be (pretty sure) fiancé, his brother, and father move her in. Donald and I buy her the necessities—shower curtain, towels, kitchen utensils, and a vacuum cleaner. My advice, "Live by yourself for at least a year, figure out what it costs to run an apartment, make a budget, do your own shopping and laundry. Do that and you will never have to panic about taking care of yourself." Donald's advice, "You can always come home." T's plea, "Now can I turn your room into a gym?" With these pearls of wisdom, we abandon her in Alameda, surrender her to adulthood, and head home. Once again we have no doubts that our good girl will be just fine.

*****

"What is that bird yelling about now?"

Mandy stretches out on the sofa, disturbing Amos and Andy from their spots curled up against her back.

"I don't think he's yelling as much as announcing that Kathy is home," yawns Amos.

"Well, whatever he's doing, that sound makes my teeth ache. I wish they'd put him in the den and shut the door." Andy slinks off toward the kitchen.

"I don't think that will work. I think he'd only squawk until someone rescued him from being alone." Amos paws Mandy's nub of tail. Mandy groans and throws Amos an annoyed look.

*****

Kim flies home for Thanksgiving. I pick her up at the Burbank airport. She pushes her duffel bag into the back seat and slides into the front.

"How are you, sweetheart?"

"Great, Mom." She takes a hold of my right forearm with her left hand. "What do you think?"

I think I was right. She is glowing as is her ring finger. The ring suits her delicate bones and clean style, a princess-cut solitaire. She's engaged to Matt, the boy who showed us the way to the laundry room the day we moved her into her freshman dorm. Now they will be man and wife; we have a year to make it happen.

I don't know what to do first. I'm accomplished at planning office retreats and client receptions but a wedding? Donald suggests I find a wedding planner, take some of the pressure off. I'm resistant, not wanting to shirk my maternal duties, but more than anything, I want this to be perfect for Kimberly. I relent, we find Ms. Wendy, our wedding planner extraordinaire.

Before the wedding we have T's eighteenth birthday and then his high school graduation.

His friends take him out for his birthday. Donald and I are curious but manage not to ask. T mentions the lap dance and tries to hide the tattoo. Obviously, cake and family time are no longer adequate. Donald cautions me not to overreact, reminding me that being eighteen legitimizes TJ's independence; he's going to test it.

"Kathy, did TJ tell you we went to the Marine recruitment office the other day?"

"No, but I overheard you two talking about it. I know he's been interested in the military, even talked about West Point for a while. Guess one of his teammates had a sponsor and got in. I think it might be a valuable alternative to college for him. But I'm not sure how he'd do with someone telling him what to do twenty-four hours a day. Might be good, might not be. Of course I'm not keen on the danger element, but I'd be so proud. And what about his asthma, that might be a showstopper."

"Well, it was. They wouldn't even discuss it. T put up a brave face, but I think he was more than disappointed."

"Oh God. Anything we can do?"

"No. Let's just move on. It is what it is."

I refocus on T's graduation. I check and double-check that required credits are earned. I swallow my guilt as I hand him his completed senior economic project. I hate that I'm one of those parents. But I need to get T out of high school. I need to get out. Like the reading, economics wasn't not knowing how; it was a matter why should I. It's June, we don't have time for that discussion. Next hurtle, getting enough tickets for the extended family to watch T cross the field one more time, not to block the quarterback but to accept his diploma. We succeed in getting six tickets, enough for Jim and the girlfriend, Kim, Nonie, Donald, and me. I'm relieved Jim is making an appearance and Kim was able to get time off work. I'm pleased that Nonie feels like venturing out from her apartment for this event. I'm ecstatic that by the end of the evening we can call T's (and my) high school days done.

*****

"What is that little yapper? Is that a pigtail on its head and a bow? Why's it in our house? Oh holy cow, there are two." I have no choice I'm going to bark and bark and bark.

"That dear Mandy is the reason Andy and I are here. Those little rug rats belong to Jim's girlfriend. She insisted Jim get rid of us. She and her pouches couldn't stand the competition."

"But why are they here in our house?"

Andy comes down the stairs and joins us in the den. "Okay, guys, here's the deal. Kathy is livid, those little dogs weren't invited to T's party. Kathy told Jim the dogs have got to go. She said, "Get them out and get them out now. They are driving my animals crazy."

"Well, I don't know if Jim can get the girl to take them out." Amos spots Teaser watching from his perch in the family room.

"Hey, Tease, we need a little help here." Teaser cocks his head, puts his crest on high, and lets out a blood-curdling squawk that cuts to the bone.

Minutes later Jim and the girl with yappers-in-purse say good night.

Saved by the bird.

*****

This is the first summer in four years that hasn't centered around football practice and transitioning Kim from one apartment to the other. We are wedding planning and enrolling T at the College of the Canyons, COC.

We have Kim's dress and are close to having a venue. We found the dress in Walnut Creek near Kim's office, and the venue will be here in Southern California. Thanks to the wedding planner the process has been low stress for me, and Kim has a clear vision of what her day should look and feel like; that's a huge help. I'm happy to tag along with Kim and Wendy to check out all the vendors. It's a relief to follow instead of taking the lead.

COC is a junior college; it has a great reputation, is inexpensive, and five minutes from home. TJ will be taking a general education path toward his associate degree. He has decided to take advantage of the school's partnership with the University of California at Los Angeles, UCLA. He will transfer to UCLA as a junior and major in philosophy. I am over the moon, surprised, no speechless, anxious, hopeful, once again acting like *that* mom.

I've decided to start job hunting. I'm going to take my time, find the right fit. I want to love my job again, like at the bank. The little firm is a dead-end. Their management style is autocratic; although they insist they are progressive. Like many law firms they hold tightly to the partnership model and are slow to embrace business acumens. I need to find a more forward-thinking organization. If I tarry much longer, I'm pretty sure I'm going to tell them what I really think. Or worse where they can go, I'm sure they won't be receptive.

The wedding. Perfection. Outside service, grape arbor, wishing well. Inside reception, welcoming, inclusive, tabletop topiaries, scattered acorns baked to rust and golden hues. Time, sunset. Bride— exquisite, adored, clutching roses of an indescribable burnt orange with pink undertones. Groom—handsome, adoring, composed. Proud families, loving friends. Monogram, oak leaf with acorn.

My mother, Nonie, didn't attend her only granddaughter's wedding. She wouldn't go. I had a lovely plum outfit picked and altered to fit her tiny-aged frame. I had a corsage made for her wrist. I hired a companion to escort her to the ceremony and take her home when she tires. But Nonie wouldn't go. She didn't want to leave Bruce. Weeks earlier Bruce had fallen through a plate glass window in her apartment. He'd been drinking; he's not supposed to drink, and as Nonie explained, "he had a *spell*." He passed out and was hospitalized. He returned just a week before the wedding. I told him he couldn't come, that there would be alcohol, and I felt the temptation would be too great. I couldn't risk his *falling* at the reception. He understood. Nonie didn't. She couldn't leave him alone; she just wouldn't. Kim was crushed, of course. My fault, my cowardice, I should have found a way.

Life slows. Donald and I relax into our weekends. Kim and Matt return from Italy to take on married life. T commits to his education and is planning a semester in London. I suspend my job search. The holidays are close, I can wait. Bruce becomes Nonie's attendant, allowing him to live with her indefinitely and make a small stipend. We hear little from Jim. Mandy spends her days napping under her favorite bush. We move Teaser to the den; I think he actually likes the quiet. Amos and Andy entertain us with their brotherly antics; chasing up and down the stairs and fighting just to make up in time to nap back to back on the sun-bathed couch.

*****

They finally got the message. They finally moved me. I thought they'd never listen to my shrieks. I didn't like being in the center of things. I didn't like hearing the water in the kitchen; it was always on like the shower in the dorm where that boy insisted on taking me Saturday mornings. Mandy was forever bumping my table, splashing water, and spilling seeds. I actually like Amos and Andy; I know they are cats, but they are good conversationalists. But I didn't like them sitting next to my cage and pawing my bell. That was a little too friendly. And the fur, it was everywhere.

I like the den; no one comes here unless they want to read. It's quiet, and my new, huge cage hangs from the ceiling close to the French door where I can see the wavy trees. T checks on me during the day. He is teaching me to whistle the "Colonel Bogey March" (from "Bridge on the River Kwai") I've almost got it. Kathy puts my cage cover on each night. When she has time, she ducks below the seed shield so I can't see her (I can but don't tell her) and asks, "Teaser? Where's Teaser?" I dip my head up and down and say, "Peekaboo, peekaboo." We have such fun!

*****

"Kathy, I think something is wrong with Mandy. She's tender around her muzzle. She won't let me trim her there."

I call Mandy's vet, tell them what my groomer told me about the tender spot. I take her in after work. I have to leave her. She's not happy; she's never spent the night at the vet's before. The only ailment that required the vet was when a bee stung her in the eye, it was swollen shut. I kiss her velvet head. "Night, sweetie."

"Okay, guys, Mandy is spending the night. She has a lump on the side of her neck. It's could be benign or not. They are going to do a biopsy. The doctor will call me when he has he results so we can discuss what to do next."

Donald rubs his face. "I think I'll go to the house, call you later, babe."

T disappears upstairs.

I tuck Teaser in and herd Amos and Andy into the family room. It's too early for bed. I want my Mandy home. I opt for *Law and Order* and insist the cats join me.

As promised the doctor calls, well, his assistant calls.

"You can pick Mandy up tomorrow after three. The tumor was cancerous, and they removed it. They are not sure if they got it all, they think they did."

"Can I speak with the doctor? I need to know what this means." I'm livid they went ahead with the surgery without consulting me.

"I'm sorry he's with another patient."

I pick up Mandy. She's happy to see me, eyes bright, tail wagging. She has a cone around her head.

"Bring her back in two days, and we will take the stitches out." The assistant gives me pain pills and antibiotics.

"I want to talk with the doctor, I want to know where we go from here."

"He's not here today. You can call and make an appointment."

Sweet Mandy navigates as if she's always had a cone around her neck. She eats well, follows T around the house, and annoys the cats. I fix her a spot on the den couch. Teaser keeps her company. Donald brings her a new tennis ball; she scoots it around with her cone. Maybe it isn't as bad as it sounds.

I finally get to talk with the vet. I grill him. It's like playing the shell game, I can't pin him down. He doesn't know if he got it all or if she'll recover or how long she has if she doesn't. He is clear; however, there is nothing more we can do, and "yes, he understands I don't want her to suffer. Do you need more pills?"

Mandy won't let them take out the stitches. They are so annoyed. I'm more than annoyed. "Don't worry they will dissolve. We took the cone off for you." They hand me the leash. As Grandpa would have said, "Here's your hat what's your hurry."

For a week Mandy seems like Mandy. She is enjoying her nest in the den. The cats sleep next to her, Andy on the back of the couch, and Amos as close to her as he can get. Teaser sings all his songs for her, over and over and over; Mandy doesn't seem to mind.

"Donald, Mandy's not doing well. We need to go back to the vet. Not the jerk that wouldn't talk to me, but one that gives a shit."

I take the day off and call around. I find a vet sympathetic to my situation. I give him my permission to call and have Mandy's records transferred. He will see us this afternoon. TJ and Donald go with us.

The doctor explains that Mandy is in shock, and her pain level is high. (She is trembling.) He's reviewed her records; there is nothing to do but make her comfortable.

"You mean put her down."

"That would be the kindest."

Donald, T, and I step out to the waiting room. There is little conversation; we make our decision. We take turns saying goodbye. I can't leave her. Donald gently insists.

Donald removes Mandy's things from the den, and when I'm at work, he takes down the doghouse and removes her water faucet.

I save her collar, tags, and leash in an antique tin advertising dog biscuit; there is a spaniel on the front. I have a stone carved with *Mandy's Spot 1985 to 1998*; I place it in front of her favorite bush.

*****

"Kathy was blowing her nose and sopping up tears with a paper towel. It was hard to hear the whole story. But Mandy is not coming home." Amos is sitting in the doorjamb between the den and family room.

Andy is silent, hanging out under Teaser's cage.

Teaser gives his bell a horrid hard shake. Raises his crest to its very tip-top and spreads his wings like Batman and screams. A scream meant to raise the dead.

T scoops up Amos and peeks in the den. "Everything okay, guys?"

*****

"So when do you think we'll have some babies?"

"Babies?"

"Matt and Kim, when will we be grandparents?"

"Are you kidding, they just got married. I'm sure it will be a while. Besides, you still owe me a couple of kids."

"Guess that ship sailed. Anyway I consider yours mine. I should have married you and adopted them. Guess Jim wouldn't have gone for that. We could have kept your last name. Or hyphenated, Hauck-Whang."

"Well, I'm not sure. Jim seems to have fallen off a cliff. He's busy being busy. I guess he's in touch with Kim and Matt, but T hardly sees him. Something's going on, I don't know what. I think we should adopt you and just make it Mr. Whang the second."

"I might go for that. Just as long as we're together forever, sweetheart." Donald winks. "You know someday I'm going to have to marry your bones. Someday when I'm sure you'll say yes. Until then I'll be content letting you and yours make me a pseudograndpa. I hope it doesn't take too long. We're getting old."

"Speak for yourself."

Funny, fifteen years ago I couldn't wait to be remarried. To reset. Start over. In retrospect marriage wasn't the issue; having Donald want to was. My notion of marriage was a product of my age and rearing. A formula for happiness: love equals marriage equals security. Just like divorce equaled failure. Now that I've evolved (for better or worse) I see it as a surrender. A loss of control of my home, income, children, even of myself. Like me, Donald is a product of his upbringing. As a husband I'm sure he would insist on being what his dad was *the king of the castle*. As unmarried individuals we aren't defined by traditional roles or expectations. We are both free to compromise or acquiesce as our preferences dictate. No one has to be the boss. No one has to be the slave. Selfish? You bet. We may fantasize time to time about the ideal marriage, where two become a better one and saunter into the sunset, but neither has the courage to actually do it. We remain hopelessly in love, selfishly protective. Single.

We take T to the airport. His trench coat underarm, collapsible umbrella in his backpack. A gift for his host family tucked in his suitcase, the recommended See's candy. We press against the terminal window and watch the 747 take flight. The jet propulsion fumes waft in thermo waves creating a mystic veil over the horizon. Up. Up. The jumbo jet disappears into a cloud bank taking Thomas James off to London. "It's just a semester," Donald comforts, but his eyes are wet too. It's hard to let go. Harder to be left behind.

I've renewed my job search. I just completed my third interview with a large firm blocks from my current one. I've been able to interview on my lunch hours. I'm hoping this is the one. They have offices across the country. Their headquarters is in San Francisco. I would be the administrator for their LA office which houses fifty-plus attorneys and sixty staff. If selected I'd be part of a team again, no longer left to my own devices. I would have support on all levels. What a relief that would be. This week I interview with the LA equity partners, all twelve of them. Next week I meet with the managing partner of the firm. Then?

TJ manages to call from London every few weeks, and we email. He is immersing himself in all things British: history, literature, pubs, theaters, landmarks, and his favorite homes and hangouts of renown authors. In addition to his studies, T is up against the deadline to apply to UCLA for fall quarter. His COC adviser is coaching us through all required paperwork. It's a real across the *pond* effort. His other challenge is relating to his host family; they couldn't be more different. But that's the point of exchange programs, right? Right.

*****

"Where's the boy, haven't seen him in a while. I finally have that song down that he taught me. Want to hear?"

"Not really." Amos teeters on the couch back and paws at Teaser's tail feathers as they poke in and out of the cage wires as he moves from perch to perch.

Teaser rings his bell and begins to sing.

*****

"Donald, I talked to Kim today. She's not doing so good. She's depressed, clinically depressed. She's seeing someone. I had no idea."

"What? You're kidding."

"Wish I was. I guess it's so bad she has trouble getting out of bed in the morning. Doesn't want to go to work. All the classic symptoms. She tried being reassuring, but she sounds bad."

"What's next?"

"Therapy and trying to find a drug that might help. So far they think it's a hormonal imbalance. She's pretty discouraged. I offered to come up, but she doesn't want that."

"What do we do?"

"Pay attention. Stop assuming all is well and pay attention."

CHAPTER 15

Molly

Description: So small, reminiscent of Ebony. Black, longhaired, but rod-straight tail. We inherit her like Amos, Andy, and Teaser the Bird. She's skittish. Big round green eyes. She has unusually sharp claws, like pins. I trim the tips with baby clippers. She likes to sleep in small spaces—breadbaskets, hats, old Pooh's lap, any warm dent in any unmade bed. She has a funny squawky meow.

I take Nonie grocery shopping every Sunday morning. We go to Ralph's. We both get carts. She leads. At ninety-one she insists on doing her own shopping. Not only won't she let me do it for her; she won't let me join her as she goes up and down the aisles. I always have a little list of things I forgot on Saturday. So I take my cart and linger long enough so I'm out of her range of vision. This way I can keep my eye on her without being obvious. I usually finish first and wait at the front of the store. The cashiers know us; they keep their eye on her too. Nonie won't use a debit card. She writes checks; this takes a fair amount of time. First she has to "unrubberband" her checkbook, find the pen that lives on the bottom of her purse, and then fill in the blanks. This ritual is slowed while she adjusts her bifocals. No one hurries her. She and the clerks chitchat through her preparations. If I apologize, they wink and say, "Oh, I'm happy to help, she reminds me of my mom." Once we load our bags into the car, we walk a few stores down the mini mall and have coffee and a pastry. Her favorite strawberry tart. I like a cinnamon twist. We no longer discuss world events or domestic plights; we don't even gossip. We sip our coffee in quiet. I hold her hand as we return to the car. At her apartment I park at the side entrance, that way she is close to the elevator; she lives on the second floor. She insists on taking her groceries in by herself. We load her little pushcart, and she makes her way to the door, turns, and waves.

"Call me when you get home, Kathy."

"I will, Mom." I used to argue, I don't anymore. I'll be home in less than five minutes, and before she calls me, I will call her.

From what I can tell, Kim is doing better, not great but better. It sounds like a lot of trial and error finding a drug that will work. Her therapist and doctor are working together. I think that's good. I understand there's no quick fix; why would there be its an insidious disease. Matt's been a brick. Donald and I remain useless.

T made it back from London. We watched him make his way through customs, I didn't recognize him at first. Donald had to point him out. "There, Kathy, right there." He had a full beard and shoulder-length hair, dark blond now no longer streaked by the sun. Much thinner than the boy-man that played ball. Gone just a semester, but I suspect more like a lifetime for him.

It's spring 1999. The elephant in the room is the excruciating wait for college acceptance letters. My friend and I spend lunch hours examining our kids' possibilities. Her daughter is waiting to hear from Tufts, and T is waiting on UCLA. Maureen and I remind each other that this may be the kids' waterloo, but it is not ours. We need to be strong for them, no time to lose ourselves in their lives.

"Mom?"

Something is wrong, I can hear it in his brief greeting. I pull the phone closer, listen hard.

"Do you have a TV there?"

"No, what's up?"

"There's been a shooting at a high school in Colorado. Mom, they are crawling and falling out of the windows. Mom, it's right on the TV. Kids are running everywhere. Can you come home?"

(The Columbine High School massacre, a school shooting and attempted bombing occurred on April 20, 1999, in Columbine, Colorado. The perpetrators, twelfth-grade seniors, murdered twelve students and one teacher. Ten students were killed in the school library. Twenty-one people were injured by gunshots. Three people were injured trying to escape the school. At the time, it was the deadliest school shooting in US history.

In addition to the shootings, the attack involved homemade bombs. Two of these were placed in the cafeteria, powerful enough to kill or seriously injure all people within the area; they failed to detonate. Cars in the parking lots were made into bombs; one bomb was in a location away from the school, two bombs were set up as diversions, only one was partially detonated. The massacre had been planned for about a year. The perpetrators hoped the massacre would cause the most deaths in US history; this meant exceeding the death toll of the Oklahoma City bombing. The culprits committed suicide in the school library.)

"I'm on my way."

TJ and I are glued to the television. Black-and-white images of Kennedy's funeral flash across my mind. That mournful feeling resurrected. Donald joins us on the couch. We watch, all we can do is watch.

The universe tips and dips and rolls over. Despair and joy exchange places.

"Mom! I'm in, my letter came. No, it's a packet. Mom, I made it I'm in!"

I buzz Maureen. They heard from Tufts last week; they made it too. She sends hugs to T and comes to my office to give me one.

I thank God, call Donald, and dance around my desk. Hands up, hands down, shuffle, shuffle, shuffle. Whahoo!

*****

"Did he like it, your song did he like it?"

"Indeed, first I sang it, then we sang it together over and over and over. I still have a little trouble at the end, but he didn't care."

*****

I'm going to meet with the managing partner of Sedgwick's LA office on Wednesday; it's been over two months since our last meeting. There were five contenders for the position; now it's down to me and one other. This interview should be the one before the offer…or rejection.

As with any potential change, Donald is anxious. He appreciates why I want to change jobs but is fearful about me leaving the known for the unknown. He's not much on seeking out opportunity. But I've learned to use his pessimism as ballast. He forces me to think things through, weigh both sides; it can be irritating, but when I make a decision, I'm prepared for all consequences.

I meet with Elliot Olson. I'm prepared to answer any outlying questions he might still have. The receptionist directs me to his office, not the conference room. He greets me at the door, and I take a seat across from him at his desk.

I literally float back to the firm. I call Donald. "You are speaking to the office administrator of Sedgwick's second largest office."

Donald's angst turns soft. "Oh, babe, I'm so proud. Come home we'll celebrate."

*****

Amos is watching Teaser take a bath. Teaser splashes and preens, splashes and preens.

"Why are you taking a bath in your water dish?"

"Why do you use your tongue?"

"Point. I miss Andy."

"He hasn't been around. Where is he? Has Kathy said?"

"No, I heard her tell Donald she didn't want to talk about it. She said, she's tired of her kitties getting sick. Donald let her sit on his lap. It was sad, I had to leave."

"Oh, sounds like Andy must be with Mandy. I'm sorry, Amos. Guess it's just you and me now."

*****

I do better writing than talking. I should of course do this in person, but I've decided not to. I get into work before anyone else. I insert my disk and print out my resignation letter. Jack's office is open; he's the firm's president, my direct boss. I lay the letter on his chair. I'm such a coward.

"Kathy, anything we can do to make you stay?"

"I appreciate you asking, but this is an opportunity I can't pass up."

Sedgwick is everything I had hoped for; a large organization where there is expertise and support in finance, operations, and human resources. I will be part of a management team that the firm respects. I won't be just a figure head carrying out the whims of the highest-paid partner. I will have the opportunity to contribute. What finalized my acceptance was Elliot's definition of his management style. "I'm a lawyer. I want to be a lawyer, not a manager. That's your job. If you need me I'm here, but you manage, and I'll lawyer." I couldn't ask for more.

TJ gets a high school buddy to help move him to his UCLA-sponsored apartment. It's on Gayley within walking distance to the campus. As a junior he doesn't need his parents moving him in, we get it. He sold his truck and is driving one of my hand-me-down Honda sedans. The guys load it up. He takes the bare necessities, no interest in setting up housekeeping like Kim was. They pull out of the drive, and he waves. Not the bon voyage I had anticipated. I resist asking him to call me when he gets there.

Donald gives me a squeeze. "Well, it's just us and the cat and bird now. Empty nesters, no offense, Tease. Any news on the baby front?"

"Oh, for heaven's sake. No babies but they are talking about getting a dog. That might be a good first step, don't you think?"

"Well, it's a start."

Donald hasn't been feeling well. Aches and pains here and there. General malaise. He's been to the doctor, but nothing specific has come of it. I'd like to think it's his hypochondriac leanings, but I can't convince myself.

Kim and Matt are in town. I'm babysitting Murphy while they have a night out. Donald went home early. Murphy is a three-month-old golden retriever. He looks like a bear cub. At this moment in time his fur is goldy white, it's fuzzy and thick. Right now, he is sleeping. I was chasing him around the yard; he managed to climb on a lounge, and by the time I caught up to him, he was asleep. I'm going to take him in; it's getting chilly out here.

*****

"What's this thing? A Mandy baby? Okay fella not too close. Don't be putting that cold black nose on me."

I stand my ground, after all this is my family room. I suspect this is the puppy they all have been raving about. They call him Murphy, Murphy the dog. Like we can't tell he's a dog.

"Step back if you know what's good for you. Seriously we aren't friends yet. It'll take some time, buddy. You are such an overgrown fur ball. Where are you going? Oh no, that's my pillow, put it down."

"Teaser, watch out he's headed your way, hold on to your perch!"

Kids.

*****

Donald and I, Kim and Matt are headed to Westwood to pick up TJ. We are going to a Bruin football game and to check out his apartment. The game was a last-minute idea of mine so we are sitting in the endzone.

TJ meets us at the curb; he's been holding a parking spot for us. We follow him through a maze of staircases and halls to his place. His roommate is not there. I had forgotten the spareness of the male college apartment. Kim teases Matt about his.

It's the end of October, it's so hot that I don't even have the energy to reminisce about my UCLA days. I hope my family knows how lucky they are. The game is not as fun sitting in the endzone as when you are nearer the booster section. T hangs out with us until halftime then he leaves to join friends. We agree to meet at the car after the game. The plan is to go for Mexican food. We could all use a pitcher of Margaritas. Donald's fidgety, his legs are bothering him; it's hard when you are six-four to fold up into stadium seating. By the fourth quarter we are ready to go. We leave UCLA winning and head to the car to wait for TJ.

My first week at Sedgwick is behind me. Elliot has filled me in; my priority is to mend fences between staff and management. There was a bit of a coo when Elliott became managing partner last year. The firm installed term limits thus forcing his predecessor to move on. He was a fixture for years with no desire to try things a different way. He ruled with the support of a handful of "yes sir" staff and attorneys. A real power clique. I was introduced to the attorneys at a welcome lunch, and I've held my first staff meeting. There's a lot of mistrust here. Folks feel they don't have a voice. I gave my *first thing I'm going to do is listen* talk, invited people to ask questions in any form they are comfortable with—email, office visit, paper note, or over coffee. I promised my door would be open. (I understand that my predecessor's was mostly shut.) Folks have walked by and peeked at me, a few have emailed. I realize this is going to be a long process. The icebreaker as always was my last name; they had to laugh when I told them I understood it may take a while before they could trust a blue-eyed, blonde Korean. I think they are most interested in the fact that I have experience in both legal and nonlegal environments. One secretary shared she had worked at Security Pacific Bank; she touted the bank's management style—she's my first ally. My admin staff, Rose and Wendy, are true professionals, open and honest, knowledgeable, and anxious to make Sedgwick LA the best it can be. I'm blessed.

I take a deep breath and rerun the conversation Donald and I just had over the phone. Donald's discomfort at the football game convinced him to return to the doctor. He just called and said it was not good news. He refused to give me details over the phone, said it could wait until I got home. I pushed; I don't like driving into the unknown. Donald has metastasized prostate cancer; they told him to get his affairs in order.

"Donald, this can't be the only answer. Not in this day and age."

He hands me a lemon drop martini, and I find a bottle of Ativan from some other crisis. I take the small wonder pill, and we settle on the couch. He's not drinking, no afternoon champagne, not even a beloved Diet Pepsi. I wait for him to fill in the blanks.

Donald refuses me the litany of his medical journey that led to today's diagnosis. He's protecting me or guilty. From what I can ascertain there have been a number of doctor visits involving PSA (prostate specific antigen) tests, physical and imaging examinations. His PSA is over three hundred, normal is between one and three. The imaging shows the cancer is throughout his skeletal system. How the cancer got to this point without medical intervention is not open for discussion. Donald's not telling. I suspect denial and postponing doctor-directed procedures. And not listening, no not hearing. I'm so angry, so betrayed, so selfish. I'm not dying, he is. Where's my empathy?

"I go back tomorrow. I have some options. But, Kathy, I'm telling you right now there will be no cutting or maiming. I'd rather be dead. It sounds like there's some success with hormone therapy. That's what we are going to talk about tomorrow."

"Do you want me to go with you?"

"No, I'm not going to do that to you. I've watched my mother spend half her life sitting in hospital rooms waiting for my father to come back from one procedure or the other. Fetch him this, fetch him that. No, I need you here, not wringing your hands in some hospital room or doctor's office."

Donald pursues hormone therapy. If successful this will reduce his testosterone to castration levels. It will starve the cancer, minimize symptoms, and extend life three to five years. Who knows what can develop in three to five years? Donald is cautiously optimistic, his newest concern: "I'm going to turn into a goddamn woman."

We let the kids know.

Donald has always been effusive with me. Romantic, sentimental, sensual, attentive. At least when he's not pissed about one of my illogical antics. Cancer has turned his anger toward God, the universe, himself. It has accentuated his regard for me. I seem to be on a pedestal, flailing to maintain perfection, keep my chin up, my desperation down.

"How's Kathleen taking it?"

"Not well. I'm surprised. She's really upset."

"She loves you. You are more than a friend. Not just a landlord. Surely you understand that by now."

"You're probably right. I didn't intend that to happen."

"I understand that. As you would say, 'It is what it is.' Be gentle, she's family."

*****

You have to be patient. Wait until Kathy returns to the kitchen. Then amble toward the couch, jump unto the arm, then the back. Can you smell it? It's right there, center stage sofa table. The cheese platter—Cheddar, Swiss, Gouda. Nice little cubes. I don't need a toothpick; I'll just use my claw.

*****

TJ is withdrawing from UCLA. It's April, just six months in and he's out.

T and I talk for hours on the phone. He's still at school; it will take him a week or two to process out. It becomes clear to me that UCLA was not TJ's idea; it was mine. He needs to get away. Away from me, us, California.

Donald is not surprised. Once again, he gets it, having gone through a similar exit with his parents.

My nightly cocktail becomes one Ativan, one Benadryl, and two 500 mg ibuprofens. Sleep is my relief. A time to put *my life* on hold. When morning comes, I wallow in those first seconds of consciousness, that space of time where everything is fine. I embrace this brief euphoria, hold it close.

TJ is released from school, gives up his law clerk position in my friend's firm, sells his car, stops home for goodbyes and clean underwear, gets on a Greyhound bus, and heads East. Jack Kerouac inspired.

We hear from him state by state. He beguiles us with his adventures. We follow him with worry and wonder as he wanders through the Caverns of Sonora, bars of New Orleans, youth hostels in DC, and the subways of New York. He charms his way onto Wall Street as a runner. I see him one morning on TV, darting around Maria Bartiromo during her morning stock report. He calls to let us know that he now smokes Cuban cigars, drinks Glenfiddich, and is being mentored by the brokers in the back room.

Donald is living vicariously through T's adventures. Not a risk taker, he is mystified by T's bravery. He hates to travel, but he's thinking we should take a trip to New York. "We should check on the boy, see if he needs anything."

As quick as it starts it ends, the stock market no longer holds TJ's passion. He sees a billboard ad and walks into an armed services recruiting center. He still wants to be a Marine. He's going to see what they say about his asthma. Three days later he is sworn in. Manhattan recruiters are not only interested in "the few, the proud" but in their signing bonuses. "Asthma what asthma?" He calls home, we're speechless.

Donald has an excellent response to hormone therapy. PSA levels are in the single digits, and scans show the cancer has retreated from his bones. Few aches and pains remain, and to his relief he has not become a girl.

We go to Carmel, stay in our favorite lodge, sit on the beach, dine under the stars, and fall asleep in front of the fireplace in our room. We walk the craggy streets and poke around antique shops. We follow the 17-Mile Drive. We admire the Lone Cypress and the massive rock formations that comprise the cliffs of Point Lobos. We watch the gulls as they dip in and out of turbulent gray-blue sea.

From Carmel we go to Alameda to see if the silence we hear from there speaks that all is well or at least all that can be. Kim has planned a girl's day out. First the mall then lunch and we'll end with an indulgence at See's. Then dinner with the guys and a walk with Murphy. I'm encouraged, she's embracing normalcy. Donald and I want to do something to thank Matt. Without his unwavering support…no words. Donald orders Matt a dishwasher. While Kim and I were shopping, the guys were watching football. Matt was doing dishes by hand during halftime, Donald was horrified. The dishwasher was something immediate he could do. Well, it's a start.

Work is my haven. There are enough problems to give me purpose but not enough to overwhelm. I'm comfortable here. I know what's expected, and there are few surprises. For eight to ten hours a day I lose myself in the peripheral. Donald has returned to his contract job. I think it gives him the same relief my job gives me. We take a breath and breathe out, slowly.

*****

"Awwwk, awwwk… Hey, somebody help me."

"Teaser, Teasy, where are you?"

"Here, over here. On the floor. Amos, on the floor."

"Where? Oh, what in the world are you doing?"

"Kathy left the door open. She put new seeds in and didn't shut the door. I thought I'd just go sit on the cage top like I do on Saturdays and wait until she remembered. I was watching the trees through the window. The wind was blowing them, and the outside birds were diving and darting in and out of the leaves. I just took off. I forgot I'm not an accomplished pilot. I flew around and around and then aimed for the cage top but hit a wall instead. I landed under the cage. I tried to take off again, no luck. So I took a walk which was exhausting. Do your nails get caught in the carpet? Mine do. I found this corner and was taking a nap. Then I heard you."

"Well, I could eat you or chase you, but I can't get you back in the cage. I suggest we just wait until a person gets here."

"Would you really eat me?"

"Nah."

*****

"Morning, sweetheart, Happy Birthday." It's Donald's fifty-nincth. It's September 11, 2001, 5:00 a.m. I can tell I woke him, but it's important for me to be the first to wish him Happy Birthday. "Go back to sleep, sweetheart, I'll see you this evening."

I spend a few minutes enjoying the warmth of my bed, force my way out and shower, clear up the mascara under my eyes, dress, and head downstairs for my first cup of coffee. It's 6:30 a.m. The phone is ringing.

"Hello. Hang on, I've got to let the cat out."

"Mom."

"Kim, what's is it?

"Mom there is something wrong with the world, seriously wrong, turn on the TV."

I take the phone to the couch. Katie Couric is saying something; she looks grim, she never looks grim. Her image is replaced by what I think is a scene from a disaster movie. But it is not a movie. It's New York. The World Trade building.

"Kimmie, stay home, you and Matt stay home."

"You too, Mom, promise you won't go to work. Please, Mom."

"Kimmie, I have to go. Jerome, our computer engineer, is there, at our office in the World Trade Center. I have to find… I need to call his wife. I need to check with Elliot and the other administrators. There are things we'll need to do. I'll keep you posted, promise."

I call Donald, repeat Kim's desperation. TJ flies through my mind. What does this mean for him? I call my brother and Nonie. She's just home from the hospital, recovering from a second hip replacement. My brother answers, he's been watching, his voice is calm, reassuring, "Just go do what you have to do. I have Mom, we'll be fine."

The freeway is empty. No traffic on the surface streets. The parking garage gates are up. Security hasn't changed shifts. The night guard walks me to the elevator and punches the eighteenth-floor button.

I flip the lobby lights on. I hear the elevator bell. Elliott comes in behind me; he's been in contact with firm management.

The office will be closed until further notice. Headquarters will use email and phone trees to communicate. Our NY office was evacuated; all members are safe. Jerome was instrumental in getting folks out of the building and across the Brooklyn Bridge. HR has contacted his wife.

"Kathy, there is nothing we can do here. Get home to your family. HR will keep us posted. And thank you so much for coming in. Call if you need me."

I go to my office, pick up files I might need at home. I glance down at the empty streets. The sun is casting long shadows down Figueroa. There are a handful of folks on the sidewalks. The red and green lights are directing no one.

9/11 revives patriotism. We attach flags to our cars and houses, stores, billboards, they are everywhere. TJ is waiting for his first overseas assignment. He's one pumped Marine, ready to defend. He is selected for an insertion team. Waiting for the "go" is driving him crazy.

Nonie passes a day before my birthday, October the sixteenth, a month and five days after 9/11. Just ninety-three, just. I can't explain her last confused helpless months, what did her suffering accomplish? Was she afraid to leave my brother, me, this corporal plain? Maybe it was the unknown that kept her here. Three days before she died Bruce called me, "Kathy, I told Mom it was okay, I would be alright, we would all be alright." Maybe that released her, maybe. When I got to the apartment to wait for the coroner, my brother had Mom tucked in with her favorite comforter. I didn't want to look, but I did. Her countenance was angelic, the lines of age had disappeared, worry was gone. She was Dorothy Amanda, Dot, Dottie, Mom, Nonie. She was at peace.

The holidays are bittersweet. I'm thankful for our good fortune, that we weren't in those buildings, that our lungs aren't full of God knows what, that T made it home for Thanksgiving, that my mom and dad are side by side, that my brother has found a home, that Kim is managing, that Donald's PSA is under three, and that Nonie's kitty Molly is now ours. I'm thankful that Christmas is close and that there will be a New Year.

Molly was given to Nonie by Bruce. A friend convinced him that a pet would help cheer her up. He found her at our local pet store. Mom named her. Molly was the queen of their apartment. She slept in a bun basket and spent her days darting across the couch and watching TV. She nibbled on Oreo's from Mom's purse and dined on Bruce's Big Macs. I tried to address the dietary problems both human and feline. But each time I'd visit, they'd be lined up on the couch watching TV engrossed in game shows or old black-and-whites. Sometimes happiness outweighs nutrition.

When Mom passed, Bruce no longer had the right to live in her HUD apartment. He didn't want to go through the paperwork that would allow him to stay. He was given thirty days to move. He decided on an extended-stay hotel, and Molly came to live with us.

"Here we go again, I hear what you're saying, but it's not going to happen. Bruce is not going to find a place that will let him have Molly. She's ours now, you know it, Kathy. Just admit it." Donald picks Molly up. They are eye to eye. She gives his beard two tentative whacks; he gives her head a pat and sets her next to him.

Bruce and I visit every Sunday morning. We have brunch and talk. He is enjoying the hotel; he feels pampered and very much likes the housekeeping service. He has many unlikely friends, bus drivers, cabbies, nuns, even a sheriff or two, and now the staff at extended stay. He has a community, not typical but inclusive. Sometimes he comes by the house to visit Molly. He plans to board with a new friend from the hotel in a few months when his "vacation" is over. He hopes to do some handyman work.

*****

"Hey, you. Hey, you big cat. You there with your paw in the water. I'm Molly, what's your name? What's on that plate? Can I have some, can I?"

Oh my, she's just a baby. She looks like she could be Ebony's baby.

"I'm Amos. This is tuna, people tuna. Kathy fixed it for us to share, to help us make friends. You'll like it. Come here. You take this side of the plate, and I'll take the other. That's right. Do you like it?"

"Oh yes, it's wonderful, very stinky."

"When you're done, I'll introduce you to Teaser. He's our bird."

"What's a bird?"

CHAPTER 16

Riley

Description: She's feral from a backyard litter fostered by a friend. She's skinny and scared. She's white with a cape, hood, and leg warmers of orangey fur highlighted with rust. Her cape covers her tail almost to its tip. Her white fur is like a mink's fur. The orange is not as soft. Her eyes are gold lime. Her paw pads, nose, and inner ears are pink. She has white whiskers. My first reaction to her is that we need to fatten her up and teach her to trust us.

TJ is on an aircraft carrier, destination Pakistan.

I move Teaser back to Kim's bedroom. I put him in the corner on the hook where he was when Kim was in college. The cage will be far enough from furniture so Molly can't torment him by sitting close and staring him down.

Home, made it in four and a half hours, wonder if that's a personal record. I'm always glad to make the turn onto Mill Valley after a road trip and pull into my garage. I've been to Kim's for Easter, and in a few hours Donald and I will have dinner. I hope he had a good time at his parents, that always stresses him out; maybe this time was different. I can see my mailbox marking the curve of the street as it dead ends into our cul-de-sac. And… I see Donald's car in the drive. I enjoyed being away, but just like home, I'm happy to see him, happy he's here.

He's waving to me from the garage.

"Hi, sweetheart, welcome home."

"Have you been here long?"

"No, just a few minutes. Wanted to let the cats out. The neighbor was here, said the sheriff stopped by Saturday looking for you, something about Bruce. Did anyone call your cell?"

There it is that despair in the pit of my stomach, that "what's wrong now" anguish that seeps through cells and organs and threatens to strangle.

"No, no one other than you. But I wasn't able to reach him to remind him I was going to Kim's. I left a message."

The message light on my house phone is blinking. I hesitate, maybe if I just turn and walk away everything will be all right. Maybe it's just a telemarketer, maybe… Donald hits the Play button.

It's Detective Somebody from somewhere. "I am calling regarding Bruce Locke. We believe he is your brother. Can you give us a call back at…?"

I call the number, I identify myself.

"What? Can you stop? Just a minute." I shove the receiver at Donald.

My brother died of a heart attack Friday night after having dinner at Outback. The housekeeping staff found him Saturday morning. There was no foul play. His body is at the LA County coroner's office. Once arrangements are made I'm to call, and they will release the body to the funeral home or burial service. His belongings can be picked up at their office any weekday. I have to call first.

"Jesus, Kathy."

"Jesus, indeed."

I remember when I told Bruce about Donald's cancer. We were on Nonie's couch; she was napping in her room. Bruce was "clear" just as clear as any sane person; well, what we call sane. I was weeping. I hadn't wanted to, but I was. My brother handed me a cup of tea, milk tea like when he brought me home from nursery school. In a calm reassuring voice he said, "Kathy, we will be okay. You take care of Donald, and I'll take care of Mom."

"And then what? Then what will we do?"

"Well, I'm going to sit on a curb with a pint of Jim Beam."

"You aren't supposed to drink. You'll pass out and God knows what."

"You know there's only one way off this planet."

That's not quite what went down. But close. I retrieved Bruce's belongings. Donald called the Neptune Society; he knew exactly what to do having just made his own arrangements. We went through Bruce's duffel bag; we were stunned by his organization. His life was meticulously filed in Baggies. His correspondence kept by date received in their envelopes severed neatly at the ends. Every receipt kept. We could trace his demise, dinner after dinner, prime rib and steak, highball after highball. Did he remember he wasn't supposed to drink? Did he? Or was this his planned vacation? We found list after list detailing the activities of his days. Donald concluded this was how he remained in control, sane, clear. He had carefully wrapped my parents wedding bands, Mom's diamond and Dad's masonic ring in a patch of flannel. There was a collection of keys, all tagged. Clothes clean and folded, military fashion. He had organized his struggle and then let it go. Donald and I sat a very long time mourning what we didn't know, what we never will.

The death certificate is mostly facts: date of birth, of death, cause, when, where. There's a blank we need to fill in, profession _____. Caregiver, house painter, small business owner, handyman, homeless? Donald and I decide on *musician*. We check the box for veteran; the man at Neptune says the government will send us a flag.

Kim, Matt, and Murphy come, second memorial in six months. I've written TJ this time; when Nonie passed, we worked our way through the Red Cross, found him in the field in the middle of some kind of war game. They made it pretty clear sending him home was not an option; we understood I just wanted him to hear it from me. This time he's oceans away, and uncles don't really qualify for Red Cross protocol. We only got through about Nonie because I convinced the agent that she was more a mother to T than I had been.

Donald and Matt are barbecuing, steaks. We have a fifth of Jim Beam. We will have a toast before dinner. Kim and I are in the kitchen.

"What is going on now?"

The bird is screaming, we can hear his wings flapping. Screaming and screaming and then there is caterwauling. Kim and I sprint up the stairs. The sound is deafening. We push each other through the bedroom door, and there's Molly hanging by her front claws on Teaser's cage. It's swinging wildly. Her back legs are pumping the air. Teaser is hysterical. Yes, he's hysterical. His wings are fully extended, and it looks like he can't catch his breath between shrieks. Kim stops the cage, and I pry Molly off; she takes a swipe, I have to drop her. She's out the door. Tears are streaming down our faces. We are at a loss as to how to calm the bird. He's all fluffed up, feather tuffs everywhere. "Shh, shh, Teasy," Kimmie whispers. All I can say is "Poor Teaser, poor Teaser." He sidesteps to the corner of his cage and looks us in the eye and screeches, "Peekaboo. Peekaboo. Peekaboo."

*****

"Molly, you can't do that. Teaser is family."

"I know, Amos, I know. It's just that he's a bird too. With wings and that long, long tail. It's so enticing when it pokes out of the cage. I won't do it again, I won't."

"I should hope not."

*****

Donald's PSA is creeping, up and scans indicate he needs to start radiation. He enrolls in a medical trial for late-stage prostate cancer, chemotherapy based. It slows the cancer but decimates the body's defenses.

On weekends we run errands and tackle to-dos. Home improvement is a welcome diversion. We are driving through Target's parking lot. Donald stops mid-aisle and addresses the windshield, "I don't believe in God, Kathy, there can't be a God if cancer happens."

I'm stunned. I have no counter.

I double up on my prayers. I find my childhood Bible and turn to Psalms. I watch evangelists at three in the morning. I pray prone on the floor like Audrey Hepburn in *The Nun's Story*. I obsess over Mark 11:23–24.

> 23 "Truly I tell you, if anyone says to this mountain, 'Go, throw yourself into the sea,' and does not doubt in their heart but believes that what they say will happen, it will be done for them. 24 Therefore I tell you, whatever you ask for in prayer, believe that you have received it, and it will be yours.

I make Donald promise that if he sees a bright light he'll walk toward it, not turn away. I beg him to reconsider. He won't. His God is dead. I don't think mine is listening.

There's a rally, a sweet spot. A weekend where Donald returns to me. Where we daydream about what will *be* when the trial is a success and we return to life. We will marry and live in Carmel by the Sea. We will walk on the beach where our grandchildren will make sandcastles. Amos and Molly will sleep all day in the sun curled up by pots of geraniums. Teaser will have a warm nook far from Molly's reach. We will put the top down on the Mercedes and ride the coast to Monterey. We will have a dog, a big one, but not as big as Murphy. We dance in the kitchen.

Our reverie is short-lived.

I haven't heard from Donald for days. His almost hourly calls have dwindled to zero. I've called and called. The ring of my phone startles. I fumble for my cell. I'm on my way to work.

"Hi, babe. I'm in the hospital."

"What's going on? Where have you been? Why didn't Kathleen call? You promised she would call if something happened."

"I know, I didn't want to worry you. I've had a time. My legs are shot. Kathleen had to find a way to get me down the stairs and to the hospital, it was a mess."

"My God, Donald, I should have been there." I'm so angry, so relieved.

I stop by the hospital on the way to work and again after. Days slide by. The medical situation is foggy. Donald is removed from the trial. It's all about pain management now. An intrathecal pump is inserted. We don't talk about it, but the damage to Donald's pelvis is irreversible. His ability to walk even stand diminishes.

Donald comes home to my house. No one has said hospice. But I'm familiar with the routine. Doctors, nurses, therapists come and go. A caregiver comes over as I leave for work, Kathleen takes over from her midafternoon until I return from work. Donald is never alone.

Donald's parents come in from Palm Springs. His dad makes it clear to me it won't be long. They stay for the day. His dad isn't feeling well he needs to get home. What did I expect?

We call the Red Cross and try to reach TJ. The best we can do is leave a message. Donald shifts in and out of consciousness. Lucidity offers bits of reflection and bittersweet musings. We are able to say everything...

He passes Sunday morning. Kim is here. I hold his hand and feel the life flow back toward his heart. I watch his skin go from ashen to the flesh color it's meant to be. His countenance becomes my Donald. I watch death step away and Donald move on. I whisper, "Move toward the light."

Our caregiver comes to call time of death. I call the hospice coordinator. I call Kathleen. She calls Neptune and Donald's parents.

Kim and I wait in the kitchen for Neptune. Something is pressing against me, holding me. I can't catch my breath. I'm not sure I can move.

"Kim," I gasp, "did you bring your inhaler?"

"I think so, let me go check. Here drink this water I'll be right back."

The sensation passes, I'm let go.

I stop her. "It's okay, I'm okay."

It's June 16, 2002, Father's Day.

*****

"Molly, Kathy's moving Teaser back downstairs. Guess she misses hearing him when she comes home. You won't fuss with him, will you?"

"No, I'll behave."

"And you have to stop clawing on the chair in the living room."

"Okay. What can I do?"

"You can climb trees and chase blue birds, lizards, and mice. Just keep the hunting outside. And come in when Kathy calls. Don't make her worry."

*****

Kim stays with me for a few days. We have a unique way of approaching grief. We start by rearranging the furniture and then we move to ice cream sundaes and M&M'S. We hit the mall. She focuses on shoes. I'm a sucker for white blouses. One night we do Asian, the next Mexican, and of course morning demands IHOP's pancakes.

"Mom, I'll call you when I get home. You should take a few days before you go back to work."

"I can't stand staying at home with nothing to do but think. I'll go back tomorrow. I'll feel better if I go in."

I write TJ. I go over our efforts to reach him. I hope to comfort. I want to look him in the eye and know he's okay. I find a website for the carrier he's on; there's bits and pieces of info on his unit. I reach out to the ship's chaplain via email.

I get several letters. Where did he get the stationery? It's tissue thin like the kind I used when I was a girl to send a letter airmail to my Aunt Bernice. The letters confirm he's received all of my communications. His letters are short, there's not even enough to read between the lines. He will be back on the East Coast soon. Then maybe here.

Work confines me to a narrow universe. *Manageable.* My five senses guide me. *No need for emotion.* People offer condolences. *I smile and say thank you.* They watch me from the corner of their eyes. *I shut mine.* Others try to pry. *I'm dumb.* I ask a friend what are the five stages of grief or is it seven, no matter I'm pretty sure I'm headed directly to anger and may be stuck there for a while.

I wander at night. Through the empty rooms straightening and remembering. I peek out the front door to see if other insomniacs are about. Sometimes there are lighted windows or someone in a robe and slippers having a smoke. I'd like to have a good cry; a wail would be even better. I'm amazed I'm still standing. During one of these treks, I see Amos and Molly sitting at the top of the stairs. Amos has been so good with her. Kind of a big brother. He is leaning toward her, sharing a secret? I remember when we first had her and she dashed out the back door headed straight to the pool. Amos flew out the door and laid on top of her until I could scoop her up. Such a good cat.

T comes home on a ten-day pass. He is full of stories of his experiences on and off the ship. I'm taken aback that a carrier can be a place of boredom and isolation. Not at all how it is portrayed in John Wayne movies. It sounds like there was maybe too much time to read and reread his small collection of books. He mentions reading a Spanish bible. I ask about the Bible. A gift from a girl.

"A girl? Who? Is she special?"

"Jackie. Her brother is my best friend. He was in my unit. He took me home one weekend. They live in New Jersey, Belleville. Love at first sight. Can't believe it. She gave me the Bible before I shipped out. She was born in Peru. She and her brothers came to the States when they were kids. Her stepfather sent for them. You'd love Jackie's mom. Jackie is teaching me Spanish, not high school Spanish, Spanish. I'm pretty fluent now. I'm reading Spanish novels, and I've tried a little writing too. Can she come here, to see where I live, to meet you and Kim and Matt? It will be just for a few days then she'll have to get back to work."

"Of course!"

TJ picks Jackie up at LAX. She arrives around 10:00 p.m. Determined to be the cool mom, I've gone to bed. I want to give them some time alone. I've talked to Nancy, her mom. T's right, I like her. She's so excited for Jackie; this will be her first time to the west coast. I assured her we will take good care of her girl.

I hear the garage door open. They come through the laundry room. I hear them giggling. To hell with cool. I meet them in the family room.

TJ has told me they are the same age; she looks younger. She reminds me of the storybook dolls my dad would bring me from his sales trips. Big, round dark eyes, rosy cheeks, charming—she is charming.

Kim and Matt come a few days after Jackie's arrival. We barbecue, swim, make Margaritas, hang out, catch up. T takes Jackie to all the tourist traps. I'm sure we overwhelm her with our desire to make her like us. She has a Jersey girl's accent when she's excited. We love it. I can't imagine what she must think of SoCal. New Jersey to California must be as drastic as Peru to New Jersey. She has to get back, she's a stylist in New York City. She tells us she works in three-inch heels; it's all about the right look when you work in an NY salon. All day on her feet in three-inch heels, ouch. It's obvious T wishes he were going with her. I'd suggest it, but I can't let go. In a few days he'll head back to Camp Lejeune.

Kathleen calls to ask me if I want Donald's ashes. Donald and I had discussed this. He thought it would be funny to put his ashes in a mantel clock; he collected clocks. I didn't like the idea then, and I haven't changed my mind. Kathleen laughs; she promised him she would ask. She's decided to have his ashes spread over Santa Barbara, Neptune was thinking LA, he would have hated that. We agree to have lunch, the two Kathleens toasting their guy. Weird.

By the time I understood Donald's relationship with Kathleen and hers with him, it was too late to be friends. When Donald became ill, I thought it would be a good time to give it a try. Donald was skeptical.

"Kathleen is afraid of you. Your success and independence intimidate her. And of course our relationship. I'm sure if she could avoid you she would prefer that."

Until lunch Kathleen and I have only nodded as she leaves from my house. After Donald passed there were a handful of phone calls. Donald had entrusted her with all the transactional aspects of his death. His way of protecting me. I'm still cogitating on that plan.

Lunch. Surreal. I go back to their house. There are pictures he wanted me to have, a clock, and I ask for a ring I had given him. She refers to it as his wedding band. We exchange anecdotes, compare notes, chitchat. Will we see each other again? No.

"Kimberly."

"Mom, if you've called to tell me another one of our people has died I'm not going to speak to you."

I have to laugh at the disdain in her voice.

"No, no one has died. I can't find Amos."

"Oh, Mom, I'm so sorry. How long has he been gone?"

"I've been looking for three days. He's just disappeared."

"Well, he's pretty old right? Maybe he's doing that thing where they go take care of themselves."

"I think he's around ten. Not so old. He's such a friend. Molly's at loose ends. Me too."

*****

"Hey, Teaser. It's me Molly. Don't be scared I'm not going to pounce or anything, I was wondering if you knew where Amos is."

"I don't, he hasn't been around to check on me. I was going to ask you the same thing."

"Do you think he's gone?"

"Could be, cats come and go around here. I never know exactly what happens to them, here one day and gone the other."

"I miss him. He taught me so many things."

"Don't worry, I'll watch out for you. You're a pretty good cat, nothing like when you were a kitten."

*****

TJ calls to let me know he and Jackie are sharing an apartment with her brother Oscar in Jacksonville, North Carolina. (Military sponsored.) *And* Jackie's pregnant. They are thrilled. I think I am.

My cell rings. I'm in Alameda helping Kim and Matt move; they've just purchased their first house. TJ has proposed to Jackie while waiting at a red light. They were headed to a romantic dinner. He couldn't wait. She said yes. I'm thrilled times two.

Kim, Matt, and I head to Jacksonville. We want to celebrate. Kim and I secretly want to orchestrate a mini wedding, a little cake, flowers, you know a small party.

Too late, three days before our arrival they, T and J, find a chaplain. They knew we'd fuss. Jackie does not like fuss.

Their apartment is bright, sparse, and immaculate. T introduces us to Camp Lejeune, Jacksonville, and Wilmington. We go to the MCX (Marine Corp Exchange) mainly to say we've been. Kim and I go to a Walmart the size of a city. We buy household goods for the apartment. It's all "sir" and "madam," crew cuts and fatigues, young men and even younger families. Kim and I are mesmerized. We find a furniture store and buy a mattress; T and J have been sleeping on the floor. You can't be pregnant and sleep on the floor, my rule. We experience a rainstorm of biblical proportions. T and Jackie laugh at our reaction. We don't see real weather in California.

One long weekend, a different world, a new beginning. I'm going to be a grandmother. All I can think is *Who me?*

It must be in the water... Several women on my admin staff have recently become grandmothers. We become a club. They already have *their* babies. I'm still waiting and not at all sure what's expected from me. They coach me along. I'm sure our coffee break chats of cloth versus disposable diapers bore those around us; we don't care.

On December 17, 2003, Eva Michele Whang is born.

I take T's call as I come out of the parking garage. I lose the signal on my way to the lobby. He has called to include me at the birth. I wave wildly at the guard; he holds the elevator for me. No signal, no signal. I run past reception, an attorney is flagging me down, I ignore him. I run past accounting. I trip into my office and lean against the window. Bingo. I have a signal. She's here, she's already here. Grainy pictures filter through. She has a full head of black hair and my nose, my God she has my nose. Jackie's family is there. Both coasts are crying and laughing.

Kim and Matt announce they're pregnant. We tease them that it was the pressure of having your baby brother beat you to it that will result in grandchild number 2.

I meet Eva when she's three weeks old. It's my first trip to New Jersey. TJ and Jackie live in Harrison. T has processed out of the Marines. Their apartment is barely big enough for two plus a tiny one, let alone adding me. So I'm in a hotel waiting in the lobby. Eva is with her great-grandma waiting for Mom and Dad to pick her up after work. I have a view of the entrance. A young couple comes through the automatic doors pushed in by a cutting cold gush of NJ January air. It takes seconds, forever, for my brain to register. A handsome young man, a beautiful young woman, a baby carrier in between.

"Mom, it's me. Meet Eva."

Jackie pulls back the corner of the blanket. Oh my.

They leave me with Eva, a diaper bag, and bottles. They need sleep and want us to bond. Scary to be so trusted.

"Oh, sweet baby, I'm your grandmother from California, we will be such pals."

Eva stares at me. She's very serious, reminds me of Kim. I make a nest of pillows on one of the double beds, cover it with her blanket, and place her little bundled self in the middle.

"Okay, I think next is a diaper change and then we'll get a bottle."

She waves her fists. Coos. I guess I'm on the right track.

"This is our first sleepover. I hope your mom and dad know what they are doing leaving you with me. I haven't done *baby* in a long time. Speak up if I'm doing something wrong."

She's hungry. She eagerly sucks her bottle. I gently pat her back when she stops to catch her breath. I recall the importance of that first burp. Oops. She fusses. Maybe I should pat a little harder. I sit her on my lap and tilt her forward. Pat, pat, pat. Oh boy, formula everywhere. What have I done? I wipe her up, change her jammies, and apologize profusely.

She grins or has gas. Is she winking at me? A milk coma follows.

Kim is due in September. I'm planning a couples shower for her and Matt's Southern California well-wishers. Theme: red, white, and pink. We will take advantage of the long Fourth of July weekend. I have included my work friends; they have adopted my children and I theirs. They are so excited for me and anxious to meet Kim and Matt. Kim worries I have taken on too much; we are expecting around sixty. I'm not worried, my friends will help. They are the four most capable women I know. I assure Kim I'll just stand back and watch the ladies make it happen. (They don't disappoint.)

In addition to the shower, I'm waiting for a new kitten. He is orange and white. Won't he and Molly be festive at Halloween? The shower is Saturday, he's coming Sunday. I've already named him. Riley. A good Irish name for a very orange kitty.

Riley is scared and skinny. Kim and I put him in her old room. We try and bribe Molly to come up and meet him. Even people tuna won't lure her. Riley eats both portions.

"Molly, I got him so you would have a friend. I thought you could take care of him, like Amos took care of you." She gives me a blank stare.

I take Riley to be neutered. As I'm completing the paperwork, the vet brings Riley back out. He has a funny look on his face.

"I thought you said Riley was a boy. He's not, he's a girl. We will be spaying *her*; the recovery will take a little longer. Just thought you should know now instead of later."

"Seriously? I was assured he was a male. I wanted a male. I was told a male would be better to pair with a female, especially since they aren't littermates."

"Yes, that does work best. But I'm sure you don't want to give her back."

"No, she's family now. We'll make it work. I insert a *Ms.* In front of *Riley* on the form."

Kim is scheduled for an emergency C-section. Her blood pressure is sky high. I get on I-5 at dusk. I'll miss the birth, but I'll be there around 10:00 p.m. T calls and keeps me company on the drive. He points out that his niece will be born on September seventeenth. I almost drive off the road. My birthday is October seventeenth, Jackie's is November seventeenth, Eva's is December seventeenth, and now Amanda will make it *four of a kind*. What do you think of those odds?

The hospital is softly lit, hushed. Matt told me to come to the recovery floor. It's a maternity hospital so the rooms I pass are spotted with dad's in recliners, mom's trying for sleep, and grandparents whispering advice. Family is welcome, encouraged. It's a happy place. There it is *Recovery*. I push the double doors open; Kim is half shaded by a curtain, smiling, waving. Matt bends down and takes the baby from Kim and, with no hesitation, hands her to me. "Kathy, meet Amanda Paige McGowan." He puts the bundle in my arms. Her eyes are open, she's wide awake. She looks fearless for someone so new or maybe it's because she is new. She favors Kim. "Hey, baby." Such a sweet innocent, correction, innocents.

Eva and Amanda are christened together in Alameda. Matt and Kim have worked hard to make this nonconventional event happen. Matt's priest bends a few rules for the East Coast Protestants. The girls are angelic in their white gowns. Amanda's is a family heirloom; Eva's is new as are her white Mary Janes. No one cries or fusses. We celebrate at Kim's. "Here's to Eva and Amanda, to cousins, to aunts and uncles, Grandmas and Grandpas, to family!"

*****

I guess I'm going to have to be a big sister to Ms. Riley. I guess Amos is gone forever. I guess I gotta stop pouting.

"Riley, where are you? Still under Kim's bed? You can't stay there forever you know."

Riley sticks her head out from under the dust ruffle. Molly creeps up. They are nose to nose. Riley jumps back and hits her head on the bed frame. Molly sticks her head under the ruffle.

"You okay? You can't spend your life in here. Sooner or later you'll meet the vacuum, trust me you don't want that. Come out. We have bird you know. He's cool."

"In the house, a bird in the house?"

Molly leads the way down the stairs.

"What are you two up to? Glad to see you downstairs, Riley. Molly, don't teach her any bad tricks."

*****

Kim and TJ have reconnected with their father. Jim and his wife have been flipping houses. They work out of Nevada. From what I learn from the kids, they flip and travel, buy, renovate, flip and travel. It sounds pretty glamorous to me. I'm glad Jim is back in their lives; everyone needs a dad. No matter their age or circumstance, I could sure use mine if only to pull flowers magically from behind my ear. Eva and Amanda both have wonderful grandfathers, but it never hurts to have a spare. The girls are also blessed with grandmas. Eva has Nancy and Amanda has Betsy. And me of course. I think the three of us are enough.

Kim and Matt go to see Jim's house and properties near Las Vegas. He is cashing in on Vegas's real estate boom which I understand is one of the most exaggerated in America. I worry about Jim's innate optimism; it might get him into trouble. I hope he'll know when to get out. The kids' report things are pretty crazy there.

TJ has completed his bachelor's degree at Montclair State University in New Jersey. His degree is in linguistics, but his passion is writing. He and Jackie work numerous jobs to keep afloat. Jackie keeps her passion alive by spending Saturdays in the saloon. Eva is in preschool/daycare. The school is sponsored by a Portuguese Protestant denomination. I was able to visit and see Eva's *babies*, she (just three) loves to help with the *babies* at snack time. They are captive in sling seats at a semicircular table; the teacher and Eva sit in the middle doling out sliced bananas and cheerios. The school is bilingual, so is Eva or would that be trilingual? I learn that Portuguese and Spanish are similar but not the same. The school's holiday programs are Hollywood worthy. Such a wonderful place for our Eva.

T is exploring real estate with his dad. Jim is looking at Detroit as a possible next market to explore. Maybe T can be his East Coast guy. Maybe this will be T's niche or at least give him an opportunity to write and work at the same time.

Kim and I use the I-5 like a private road. She and Matt tuck Amanda and Murph into their Audi hatchback and make the trip to my house about every other month. I go up to Alameda in between. At Kim's house I sleep in Mandy's room. Mandy and I are early risers. We try not to giggle; Mom and Dad are just down the hall. We hide under the covers in my daybed. I tell her stories about pixies and butterflies. She offers me her suck-suck and blank-blank. Like Eva, Amanda is in day care. There are seven other little ones that join her. Day care is a family affair lead by a husband-and-wife team, their school-aged daughter is their afternoon helper. Mister is retired military. It's a sight watching him take the kids to the park; he instructs the ones who walk to hold hands, "Don't let go." The nonwalkers are strapped into the longest stroller I've ever seen. He leads with the stroller, and the toddlers follow. A baby train. When they return, missus serves Filipino chicken and rice in bright-colored bowls. Then there's naptime. When daughter comes home from school, she helps with crafts and then it's cartoons until Mom and Dad pick up. It's Amanda's weekday family. The happiest place on…in Alameda.

*****

"Riley, come over here. See that, that little human. On the blanket. That's the kitten, I mean baby that arrived just a little after you did."

"Oh, does it want to play?"

"You stay here, I'll go see."

Molly peaks from under the staircase. Assesses the situation. Matt and Murphy are watching TV, and Kathy and Kim are in the kitchen. It appears the baby is doing nothing. Just sitting on the blanket in the middle of the family room.

"There you go, sweetie, your sucky is all clean." Kim pats her baby and returns to the kitchen.

I wonder what a sucky is; it looks like the rubber plug in the bathtub. Baby pops it in her mouth. I guess it's safe now to go over and introduce myself.

Ahhhhhhhhhhhhhh!

I air walk back across the family room, turn and fly up the stairs, and cower under the bed with Riley. "Guess baby doesn't like cats."

Ahhhhhhhhhhhhhh!

*****

311

Matt and Murph come running from the den, and Kim and I sprint from the kitchen. We surround the blanket. Amanda is screeching, Teaser-like. She is inconsolable, her face all red and globs of tears and other baby goo run down her checks. Murph offers to clean her up. Kim puts a stop to that. In between sobs Mandy gulps for air. Kim picks her up. "Well, so much for being friends with Molly."

The firm is growing. I'm involved in the LA office's expansion and renovation. I enjoy this aspect of my job almost as much as the finance piece. My path crosses with several of Kim's design cohorts. It's a small world. It's fun to have a closer look into Kim's career. Kim's role in design has expanded to project management; she's currently at Gensler, the world's largest design firm. (Yes, I'm bragging, unabashedly.) She has managed a number of build-outs. She's a valuable resource, helping me ask the right questions to get to the best solutions. Our LA attorney head count is at eighty, which translates to a total staff count of around one hundred seventy. We occupy four floors, around thirty thousand square feet. Accommodating and then reshuffling that number of people is a logistical nightmare. I'm loving the challenge.

Jim has been coaching T in the art of flipping. TJ has found a house, a converted fishing cabin, in Highland Lakes, New Jersey, about an hour and a half from Harrison. He thinks it would be a good investment for me. He would replace the roof, floors, paint, etc., and in three years we could flip it and make a profit. Funny I've always wanted a house in the woods, a getaway buried in the trees. TJ's family could stay in it during the summer as he works on it. As owners we would be members of the Highland Lakes Country Club, which owns the community lake and recreation center. There is a large summer crowd, lots of fishing, swimming, and nonmotor boating. If you prefer winter sports, there are ski areas just down Breakneck Road. A wonderful rural kind of place.

The cabin is just that, a cabin like in *Goldilocks and the Three Bears*. It's tiny, just two bedrooms. There's just one bath and an excuse for a kitchen. The main living area is what we refer to in California as a great room, maybe twelve-by-twenty feet. There is an enclosed porch that runs the width of the house. All the walls are knotty pine. It's a fifties classic. The house is not insulated, but it has central heating and air-conditioning. Strange, I guess we want the bears to be comfortable. The lot is large, maybe half an acre. Trees, trees, and more trees. There's no fencing, and neighbors are scattered along a very narrow asphalt road, which they snowplow in the winter. Deer, bears, and chipmunks are common fauna. I'm intrigued by the possibilities. It would be a great backdrop for a Steven King mystery or a Norah Roberts's romantic tryst.

"Okay, let's do it."

Year 2007 explodes the Las Vegas real estate bubble. *Crash* is a mild term. There are sweeping foreclosures, huge job losses, plunging prices, and evaporating development. It's dubbed one of the most devastating real estate debacles in the country. The flip has flopped. Jim retreats. We worry.

Los Angeles real estate slides and with it California's economy. Alameda seems to dodge the bullet. Kim and Matt are safe for now. The firm shrinks, salaries are frozen. The cabin becomes home for T, Jackie, and Eva. Kim is pregnant, it's a boy.

Jim is in over his head, that's my conclusion. We haven't talked in years. I only know what the kids feel like sharing. I often don't recognize the Jim they describe. A man moved more by what he wants than by what he has, a captive to accumulation, a man with monogramed shirts, and houses not homes. What happened to the guy with dreams of boats to skim across the waves, of ski chalets to be hip deep in powder, of cars to master hairpin curves, of travel to taste the foods of the world? Where did he go? The guy that could be too gullible, too open, even too kind but who could turn defeat into a reason to try again. Where is he?

Jim commits suicide in February 2008.

Kim is six months pregnant. She's walking to the ferry, homebound when her cell rings and her aunt delivers the news. I'm not clear where or how TJ finds out. The horror is not so much the deed, but that it is done. The horror is that this attempt succeeded; it wasn't deterred, stopped, waylaid, or even undone. The horror is the missing dad, the missing grandfather, the missed.

The kids go to Henderson. Other than his wife, Kim, Matt, and TJ are the only mourners. Jim's sisters and mom opt out. They are hostage to years of alienation, unresolved feelings and closely held grievances; all valid but not now. So my daughter and son say good-bye to their dad at a county coroner's office and begin years of asking why.

I wonder what I could have done. What can I do? I did call Jim before the deed was done. I asked what was going on. He shouted "nothing." His pain was palpable. I acquiesced. I join the guilty.

Donald would say, "It is what it is." I wish it weren't so.

Reed Thomas McGowan is born May 3, 2008. Best name ever. Reed after Grandma Betsy's dad. Thomas after his two uncles, Tom McGowan and TJ Whang.

Fall approaches. Highland Lakes is covered with red, gold, orange, and yellow leaves of every size and shape. We hire a yard man to dig out. I imagine the rolling hills are heavy with golden foliage. Maybe next year I'll go and see the colors. TJ, Eva, and Jackie are somewhere in Canada. Jim's wife is holding a memorial at one of his favorite spots. I wonder how that's going.

"Mom, what's up? We're back."

"How it go?"

"It was nice. Glad we went."

"Good, did the girls enjoy it? Give me some details."

"I can see why Dad like it there—woodlands, river, blue sky, white clouds. No one around but fishermen, fly-fishing in those crazy hip boots. We met his in-laws; they were very warm. We barbecued his favorite steaks and toasted with Jack Daniels. We rented a small boat and motored to a wide area in the river. His wife asked me to do the honors and scatter his ashes. I couldn't get over how small the urn was; how that could be Dad? I didn't want to dump them, so I tried to be ceremonious, a slow pour. Bad decision, we were moving upriver. Eva was drenched in ash. Jackie was pissed. I stifled my weird sense of humor."

"Oh my god. Poor Ev."

We wiped her off. She looked at me and said, "Well, there goes Grandpa."

If life would pace itself, then so could I. But there is no stopping it. I try to adopt the Alcoholics Anonymous Serenity Prayer:

> God grant me the serenity to accept the things
> I cannot change; courage to change the things I
> can; and wisdom to know the difference.

The key is knowing the difference, that's the tricky part.

I'm propelled forward.

Barack Obama, the forty-fourth president of the United States, is inaugurated on Tuesday, January 20, 2009. We turn on TVs in the lunchroom and key conference rooms. They will be on all day. We invite all office members to stop by and participate in this historical event. When he takes the oath, the rooms are packed.

"Rose, can you come to my office and read this email?"

I barely release the phone, and she's in the doorway.

"Look there, halfway down her *what-I-did-today* list!"

"It says I took a pregnancy test it was positive, it was old. I went to the drug store and took a new one, it was positive, just told Matt."

"That's what I thought it said. What a way to break the news."

Kim and Matt had agreed to two children. Kim wanted more, but after Reed, she had to agree that would be a lot of work. They are educated, mindful people so what happened?

Lily Annalise McGowan was born on May 26, 2010. Amanda was totally against this addition until she saw her. Reed seems curious, but at two he just wants to sit in Mom's lap. Lily is named by her dad. She completes the set. Like pepper is to salt, mustard to catsup, meatballs to spaghetti. Lily, Reed, Amanda, perfect.

I was sure the next gran would be a sister or bother for Eva. But it hasn't happened yet. I know how much Jackie wants babies. She doesn't ask for much not like the rest of us Whangs; it's all about family for her—all about her Tommy (TJ) and Eva, her parents and brothers and cousins so many cousins. I cross my fingers.

*****

"Molly, what are they doing now?"

"They're packing up the van."

Riley and Molly are down the street, under a bush at the end of the cul-de-sac. They have been hiding out for a couple of days.

"What's Kim saying, can you hear?"

"She's asking Kathy if she wants her to help look for us. Kathy says no, she's sure once we realize the kids are gone we'll come home."

"Well, da."

"Hey, do you remember Murphy the Dog?"

"Do I. Remember when he trapped us on the stair landing and we jumped over him? Wow that was cool, we flew over his head and seven steps to the floor. He had a terrible time backing down the stairs. Where is he? He never comes anymore. Kind of miss the old guy."

"I heard he had cancer. There was nothing anyone could do. Broke his peoples' hearts."

"I wonder if we'll ever have a dog."

*****

The pain is excruciating. Am I overreacting? No, maybe I'm dying. I know that meatloaf tasted wrong. It has to be food poisoning, doesn't it?

"TJ, can you call Kaiser for me?"

Kaiser advises us to call 911. We do. After evaluation at the local hospital and two ambulance rides, I'm admitted to Kaiser Panorama City with pancreatitis. I'm not dying, I just feel that way. Some enzyme is wacky; it's poisoning me. I can't have anything orally not even ice chips. I bond with my pain medication. They are sure I'm an alcoholic, I'm not. I know it was that pre-prepared meatloaf. Well, my eating habits in general. It's not my gallbladder or diabetes or anything they can find. Maybe my blood pressure mediation, but why now? A gastroenterologist reluctantly agrees since it occurred about an hour and a half after eating, it could be the food. You think?

TJ is here. He'd just got into town. What a mess to walk into. He and Jackie are taking a break. California was the most practical destination for him. So he's here with me, the sicky. I'm sorry for Jackie and Eva, but selfishly happy for me. I've never needed someone like I needed someone after that meatloaf. I'm humbled, embarrassed, vulnerable. Guess I'm not superwoman after all. Kim magically appears. I'm so touched. And Rose mans the work front as the pro she is. Between the three of them I'm in good hands. I surrender to sleep, days of sleep.

I convalesce with Molly and Riley on my bed. I can hear Teaser whistling to TJ downstairs. Being a slug is just about over. Kim has left us with a clean house, and T has made it clear that breakfast in bed has got to stop. "Time to pull yourself together, Mom."

T asks his girls to join him. It will be a grand experiment. A year in California, maybe it will become permanent. Jackie and Eva are so brave. Eva will transfer to Meadows (T and Kim's grade school) in time to start the fourth grade. Jackie's employer, RLB Food Distributors, has clients in SoCal that are anxious to interview her. She's hired within weeks of her arrival by Sun Pacific; they are headquartered in Pasadena. T is exploring the entrepreneurial market. While he searches for a fit, I keep him busy with painting, woodworking, a bathroom renovation, and a patio cover redo.

Jackie's stepfather, Joe, dies unexpectedly. He was in a car accident on his way to work. He had just returned to work after a bout with kidney disease and diabetes. Jackie and him were close, the closeness found between strong fathers and headstrong daughters. Eva was the apple of his eye and he of hers. Like Nancy, Joe was a friend and parent to TJ. Everyone is devastated. I take them to the airport. That's all I can do.

I'm surprised they return to California. Over the moon, but surprised. I thought they might stay for Nancy. I've never had my grans altogether, well, not on the same coast for more than a few days. We wear a path between Alameda and Valencia. TJ takes Amanda and Eva to pick a live Thanksgiving turkey, that's how it's done in Jackie's family. Reed and Lily bask in Eva's attention. We take the ferry to SF to see the Christmas Tree at Union Square. The grans celebrate birthdays together. They perform elaborate aquatic shows in the pool. We have barbecues and more barbecues. Uncle Matt ensures a July 4 extraordinaire with fireworks smuggled in from Filmore. There's a Disneyland trip. Miniature golf. It's family time on steroids.

They are packing up. Ready for a power road trip back to New Jersey. They are going home, back to the cabin in the forest. Nancy has renovated it in their absence. I suspect that's part of Joe's legacy. It's all insolated now; winter will be tolerable. The great experiment was a success, just not for California. Once home, Jackie and TJ will unpack and repack. They have a planned trip to Peru. They won't return until after Eva starts the fifth grade, so I will be going to New Jersey in a few weeks to spell Nancy and get Eva started in school. I am looking forward to our time together and exploring everyday life in Highland Lakes. I often think it could be a retirement destination. There's a bit of Goldilocks in me.

I'm convinced it's a miracle. Jackie is pregnant. Sometimes a couple just needs to be alone. On April 30, 2015, Olivia Grace Whang is born. Eva is a big sister. The Whangs are complete.

I return from my first hugs with Olivia and notify my COO that I want to retire. It's time. The firm is changing, of course it is. Things change, but I don't like what I see, and I'm in the position to walk away, so that's what I'm going to do.

The firm is losing its financial practicality. Once lean and mean, it's now top heavy with pricey partners underpinned by vanishing collectibles. Purporting centralization as a cost-saving technique has caused collateral expenses not recoverable anytime soon. The push to make all offices the same has stifled independent problem solving and creative competition. Insisting we are all one happy content family makes it pointless to risk standing out to offer new ways to succeed. Ideas are only valuable if they come top down. As managers we are encouraged to mind our own business while we watch our business systematically siphoned away.

So I'm done. I don't say, "I can't stand this nonsense anymore" or "if I don't leave soon my politically incorrect mouth is going to take care of my exit for me." No. I'm professional, eloquent, humble, and thankful for my years at the firm. I am, it's been a good seventeen years. But my value is spent. I give a year notification. I craft a turnover plan. Rose will be my successor. I'm not sure that's kind. I do everything by the book, neat and tidy.

My Teasy is not feeling well. He still comes to nuzzle my cheek, but sometimes he stumbles; once he fell off his perch. I watch him closely. He's slowing down, one day at a time. He moves to the bottom of the cage. I read this isn't good. One night he doesn't look up when I come in. Oh, little gift from God, I'll miss you so. He's twenty-three years old. I wrap him in a silk scarf and bury him under the rosemary bush. I'll call Kim tomorrow. Tonight I'll just weep. Who will greet me when I come home?

My last day. There is a party, accolades, gifts, cake, tears, and heartfelt farewell speeches. Office services packs me up. I'm told several partners have bids on my corner office with its floor-to-ceiling glass windows, Hollywood sign view, and square footage larger than the managing partners. It pays to take an interest in build-outs. We manage to fit seventeen years in four banker boxes. I leave my keys and access card with my HR manager. We take the boxes down on a dolly. Rose and I carpool one more time. That's the only thing. I'll miss our long ridiculous sometimes soul-searching conversations to and from Valencia. We will just have to have a lot of Saturday brunches.

I place the cat carrier on the garage floor, close to Molly's nest, which is on the bottom shelf of the worktable. Her nest, a basket with her favorite towel tucked over a pillow. All cushy. Molly claimed this spot six weeks ago. I've provided a fan, food, and water and her litter box. When she is perched on her pillow, she looks like a black bird protecting her eggs. She is seventeen years old. Now tinier than ever. For the last two weeks her appetite has dwindled, and she no longer enjoys our nightly walks down the driveway and back. She is rooted to her basket, waiting for me to peek in and check on her. She looks up when I do, her green eyes searching my face as I search hers. I know she is waiting for me to do something.

The vet and I have agreed that when Molly and I know it's time she will be there to assist. I pet Molly's velvety head and scoop her up like a sleeping baby. I place her in her carrier and that in the car's passenger seat. She makes no fuss. I get in and buckle up. I reach my fingers through the grate. Molly leans into my touch, and I into hers.

There is no one but the receptionist in the clinic lobby. They are ready for us. We settle in a treatment room. An assistant invites Molly to leave her carrier. She is reluctant. I coax her out.

"What a pretty girl. So tiny. So sweet," the assistant coos. She explains the process to me. She assures me I have made the right decision. She offers us time alone.

"Here we are, Molly Cat, just you and me."

I lean over the treatment table and surround her with my arms. I thank her for each year of her life. I remind her of my mom and brother, her first family. I retell her the story of Amos, the cat that brought her up and left only when he knew she would be alright. I recall all those winter nights when she slept curled like a muff on my feet. I thank her for letting me cry into her fur with each death in our family, human and animal. I assure her that she is irreplaceable. I whisper in her satin ear, "I understand why you moved to the garage, and I appreciate your attempt to soften our separation." I tell her to be on the lookout for all our people.

"Goodbye, sweet Molly."

*****

First Teaser and then Molly. I sit in the grass while Kathy plants Molly next to Teaser. I make a promise.

"Guys, I'll take good care of Kathy. I won't scratch the couch or chew on the potted fern, and I'm going to give up chasing birds."

Kathy pats me on the head, scratches my chin.

"Riley, let's go in. We'll be all right, promise."

*****

I'm four years into retirement and on schedule with my retirement bucket list. I've learned how to knit. I've joined a gym and go three times a week. I've completed my certificate in nonfiction creative writing and have started a book. I've taken my family on a cruise to Alaska. I've replumbed and repiped. I've drought proofed the yard and installed solar panels. And best of all I've acquired Ms. Beatrice Blossom.

CHAPTER 17

Beatrice Blossom

Description: Beatrice is a goldendoodle, mostly standard poodle. If you are thinking, "Oh no, a designer dog why not a rescue?" I assure you she is a rescue—she rescued me. I chose her because of a picture in a magazine. I had to have one. I put her on my retirement bucket list and gave her to myself for my seventieth birthday.

Before she's clipped, she looks like a GUND teddy bear. I keep her fur just short enough to avoid matting and long enough to showcase her ringlets. When clean she is the color of the inside of a white peach. Right before her groomer comes, she's kind of well dirty, dirty peach. She has eyelashes so long they require trimming; we keep them at about two inches, but they can get to a swept-back five. They are rust color. She weighs fifty-nine pounds, all muscle, all love, all the time.

She has a huge vocabulary, a quirky sense of humor, and can be sneaky when it comes to stealing my dishcloth or towel. She will do anything but eat green beans for a doggie treat. She is very, very, very stubborn. We are currently arguing about where she should go—to bed, laundry, or family room…

She lives downstairs, and Riley lives upstairs. It's a house full of love.

"Hey, Bea, come in here."

She trots up to the back door, dripping wet tennis ball in her mouth. She thinks I want to play.

"Drop it, Bea, you can come in, but not with that wet ball."

She sits down to think about it. Releases the ball and comes in.

"I've finished, Bea, I've put the last word on the last page! What do you think of that?"

She does downward dog and settles onto her stomach. She looks up through her lashes, catches my eye, and yawns.

The yawn doesn't offend me; she must be tired, tired of me reading and rereading my story out loud to her to make sure the words ring true. I'm surprised she's not howling.

"Okay, sweetie, let's take a walk. A nice long one, that's the least I can do for you. Let's get out there and look for our story, it promises to be a good one."

ABOUT THE AUTHOR

Kathy Whang lives in Southern California with her goldendoodle, Beatrice, and her cat, Ms. Riley. She recently retired from a career that began in aerospace, cycled through computer software, banking, business operations, and culminated with law firm administration.

Whether sharing short stories and essays with family and friends or surprising business peers with off-beat memos or precision white papers, Kathy's true passion is writing about life, it's extraordinary and it's mundane.

Kathy is the mother of two and the grandmother of five. She has a bachelor's degree in psychology from the University of California, Los Angeles, and a certificate in creative nonfiction also from UCLA.

CPSIA information can be obtained
at www.ICGtesting.com
Printed in the USA
LVHW030856250621
691134LV00001B/73